THE EVOLUTION OF ANAESTHESIA

Without history, a man's soul is purblind, see-ing only those things which almost touch his eyes – Thomas Fuller

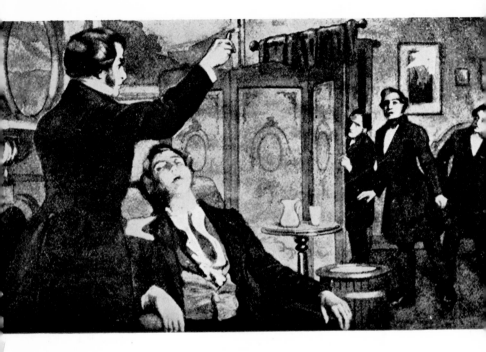

11th December, 1844. Horace Wells inhales nitrous oxide and allows one of his teeth to be extracted.

The Evolution of Anaesthesia

by

M. H. ARMSTRONG DAVISON

M.B.E., T.D., M.D., F.F.A.R.C.S., etc.

Lecturer in Anaesthetics and in the History of Medicine in the University of Newcastle upon Tyne; Sometime Vice-President of the Scottish Society of the History of Medicine

ALTRINCHAM
JOHN SHERRATT AND SON

First published 1965

Printed in Great Britain at the St Ann's Press,
Park Road, Altrincham

To my Wife,
and all other Clients of Clio

PREFACE

Although the first chapter of this book was inspired to some extent by the valuable chronology of Thomas E. Keys in his *History of Surgical Anesthesia*, the whole work is intended as a scientific and factual counterblast to the many romantic and largely fictional "histories" of anaesthesia which have been put before the public in the last half century. I also hope that someone, more patient than I, will some day find this work of value when preparing a definitive history of the most humane discovery the world has ever known.

The task of writing a history of the world in less than one hundred pages, as has been done in the first chapter, suggests an egotism which I no longer feel. The effort of compression is, I hope, worth while, because the story of man's attitude towards pain can only be properly understood when seen through a wide-angle lens, which while perhaps distorting some things, will nevertheless permit the whole field to come into one comprehensive view. Each individual will erect his viewpoint in a different place, and to this extent history must necessarily be individualistic. Those who quarrel with my intentional omissions or inevitable distortions may be more likely to forgive me when they realize that I have been depicting the scene as I see it, for Truth has many faces, and I have tried to depict that one she has turned towards me

In my attempt to show the essential unity of history I have selected for my chronology certain dates in order to impress the concurrence of these events on the reader's mind. Some dates (e.g. 1066) are included merely because to leave them out would smack of iconoclasm, while others (e.g. 1563) are inserted because of their impact.

As with all searchers, my thanks are due to those authors who have prepared my way and from whom I have taken many of the bones of my history; some of the flesh, however, I believe to be original. I particularly offer my sincere thanks to my colleagues on the Board of Management of the *British Journal of Anaesthesia* for their ready permission to make use of certain matter which first appeared in that journal. I am most grateful to the Editor of *Anaesthesia* for permission to re-publish the article on Eufame MacCalyean which appears as one of the appendices to this book.

In conclusion, I ask the reader to bear in mind that almost none of the characters in this book is entirely fictitious.

CONTENTS

Preface   7

Introduction   13

Chapter

1. Chronology   23

    A.   The Prehistoric Age (until *c.* 3000 B.C.)   23

    B.   The Magico-Empiric Age (*c.* 3000–585 B.C.)   25

    C.   The Scientific Age (585 B.C.–A.D. 200)   32

    D.   The Age of Superstition (A.D. 200–1454)   39

    E.   The Renaissance (1454–1754)   51

    F.   The Pre-Anaesthetic Era (1754–1846)   73

    G.   The Modern Period (since 1846)   96

2. Ether   110

3. Nitrous Oxide   124

4. Chloroform and Drugs Related to Chloroform   135

5. Endotracheal Intubation   149

6. Muscle Relaxants   154

7. Premedication   159

8. Refrigeration Anaesthesia   162

9. Local Analgesia   171

10. Oxygen and Helium   178

Chapter

11. Blood Transfusion and Intravenous Anaesthesia   193

Appendices

A. The Discovery of Ether   207

B. The Fate of Eufame MacCalyean   212

C. Endotracheal and Other Modern Methods in the
Eighteenth Century   216

Index   223

ILLUSTRATIONS

Horace Wells inhales nitrous oxide   *Frontispiece*

Figure No.   *Facing page*

1. Circumcision, from an Egyptian tomb   30
2. The Stele of Khammurabi   31
3. Asklepiades of Bithynia   46
4. Asklepieion at Cos   47
5. Mandrakes   47
6. Raymond Lully   62
7. Paracelsus   63
8. South American Indian   78
9. Amputation of the leg   79
10. Jean-Baptiste van Helmont   94
11. Resemblance between burning and breathing   95
12. Blood transfusion   110
13. William Harvey   111
14. Joseph Black   126
15. Franz Anton Mesmer   127
16. Antoine-Laurent Lavoisier   127
17. George Moore's clamp   142
18. Gilray's cartoon of pneumatic treatment   143

Figure No. *Facing page*

19. James Blundell's "Impellor" 158

20. Henry Hill Hickman 159

21. William Thomas Green Morton 174

22. Oliver Wendell Holmes 174

23. First demonstration of anaesthesia 175

24. First English surgical operation under anaesthesia 190

25. John Snow 191

26. David Waldie 191

27. Sir James Young Simpson 206

28. Mobile operating theatre designed by Paul Bert 207

Grateful acknowledgement is made to the undermentioned for permission to reproduce copyright illustrations.
Figures 1, 2, 3, 4, 9, 10, Ralph H. Major, *A History of Medicine*, Charles C. Thomas, Illinois, U.S.A. Figure 8, E. Trier Mørch, *Anethesi*, Munksgaard, Copenhagen. Figure 11, Charles Singer, *A Short History of Medicine*, Clarendon Press. Figures 13, 24, Douglas Gutherie, *A History of Medicine*, Thomas Nelson. Figure 14, Sir William Ramsey, *Joseph Black M.D.*, James MacLehose, Glasgow. Figures 15, 21, 28, Thomas E. Keys, *A History of Surgical Anesthesia*, Henry Schuman, New York. Figure 17, Victor Robinson,*Victory over Pain*, Henry Schuman, New York. Figures 20, 26, The Wellcome Foundation Ltd. Figures 18, 22, Howard H. Haggard, *Devils, Drugs and Doctors*, Wm. Heinemann Medical Books Ltd. Figure 25, Dr. R. G. Snow. Figure 27, H. Laing Gordon, *Sir James Simpson and Chloroform*, Ernest Benn Ltd.

INTRODUCTION

A knowledge of the history of anaesthesia has no commercial value for the practising physician, but it does have an immense cultural value. The medical student is too harassed by the need to pass examinations to find the time to obtain a liberal education, but a liberal education is essential for the proper intellectual appreciation and enjoyment of life. The history of medicine has close contact with the story of every science and art, for history is the cement which binds together all the varied activities of man. To study medical history is to make acquaintance with all the numerous subjects which comprise a liberal education, and such study is thus a short cut to a knowledge of the humanities.

The history of anaesthesia is a large subject; paradoxically, it is also true that it does not exist at all. Anaesthesia is a branch of medicine, and its history can only be understood by examining the whole subject. Equally, medicine is a branch of science, while science is only one facet of human activity: it follows, therefore, that the history of anaesthesia can only be interpreted correctly by viewing it in the perspective of other human activities, medical, scientific, and social; inventions, discoveries, wars, religious beliefs, and all the manifestations of art and culture.

It is unfortunate, therefore, that the history of anaesthesia has been mainly considered by anaesthetists, for it is natural that they have viewed the field with nothing but their own subject in mind, and have therefore emphasized unduly a number of early attempts at pain relief, without considering whether these attempts have any causal relationship to the discovery of surgical anaesthesia.

Naturally, also, we tend to project our own humanitarianism into the minds of our progenitors, even as far back as the dawn of history. If one examines any book or chapter which tries to cover the history of anaesthesia, one finds some such statement as "From earliest times, man has sought to prevent pain". At first sight, this seems a reasonable remark; on consideration, however, it begins to appear less reasonable. Direct evidence is obviously lacking, but indirect evidence is often in flat contradiction. We have only to look back 200 years, and we see that the general tendency of mankind was to inflict pain, not to prevent it. The social history of England at that time discloses a treatment of malefactors, of lunatics, of slaves, and of animals which was barbaric in the extreme; and there is no reason to believe that uncivilized people are less brutal than we were in England at a date when the arts flourished more luxuriantly than at any other period in our history.

This is not to say that there were no humane beings, that no one prior to the end of the eighteenth century ever tried to prevent pain or to discover some means of surgical anaesthesia. Such people undoubtedly did exist, but their efforts produced no noticeable effect on the general attitude of their professional colleagues; they did not influence history and their work had no part in the ultimate discovery of anaesthesia; they sank into oblivion from which some of them have only been rescued since anaesthesia became an accomplished fact.

For example, we are interested to know that Severino of Naples employed refrigeration analgesia for the operation of perineal lithotomy in the first half of the seventeenth century, but his technique passed almost unnoticed, and was not at all a factor in the recent reintroduction of refrigeration analgesia for amputation. None of the authors of the histories of anaesthesia seem to be aware of this important distinction: every event with the slightest anaesthetic flavour is seized on as part of the "history of anaesthesia", such as, for example, the story from Herodotus (fifth century B.C.) of the Scythians intoxicating themselves with the fumes produced by burning some sort of hemp (*History*, Book 4). This is obviously an attempt to make bricks without straw; the incident may have some anthropological importance, but it has no real bearing on the history of anaesthesia.

History teaches us that man has usually been tolerant of pain, especially in others; and this is very natural. Pain and disease were present long before man appeared on the earth, and the earliest man therefore accepted the ills to which the flesh is heir as a natural concomitant of life. The revolt against disease was slow : that against pain was slower still. It was not until the second half of the eighteenth century of the Christian era that a new feeling spread abroad. Humanitarianism became widespread among civilized peoples; while hitherto it had been a tender plant, rarely seen and often disregarded, it now grew to be the most important vegetation in the moral jungle. It was then that the history of anaesthesia began, nor was it long before anaesthesia itself came into being. The Renaissance had done its finest work: humanitarianism, the dislike of pain and suffering, was quickened into full life by the outwardly hateful events of the Industrial Revolution. Already the revival of learning and the development of experimental science had prepared the way; as soon as anaesthesia became a moral necessity, the knowledge and the tools being available, the discovery could not be long delayed. So the stage was set for that memorable day, October 16, 1846, when William Thomas Green Morton gave anaesthesia to the world.

THE WORD "ANAESTHESIA"

The word "anaesthesia" is generally said to have been coined by Oliver Wendell Holmes; certainly he applied it to "etherization", but the word was already in current use before Morton's discovery.

Experimental science may be said to begin with Thales of Miletus (c.624 – 565 B.C.). This Ionian Greek had studied Mesopotamian and Egyptian astronomical and physical observations: he took a tremendous step forward when he used these observations to make deductions, and to argue from the particular to the general. Thus the empirical Mesopotamian astronomical knowledge led him to predict an eclipse of the sun, visible at Miletus in 585 B.C.; similarly, the Egyptian knowledge about special triangles (those with sides in the proportions 3 : 4 : 5 units of length, which the Egyptians used for constructing right-angles in their building operations) enabled him to deduce the general law expressed in the so-called Theorem of Pythagoras. Thus science began; the study of science was a peculiarly Greek gift to mankind. In the years after Thales, Greek science rose to tremendous heights, which, in spite of the Dark Ages, left us a legacy which we still enjoy. It is natural therefore, that the scientist turns to the Greek language when he wishes to record his observations and deductions. Hence it follows that scientific terms are almost entirely Greek in origin, and the words "anaesthesia" and "anaesthetic" are no exception.

The Greek stem αἰσθε means "to perceive", ἀναίσθησις thus means "an absence of feeling", and in classical times this conveyed a moral state, rather than a physical one, that is to say "a boorishness"; the word is used in this sense by Plato. It can still convey this meaning, although it is rarely used thus in modern times; for example, Windsor (*Ethica*, vii, 338) in 1860 uses the phrase, "this cold, anaesthetic temperament". During Roman times, the great majority of physicians, even in the Eternal City itself, were Greeks, for the Roman genius turned more towards the work of the military surgeon. The physicians naturally wrote in their own tongue, which was, in any case, the language of culture; but, with the passage of time, some words had changed in meaning. Dioscorides, who probably wrote at the end of the first or the beginning of the second century A.D., uses the word in its usual modern sense when discussing Mandragora. The *Shorter Oxford English Dictionary* dates the first use of the word "anaesthesia" in English as 1721; presumably it was then used to indicate loss of sensation in one limb or a part of the body. John Elliotson (*Numerous Cases of Surgical Operations without Pain in the Mesmeric State*,London, 1843, p. 65) quotes himself as using the word (from the context, in 1838) thus: "'For a length of time she had perfect loss of sense of touch, — anaesthesia, in her ecstatic delirium'." In June 1846, four months before Morton's successful demonstration of ether anaesthesia, Elliotson delivered an Harveian Oration, in which he used these words: "The loss of common feeling, – anaesthesia, is but a form of palsy, and in it wounds give no pain. If this condition can be induced temporarily by art, we of necessity enable persons to undergo surgical operations without suffering."

Morton attempted to keep secret the nature of the substance which he used; he therfore called it the "Letheon", a name suggested by Dr. A. A. Gould. The word is derived from the Greek, λήθη, oblivion; according to Latin poets, there was a river of this name in Hades; its waters were drunk by souls about to be reincarnated, and caused them to forget their previous existence.

Subsequently, on or about November 6, 1846, Morton revealed the nature of the substance confidentially to the authorities of the Massachusetts General Hospital, and on November 9, Dr. H. J. Bigelow read a paper at a meeting of the Boston Society of Medical Improvement, in which he stated that he had identified the Letheon with sulphuric ether.

Twelve days later, Oliver Wendell Holmes, at that time in practice in Boston, and the following year to be appointed Parkman Professor of Anatomy and Physiology and also Dean of the Harvard Medical School, wrote to Morton as follows:

November 21, 1846

Dr. Morton.

My dear Sir,

Everybody wants to have a hand in a great discovery. All I will do is to give you a hint or two as to names, or name, to be applied to the state produced, and to the agent.

The state should, I think, be called anaesthesia. This signifies insensibility, more particularly (as used by Linnaeus and Cullen) to objects of touch. The adjective will be anaesthetic. Thus we might say the "state of anaesthesia", or the "anaesthetic state". The means employed would be properly called the "anti-aesthetic agent". Perhaps it might be allowable to say "anaesthetic agent"; but this admits of question.

The words, anti-neuric, aneuric, neuroleptic, neurolepsia, neurostasis, seem too anatomical; whereas the change is a physiological one. I throw these out for consideration.

I would have a name pretty soon, and consult some accomplished scholar, such as President Everett, or Dr. Bigelow, Sr., before fixing upon the terms which will be repeated by the tongues of every civilized race of mankind. You could mention these words which I suggest, for their consideration; but there may be others more appropriate and agreeable,

Yours respectfully,

O. W. HOLMES

There seems to be no evidence that further advice was sought. The words "anaesthesia" and "anaesthetic" were accepted readily by the profession, which was already familiar with them. Until the end of the nineteenth century, the original spelling was retained in America; early in the twentieth, however, the sensible simplified spelling "anesthesia", was introduced in the New World, and was fully established before the outbreak of the Great War. It is altogether unfortunate that, in the United States, the necessity for distinguishing between physicians and nurses who administer anaesthetics has led to the invention of the ugly words "anesthesiologist" and "anesthesiology". Both words are best avoided whenever possible.

FURTHER READING

Many books have been written on the subject of the history of anaesthesia; the following notes may be helpful to the student who wishes to delve more deeply. A warning, however, is necessary: the student should guard himself against believing a statement simply because it is made in an authoritative manner; belief can only be commanded when a statement is supported by a satisfactory reference, quoting an *original* document. Scepticism is the finest rein to the enquiring mind, and an attitude of honest scepticism should be cultivated. On reading a new statement, the student should say to himself, "I doubt that; what proof is offered?" If the proof seems adequate, qualified trust may be given, but the final acceptance of the statement as a *fact* must depend on cumulative evidence, with no rebuttal. In identifying fingerprints, Scotland Yard demand that two prints, to be shown from the same finger, must have no less than sixteen points of similarity, and no single point of dissimilarity.

Books dealing with the history of medicine as a whole are valuable for filling in the background. As a general rule, these books deal with the history of anaesthesia in an unsatisfactory manner, but the following are strongly recommended.

An *Introduction to the History of Medicine* by Fielding H. Garrison. London: W. B. Saunders (1913). This book reached its 4th edition in 1929 and has become recognized as the authoritative book on the subject. It is a work of reference rather than literature, and is well indexed.

A *Short History of Medicine* by Charles Singer. Oxford: Clarendon Press (1928). A well-illustrated outline of the subject; readable.

A *History of Medicine* by Douglas Guthrie. London: Nelson (1945).

A History of Medicine by Ralph H. Major. (2 vols.) Oxford: Blackwell (1954). Profusely and excellently illustrated.

Eternal Eve by Harvey Graham. London: Heinemann (1950). This book deals mainly with obstetrics, but it contains much of general interest. Not always accurate, it suffers from lack of references, but it is well worth reading.

Of books dealing specifically with the history of anaesthesia, the most important are:

The Development of Inhalation Anaesthesia by Barbara M. Duncum. London: Oxford University Press (1947). This is an outstanding book, accurate, comprehensive, well illustrated and fully documented.

The History of Surgical Anesthesia by Thomas E. Keys. New York: Schuman (1945). Another valuable book; it contains a most useful chronology of events and many important references.

Ancient Anodynes by E. S. Ellis. London: Heinemann (1946). This is a useful compilation of incidents and events, mostly in note form, with many references.

The English Pioneers of Anaesthesia by F. F. Cartwright. Bristol: Wright (1952). Deals in great detail with Priestley, Davy, and Hickman, and thus covers the "pre-anaesthetic" period. Very fully documented.

Triumph over Pain by R. Fülöp-Miller, translated by E. and C. Paul. New York: Bobbs-Merrill (1938). A "romantic" book, without references, frequently inaccurate in details, it is nevertheless an interpretation of the history of anaesthesia which makes enjoyable reading.

In addition, there are numerous biographies of people such as Sir James Y. Simpson, Sir Benjamin W. Richardson, Joseph Priestley, John Snow, and Crawford W. Long, which can be studied with profit. Special articles are also to be found in the *British Journal of Anaesthesia* (started publication 1923), *Current Researches in Anesthesia and Analgesia* (commenced publication 1922), *Anaesthesia* (started publication 1946), and in the *Proceedings of the Royal Society of Medicine*. The issue of the *Journal of the History of Medicine and Allied Sciences* (Vol. I, No. 4) for October 1946, was a special "Anaesthesia Centennial Number" and contains a great deal of important material.

As a general rule the "potted" history given in chapters on this subject in anaesthetic textbooks is of little value, but exception may be made in the cases of *A Synopsis of Anaesthesia* by J. Alfred Lee, Bristol: Wright, 3rd edition (1953), whose chronology is helpful and down to earth, and *Essentials of General Anaesthesia* by Sir Robert Macintosh and Freda K. Bannister, Oxford: Blackwell, 5th edition (1952), which is accurate and entertaining. For the history of endotracheal and allied methods, *Endotracheal Anaesthesia* by Noel Gillespie, University of Wisconsin Press, 2nd edition (1948), and *The Principles of Thoracic Anaesthesia, Past and Present* by William W. Mushin and L. Rendell-Baker, Oxford: Blackwell (1953), are particularly informative and well illustrated.

Chapter One

CHRONOLOGY OF THE HISTORY OF ANAESTHESIA

For our purpose, the main stream of history can be divided into certain fairly well-defined periods:

A. Pre-historic, up to about 3000 B.C. (Nile Valley, Mesopotamia).

B. Magico-Empiric, 3000–585 B.C. (Nile Valley, Mesopotamia).

C. Scientific, 585 B.C.–A.D. 200 (Asia Minor, Greece, Alexandria, Rome).

D. Superstitious, A.D. 200–1454 (Constantinople, Arabia, Western Europe).

E. Renaissance, 1454–1754 (Western Europe).

F. Pre-anaesthetic, 1754–1846 (Western Europe and America).

G. Anaesthetic, 1846 onwards.

A. PREHISTORIC AGE (until *c.* 3000 B.C.)

The prehistoric races which settled in the Nile Valley and the Mesopotamian region were similar to such races in other parts of the world. They passed through the usual neolithic and chalcolithic stages of development. In the absence of written records, direct evidence can only be obtained from archaeological discoveries, particularly of interments. Indirect evidence is available in the customs of recent and present-day primitive peoples whose culture has reached a similar stage of development, but such evidence must, of course, be treated with caution.

The cause of disease is ascribed by such peoples to the wrath of a god or gods, who either make use of material objects to injure the people who have insulted them, or else fire magical "elfshot" into them. Sometimes a demon or spirit may take up his abode within a man, and thus cause disease, physical or mental. By means of magic, some men may be able to make the spirits do their bidding, and thus disease may be caused by a "powerful" enemy.

The treatment of disease, therefore, consists of placating the wrathful god by means of magical rites, removing the magic "elfshot" or, if the patient be inhabited by a spirit, making him so uncomfortable that the spirit will be glad to go elsewhere. The need for special knowledge and powers to carry out the magical rites correctly led to the establishment of the witch-doctor. When medicines were administered to the patient for the purpose of driving out a spirit, they were usually unpleasant and revolting by nature, frequently compounded of various sorts of animal and human excreta; evil-smelling herbs were also employed, and perhaps plants with specific but drastic action, such as castor oil seeds, while other herbs were employed for purely magical reasons. There was no trace of rational medicine; the administration of substances to produce a specific pharmacological action was unthinkable.

Surgery existed at three levels. First, a crude knowledge of anatomy was helpful in killing and preparing animals for food. Secondly, wounds received in battle or the chase were obviously bandaged and given some sort of first aid. Thirdly, ritual operations were carried out. As the latter were, to some extent at least, tests of endurance and evidence of manhood, anaesthesia was undesirable.

In many parts of the world, trephined skulls are found dating back to neolithic times. It has been suggested that this was done for the treatment of headache; it seems more probable that it was for the evacuation of an obstinate demon, who might manifest his presence in many other ways, such as madness or delirium, or it may have been a purely magical rite: the removed discs of bone were often used as amulets. No such skulls have been discovered in the Nile Valley or in Mesopotamia.

The inevitable conclusion is that, in the pre-historic era, there was no knowledge of pain-allaying drugs; the rational basis of pharmacology was entirely lacking, and medicine was purely magical in nature.

B. The Magico-Empiric Age (c. 3000–585 B.C.)

Sometime about the end of the fourth millennium B.C., the great civilizations of the Nile Valley and of Mesopotamia came into existence. While there are many points of resemblance between these two cultures, there was one important difference: in Mesopotamia there was constant rivalry between city states, now one and now another being dominant, while in the Nile Valley the government was centralized, the whole of Egypt being under one authority, save for comparatively short periods.

The major part of our knowledge of Egyptian medicine is derived from a number of papyri, most important of which is the Ebers Papyrus, which was written in the XVIIIth Dynasty (about 1500 B.C.), but was undoubtedly copied from much older sources. From this alone we are able to form a good idea of the state of Egyptian medical knowledge, while the other papyri, earlier and later, substantiate our ideas. The continuance of a central government, coupled with Egyptian reverence for the past, led to a relatively static state of culture, and, during the period under consideration, medicine changed but little. Egypt attained a high level of culture early in her history, but she failed to show great advances afterwards.

Egyptian medicine was compounded of two elements: magic and rational methods. The action of some drugs (e.g. the diuresis caused by juniper berries) was known, but magical rites always accompanied their administration, and often drugs were omitted, treatment being by magic alone. Diseases were still personified, and thought to be due to the presence of a god or goddess in the patient. Surgery seems to have been limited to circumcision and to the first aid treatment of wounds and fractures. The use of "plaster" casts, made of gums and so forth, for the treatment of fractures was highly rational.

The knowledge of anatomy was very limited: the same word was used for veins, arteries, nerves, and muscles. There was, however, some idea of the gross details of the larger viscera, since these were removed in the process of embalming. As, however, the men who were employed to do the evisceration of corpses were considered to be polluted and outcast, the influence of embalming on anatomical knowledge was very slight.

The Egyptians used many drugs: unfortunately, only a few of them can be identified. There is no evidence that they used any anaesthetic or pain-allaying drugs, and such carvings and frescoes as depict surgical operations always indicate a fully conscious patient.

The Mesopotamian cultures developed a system of medicine that was very similar to that of Egypt. Diseases were caused by demons, special demons being responsible for definite diseases, some degree of diagnosis being made, e.g. "wasting disease", "liver disease". Apparently, the physicians were priests. Surgery seems to have been in the hands of craftsmen: in the Code of Khammurabi (about 1700 B.C.) the rewards for successful, and punishments for unsuccessful, operations are laid down, but no attempt is made to regulate the activities of physicians.

The Mesopotamian list of drugs is large, and, as in Egypt, some of them had therapeutic properties. Some crude knowledge of anatomy existed, fostered, no doubt, by the custom of divination from the entrails, especially the liver, of animals. Medicine marched hand in hand with magic, and what rational treatment was adopted was purely empiric. There is no evidence that anaesthetics were attempted or that pain-relieving drugs were known. Some authorities claim that the Assyrians were familiar with mandragora, a Greek word which they derive from Assyrian nam-ta-ira, but the argument seems unconvincing.

According to Hoffman (*De Thorace*, *1625*) the Assyrians were accustomed to compress the vessels in the neck in order to produce insensibility during the operation of circumcision. In the seventeenth century, knowledge of Assyria was scant, and the Assyrian language was undecipherable. Hoffman's remark has been copied by subsequent authors, but may safely be disregarded as without foundation.

Astronomical observations were made and recorded with great assiduity by the Mesopotamians, who developed a system of counting based on the unit 60. This is the origin of our subdivisions of the hour (60 minutes each of 60 seconds) and of the circle (360 degrees each of 60 minutes, each minute being 60 seconds). Both at the time of the French Revolution and of the Nazi hegemony, attempts were made to subdivide the circle into 400 degrees, but the hand of Sumer was not to be wrested from astronomical studies.

The Hebrew culture sprang to life in Palestine, under the influence of both Egypt and Mesopotamia. In medicine, the Hebrews made great advances in hygiene, but surgery and therapeutics remained respectively primitive and superstitious. Anaesthesia was unknown, although, at a later date, mandrakes seem to have been credited with magical properties. The great contribution which they gave to the world was, of course, monotheism.

It must be realized that the dates given in the chronology below are not final. Archaeologists frequently revise their schemes of dates, and the older the period, the greater the chance of error. The dates here given are usually in accord with Allbright (*Bulletin of the American Schools of Oriental Research*, 1942, 88, 32).

B.C.

c. 2900. Old Egyptian Kingdom : beginning of the Ist Dynasty with King Menes.
c. 2800. Beginning of the Early Sumerian Dynastic Period.
c. 2700. Tjeser (Zoser), first king of the Egyptian IIIrd Dynasty.
c. 2600. Building of the Great Pyramid by King Khufu (Cheops).

The Early Sumerian Dynastic Period began after a great flood had inundated the Mesopotamian region, and evidence of this was discovered at Ur. King Tjeser had, as his "vizier" the Priest-Physician Imhotep, who is believed to have been the architect of the first Egyptian pyramid (the step-pyramid at Saqqara). Imhotep was greatly revered in after ages, and, by the end of the Magico-Empiric Age, had received his apotheosis as God of Healing.

c. 2360. Sargon of Akkad becomes master of Babylonia.
c. 2200–1989. Intermediate period of collapse of central government in Egypt (VIIth-XIth Dynasties).
c. 2180. Babylonia overrun by the Gutians (King Gudea).
c. 1989–1776. The Middle Kingdom of Egypt.
c. 1960–1830. Frequent Elamite and Amorite invasions of Babylonia.
c. 1935. The migration of Abraham from Ur (anachronistically called "of the Chaldees" in the Bible) may have occurred at about this time.
c. 1830. The Old Babylonian Period begins.
c. 1776–1570. Intermediate period of collapse of central government in Egypt.

It was during this last period (1776–1570) that the Hyksos made themselves masters of Egypt. In the past, the word has been translated as "Shepherd Kings", but it is now known that this is an error, and that the real meaning is "Foreign Kings". Some have gone so far as to identify the Hyksos with the Israelites, but this is certainly wrong, although little is known about them. They probably originated in Asia Minor.

28

Cuneiform tablets found at Nippur in Babylonia describe the treatment of dental decay by the local application of a gum containing, among other things, seeds of henbane. It is perhaps stretching a point too far to call this, as does Major (*op. cit.*), "the earliest record of local anaesthesia". That author dates the tablets to about 2250 B.C., but this is almost certainly several hundred years too soon.

c. 1748–1716.   Shamshi-Adad I, King of Assyria.
c. 1728–1676.   Khammurabi, King of Babylonia.

It is about the time of Khammurabi that the name "Habiru" begins to appear in Mesopotamian inscriptions, and some have seen in this name the earliest allusions to the Hebrews.

A black diorite stela, some 6 feet tall, inscribed with the Code of Khammurabi, has been found at Susa, whither it had presumably been taken by raiding Elamites. The stela is headed by a relief of Khammurabi receiving the Law from the Sun-God. Underneath are nearly three hundred paragraphs, some of which refer to the duties, fees, and responsibilities of surgeons. It is difficult to believe that the brutal punishments awarded to unsuccessful practitioners can have been intended to be inflicted in ordinary cases. For instance, if the opening of an abscess in the eye were followed by loss of sight, the surgeon's fingers were to be cut off. There is no evidence of any form of anaesthesia in the Code, nor is anything related referring to physicians.

c. 1570–1150.   The New Empire of Egypt. Aames, the first king of the XVIIIth Dynasty. Thothmes the Great extends Egyptian rule to the Euphrates.

It is to the earlier part of this period (*c.* 1550) that the Ebers Papyrus is to be assigned, although the language in which it was written shows that it was undoubtedly copied from works of a much earlier date. It consists of a list of prescriptions for various diseases, which are named, but no guide is given as to diagnosis. There are many mentions of magical rites. It may have been a "Handy Home Doctor", rather than a physician's text.

Other medical papyri have also been discovered: the Ramasseum Papyri (XIIth Dynasty); the Kahûn Papyrus, which is mainly gynaecological, of about the same date; the Hearst, the Edwin Smith, and the London (all XVIIIth Dynasty); the Berlin (XIXth Dynasty); and the nineteen Chester Beatty Papyri (XXth Dynasty). All show a strong predilection for magic, and no mention is made of anaesthesia or opiates, but it must be borne in mind that translation is often difficult or impossible, especially since many are damaged and some are only fragmentary. For example, the word "Didi", at first translated as "Mandrake", is now known to have been a mineral (haemitite).

c. 1400. The Exodus is usually dated at about this time.
c. 1377. Accession of Amenhotep IV (the "heretic" King Akhnaten) to the throne of Egypt. Subbilluliuma, King of the Hittites. Ashuruballit I, King of Assyria.
c. 1301–1234. Rameses II (the Great): XIXth Dynasty. The Empire maintained by constant fighting. The Temple of Karnak, which dwarfs St. Peter's at Rome, and many other colossal building projects undertaken in Egypt.
c. 1250. The Children of Israel come into the Promised Land. (Palestinian Early Iron Age.)

It was during the reigns of Amenhotep IV (Akhnaten) and his father that the collection of "Tell-el-Amarna" letters was made. These describe graphically how the Empire was being threatened, and how, among others, the Habiru were attacking Palestine from the East.

Tutankhamen, originally called Tutankhaten, succeeded Akhnaten after a short interval. An attempt has been made to identify him with the Pharoah of the Exodus, but this is unlikely. Unfortunately, Egyptian records are completely silent about the presence of the Israelites in Egypt. Oriental-

Figure 1. Circumcision, from an Egyptian tomb. As with other scenes depicting surgical operations in ancient Egypt, there is obviously no attempt to produce anaesthesia.

Figure 2. The stele of Khammurabi (*c.* 1750 B.C.), on which the rewards for successful, and the penalties for unsuccessful surgical operations are detailed.

ists of an earlier age placed the Exodus in the reign of Rameses II, but it is difficult to fit the catastrophes associated in the Old Testament with the events which led up to the departure of the Children of Israel into the known history and pattern of the reign of a king surnamed "the Great". The problem has not been solved.

c. 1150. The decline of Egyptian power (XXIst Dynasty). The Seige of Troy may be assigned to this period.
c. 1000. David, King of Israel, makes Jerusalem his capital.
c. 950. Solomon builds the Temple in Jerusalem.
c. 950–900. The Homeric Period.

Although the Odyssey was not written down until a much later period, the poem probably altered little. The herb "Moly", perhaps the earliest ancestor of the mandrake, is mentioned in the tenth book. Kirke has turned Odysseus' men into swine; he sets forth to rescue them and is met by the god Hermes, who offers him the herb, whereby he may overcome the magic of Kirke. The plant is described with some minuteness, "It was black at the root, but the flower was like to milk. 'Moly' the gods call it, but it is hard for mortal man to dig, howbeit, with the gods, all things are possible".

c. 883–859. Ashur-nasir-pal II makes Assyria an armed camp.
847. The foundation of Carthage.
776. Greek chronology begins with the first Olympiad.
753. Roman chronology begins with the foundation of the city of Rome.
744–727. Tiglath-Pileser III, King of Assyria and conqueror of Babylonia, over-runs Palestine and deports many of the Israelites.
704–681. Sennacherib, King of Assyria. He besieges Jerusalem, but raises the seige, perhaps on account of an outbreak of bubonic plague.
c. 700. Isaiah, the prophet.
669–633. Ashurbanipal, King of Assyria.

It was Ashur-nasir-pal II who began the reign of terror which was to make the cruelty of the Assyrians a byword. Two hundred years later, the Assyrians were becoming a more cultured race. Ashurbanipal gathered a huge library, many of the "books" being copies of older texts, some very old. Among them are no less than 800 medical prescriptions, including one for toothache, a local application not dissimilar from that discovered at Nippur, but containing, among several ingredients, mustard! The prescriptions are largely magical, and incantations are scattered freely among them.

c. 624–565. Thales of Miletus, founder of Greek science.
612. Fall of the Assyrian empire. Nineveh destroyed by the Medes and Persians.
594. Solon codifies Athenian Law.
587. Destruction of Jerusalem by Nebuchadnezzar II of Babylon.
539. Babylon falls to Cyrus, the Persian; the end of the Babylonian Captivity.

C. THE SCIENTIFIC AGE (585 B.C.–A.D. 200).

The prediction by Thales of an eclipse of the sun in 585 B.C. marks the beginning of the rise of Greek science, which, in medicine, was to come to an end with the death of Galen. The attitude of the Greek philosophers to life in general was quickly reflected in the physician's attitude to disease : the natural history of disease was studied and rational treatment was instituted. Because the causation and nature of disease were often misunderstood, the treatment was frequently incorrect, although it was nevertheless rational.

Parallel with the treatment of disease by physicians, magical treatment by priests was also carried on in temples erected for the worship of Asklepios. Here, again, treatment became more rational, employing baths, physiotherapy and some degree of "mental rehabilitation", but the essentially magical nature of treatment in the Asklepieia must not be forgotten. The final defeat of the Persians ensured the success of rational medicine in its fight against superstition.

Greek medicine reached its first peak in the time of Hippocrates of Cos, and much evidence of its modernity in outlook is to be found in the Hippocratic writings, the majority, if not all, of which were written by members of the "Hippocratic" school; they certainly reflect the teachings of the "Father of Medicine". From Asia Minor, Greek medicine spread to, and flourished in, Athens during the Golden Age of Pericles, which ended with the plague and the Spartan victory. Later the conquests of Alexander the Great, whose father had brought all Greece under his rule, led to the founding of Alexandria, with its "University". Here Greek medicine reached its second peak with Erasistratus of Chios and Herophilus of Chalcedon. Hitherto, respect for the dead had prevented human dissection, although the bodies of animals had been frequently examined. Now, for the first time, human anatomy was closely inspected.

The conquest of Greece, and later Egypt, by the Romans, shifted the medical centre to Rome, but the light of Alexandria still burned, although not so brightly as of yore. The interest of Rome in war and conquest attracted those with medical leanings to the post of military surgeon, a craft which, even in those days, was considered separate from, and of a lower social status than that of physician. The physicians were mainly Greeks, and wrote in that language (e.g. Asklepiades and Galen). The only medical works in Latin which have come down to us are the *De re medicina* of Celsus and the *Historia Naturalis* of Pliny, both written in the first century A.D. It is here that mandragora makes its appearance in medical literature.

Galen was the last great physician of the scientific era, and this was in part his own fault. A prolific author, he wrote more than 100 books, and he influenced posterity to a greater degree than any other medical man. His dogmatism and the teleology of his ideas would have smothered scientific spirit in suitable surroundings: the spreading of Christianity was not favourable to science, while, in Arabia, Islam also resisted scientific advance. Thus Galen remained the supreme authority until the Renaissance.

Greeks and Romans alike seem to have had no knowledge of anaesthesia, although the soothing and pain-relieving attributes of opium were appreciated certainly in the fourth century B.C., and probably earlier. Belief in the narcotic power of mandrake sprang up towards the end of the scientific era, while opium seems to have been less and less used. Mandragora will, however, be dealt with in the next section, where it logically belongs.

c. 624–565. Thales of Miletus.
c. 580–500. Pythagoras.

Pythagoras may be regarded as the originator of the doctrine of the four elements and the four qualities, which was later applied to medicine. The four humours were Blood (like Fire, hot and dry), Phlegm (like Water, cold and wet), Yellow Bile (like Air, hot and wet), and Black Bile (like Earth, cold and dry). These humours regulated the functions of the body, disease being caused by an upset in their proper proportions. Treatment was by opposites; later, therefore, herbals listed drugs and plants as being "dry and cold", or "wet", and so on "to such-and-such a degree", to indicate the sort of complaint for which they would be suitable. The theory received much support from Aristotle. Erasistratus (c. 300 B.C.) modified the theory because he believed that the majority of diseases were caused by a plethora, or local excess of blood. His successors turned to blood-letting as a logical means of treatment.

509. Expulsion of the Tarquins from Rome and the foundation of the Roman Republic.
496–406. Sophocles, the great tragedian.
490. The battle of Marathon : the Persian army defeated by the Greeks under Miltiades.
480. The battle of Salamis : the great naval battle in which the fleet of Xerxes was destroyed by the Greeks.
c. 480–425. Herodotus, the first historian.
469–399. Socrates.

From Xenophon, a contemporary of Socrates, we learn that the latter was aware of the sedative action of opium, and this seems to be the first intimation which has reached us of the medical use of this substance.

c. 460.   Birth of Hippocrates on the island of Cos.

Hippocrates, the Father of Medicine, founded a school of medical thought which depended mainly on two points: accurate observation and recording of the signs, symptoms and progress of disease, and the adoption of such remedial methods as could do no harm, thus fostering the "healing power of nature". His followers produced a number of books, collectively known as the corpus Hippocraticum, some of which may even be by the master himself. His name survives in the "Facies Hippocratica", and the Hippocratic Oath still remains the foundation of medical ethics throughout the world. He is thought to have lived to a ripe old age.

c. 450.   The time of Nehemiah in Jerusalem.

About this time, the Hexateuch (i.e. the Pentateuch and the Book of Joshua) was compiled from earlier documents. The account of the birth of Eve (Genesis ii, 21) has been used as evidence of anaesthesia at an early date. It seems much more likely, however, that the sleep which was cast upon Adam was a device to keep God's secrets, rather than that the human chronicler had any idea of surgical anaesthesia. There is no evidence that the Israelites used any form of pain-relief.

The Hebrew word "Dodaim", translated in the Bible (Genesis xxx, 14–17) as "Mandrakes", applies to a plant which had a magical significance in connexion with fertility.

443–429.   Pericles rules in Athens; the Golden Age.
427–348.   Plato.
404.   Athens falls to Sparta.
384–322.   Aristotle.

Plato was a disciple of Socrates, and was the founder of the Academy. The views which he taught concerning the soul and the universe led to the belief that the body, or micro-cosm, and the heavens, or macrocosm, were interdependent, thus supporting the application of astrology to medicine.

In the year 342, Aristotle was appointed tutor to Alexander, later the Great, then a boy of about 14 years of age. Aristotle made great discoveries in comparative anatomy and embryology, studying the development of the chicken, and dissecting and describing the natural history of many animals and fish with remarkable accuracy. Although he had no comprehension of the theory of evolution, his "Ladder of Nature", in which he arranged plants and animals in an ascending scale of complexity, was the first step towards the evolutionary idea.

382–322.   Demosthenes, Athenian orator and statesman.
c. 371–287.   Theophrastus, the "Father of Botany".
323.   The death of Alexander the Great.
c. 300.   Herophilus of Chalcedon; Erasistratus of Chios.

Demosthenes is reported as saying in one of his speeches that the lethargy of the Athenians resembled "sleep induced by mandragora or some other narcotic". This same plant is also mentioned by Theophrastus, who also described the opium poppy.

On the death of Alexander the Great, the empire which he had created fell to pieces, the Seleucids obtaining the East, and the Ptolemies, Egypt. The city of Alexandria had been founded by Alexander in 331, and here Ptolemy I Soter began a great library, to which, in succeeding years, the learned of the ancient world resorted in large numbers. Alexandria, therefore, has some claims to be regarded as the seat of the first university in the world. It was here that Herophilus acquired fame as an anatomist, carrying out human dissections in public. He was probably the first to regard the brain as the central organ of the nervous system. His younger con-temporary, Erasistratus, recognized the function of the muscles, and tried to explain respiration in terms of the

"Pneuma", an almost non-material substance in air which was the cause of life. His theory of disease, as caused by a plethora, has already been mentioned. He emphasized the dangers of opium.

168.	The revolt of Judas Maccabeus against the Seleucids.
146.	The conquest of Greece by Rome; the fall of Carthage.
70–19.	Virgil.
63.	Pompey extends the Roman boundaries to the Euphrates.
58.	Julius Caesar makes the Rhine the Roman frontier in the North.
55 & 54.	Caesar in Britain.
31.	Octavian (Augustus) defeats the fleets of Antony and Cleopatra at Actium. Their suicide brings to an end the Ptolemaic rule in Egypt, which now becomes a Roman Province.
4.	Death of Herod the Great.
A.D.	
26–36.	Pontius Pilate, Procurator of Judea.
23–79.	Caius Plinius Secundus (Pliny the Elder).
37–c. 100.	Flavius Josephus, Jewish statesman and soldier.
c. 30–40.	Issue of the *De Re Medicina* by Celsus.
55–117.	Tacitus.
64.	Traditional date of the martyrdom of St. Peter and St. Paul.
68.	Death of Nero.
c. 100.	Issue of the Herbal of Dioscorides.

Pliny the Elder was a prolific author; among other works, he wrote the famous *Historia Naturalis*, which was dedicated to Titus in 77 and was issued largely posthumously; it was translated into English in 1601. Pliny died in the eruption of Mount Somma (the lower summit of Vesuvius) which overwhelmed Pompeii, Herculaneum and Stabbia in 79, and which was described by his nephew, Pliny the Younger. The *Historia Naturalis*, in 37 books, contains a vast amount of miscellaneous knowledge, but the author was entirely undiscriminating: he wrote down everything that came to hand from old wives' tales to personal observations. His account of the Mandrake mentions its use for diseases of the eyes, and describes, inadequately for the purposes of recognition, the two forms of the plant, male and female. He writes that "Persons when about to gather the plant take every precaution not to have the wind blowing in their faces; and, after tracing three circles round it with a sword, turn towards the West and dig it up". Directions are given for the extraction of the juice, which has the power to strike some people dumb. A dangerous poison, the juice can nevertheless be used as a narcotic before incisions are made in the body; it can also be used for snakebites and as an emetic. Pliny also notes the soporific action of opium, but he does not approve of its use.

The writings of Josephus comprise the *Antiquities of the Jews* and the *Wars of the Jews*. It is in the latter (Bk. 7, Chap. 6, Sec. 3) that he describes the plant, Baaras, which seems to be extremely similar to the mandrake, although without the latter's soporific action. The method of obtaining it by means of a dog, later the standard procedure in uprooting mandrakes, is here described for the first time.

The *De Re Medicina* of Celsus was the first classical medical work to be printed (1478); it was probably chosen so early on account of the purity of its Latin. Celsus was not a physician, and this book is all that remains of a far larger encyclopaedia of natural science, the rest of which has not survived. Celsus mentions the soporific quality of the poppy (Bk. 2, Chap. 32), and he recommends mandrake as an ingredient in an eye ointment (Bk. 6, Chap. 6).

Pedanius (or Pedacius) Dioscorides lived in Anazarba in Cilicia. There is some doubt about his date, but there is no adequate reason for believing that he was ever a surgeon in the army of Nero, as some modern authors state. His book leans heavily on Pliny and on other early writers, and his accounts of the poppy and the mandrake are obviously drawn from the *Historia Naturalis*. He was, however, a physician, and is apparently the first medical man to describe the soporific effect of mandragora (mandrake). His use of the word "anaesthesia" has already been mentioned (p. 16).

117–138. Hadrian.
c. 130–200. Galen of Pergamum.

Galen, incorrectly named Claudius Galen by early writers who misunderstood the prefix "Cl" invariably given him (for "Clarissimus", "most famous"), remained the colossus of medicine throughout the Dark and Middle Ages, and the system of anatomy, medicine and physiology which he formulated continued to be authoritative even after Vesalius and the anatomists in the 16th century, and William Harvey in the 17th, had exposed the fallacies of his ideas. His more than 100 works, all dogmatic and plausible, played their part in preventing further scientific investigation in medicine for 1,300 years. Educated at Alexandria, he came to Rome and became physician to the Emperor Marcus Aurelius. Among his recommendations was a paste containing opium as an application for toothache: opium has no local analgesic action.

D. THE AGE OF SUPERSTITION (A.D. 200–1454).

This period, from the death of Galen to the invention of movable type by Gutenberg, is contemporaneous with the decline and fall of the Roman Empire: Constantinople fell to the Turks in 1453. With the death of Galen, Graeco-Roman medical science may be said to have come to an abrupt end. What medical authors there were contented themselves with writing commentaries on the works of Galen, which were kept alive, at least in Byzantium (Constantinople) after the transference of the seat of government thither from Rome in A.D. 330. However, the anarchical state of the rest of Europe led to a rapid decline in learning, and the Greek texts could no longer be read outside the domains of the Eastern Roman Empire. Grossly distorted translations of excerpts from such classical authors as Aristotle and Galen passed current for true learning, while much ingenuity was wasted in syllogistic quibbles about these texts. Observation was no longer used: what the ancients had written was true, and, if observation differed, observation was wrong. For instance, anatomical dissection ceased and was replaced by reading the Galenic texts, although Galen himself had probably never dissected a human being. This is the period of scholastic authoritarianism.

Three other forces also militated against science at this time: Religion, Astrology and Alchemy. The spread of Christianity in Europe with its answers to all problems, spiritual as well as temporal, disposed men to think of the world to come rather than the world in being. Furthermore, the accepted implication of religion was that pain and disease, like famine or poverty, were punishments prescribed by God for wickedness, either of the sufferer or of mankind at large. There was, therefore, something sacrilegious in attempting to fight disease or to prevent pain. It must not be forgotten, however, that, in Western Europe at least, the Church was the sole repository of learning, the preservation of which was later to bear fruit. Until after the Reformation the Church had a vested interest in fostering antipathy to science, and she virtually forbade all experimental investigation; thus it was only at the risk of a charge of heresy that the doctrines of Aristotle (a heathen) could be challenged. This had a close bearing on the second factor, Astrology, for the close interdependence between Microcosm (Man) and Macrocosm (the Universe) which Aristotle had postulated came to be interpreted as meaning that wordly events could be foretold by the movements of the heavenly bodies, and there are certain passages in the Bible which will support such a construction. Such belief could not but be fatal to scientific enquiry.

Alchemy, the theoretical basis of which was laid down towards the end of the first millennium in the Moslem Empire, spread to Europe, partly as a result of the Crusades. Being a scientific investigation, it came into conflict with the Church, and, being based on false premises, weakened the cause of science still further.

The establishment of Christianity as the Roman official religion was soon followed by the growth of heresies: many of the heretics migrated rather than conform, and thus the Nestorians (Monophysites) carried into Asia Minor and the Near East the works of Galen in Greek. Later came the flood of Moslem conquest, followed in due course by the great period of Moslem culture. Galen's works were translated into Arabic, and commentaries were written on them by such men as Rhazes and Avicenna. These translations were infinitely better than anything available in Western Europe, and they were gratefully accepted when they began to appear in Latin, a further translation which was facilitated by contacts with the Moslem Empire, not only by the Crusades, but also in Spain, the southern two-thirds of which was Moorish, and in Sicily. The improved texts of Galen stimulated learning but not observation, for scholastic authoritarianism was still the ruling force and was to remain so until the Renaissance. However, a greater appreciation of what Galen and others had actually written became apparent, and schools of learning (universities) began to be founded, first in Italy and then elsewhere.

From this it can be seen that there was little possibility of an extension of medical knowledge during this period of twelve and a half centuries; indeed, there had been a diminution of it through over-emphasis on the wrong things. Furthermore, the inadequacy of the description of plants led to obvious difficulties, the more so as *Herbals* written, for example, in Asia Minor, were used in France and elsewhere where the flora was very different. The systematic identification of plants was, of course, not yet conceivable.

MANDRAGORA

We have seen the first reference to mandrakes and mandrake-like plants in Homer and the Bible. References multiply as time passes and begin to appear in medical works at the end of the scientific period, usually copied from Pliny, whose "authority", although he was not a medical man, was great. The adoption of the mandrake in medicine, chiefly as a soporific, was parallel to its use socially in magic. That no such plant exists, or ever did exist, in no way interfered with this. The finding of any anthropomorphic root blended well with earlier tales, and fantastic stories about the dangers and difficulties of obtaining specimens explained the absence of supplies. Later the name *atropa mandragora* was to be given to a plant of the family of Solanaceae, and this added to the confusion of thought about mandrakes.

As we have seen, primitive man naturally turns to magic in his attempts to master disease, and sympathetic magic, in which, for instance, a stone like a tooth can cure dental disease, is a method which has had its appeal in all ages. The outstanding feature of the mandrake is its anthropomorphism, and this human shape led automatically to belief in its magical properties. Andrew Lang has summed up well the medieval ideas about this impossible root in *Custom and Myth* (1893): "He who desires to possess a mandrake must stop his ears with wax, so that he may not hear the deadly yells which the plant utters as it is being dragged from the earth. Then, before sunrise on a Friday, the amateur goes out with a dog, 'all black', makes three crosses round the mandrake, loosens the soil about the root, ties the root to the dog's tail and offers the beast a piece of bread. The dog runs at the bread, drags out the mandrake root, and falls dead, killed by the horrible yell of the plant. The root is now taken up, washed in wine, wrapped in silk, laid in a casket, bathed every Friday, and clothed in a little new white smock every new moon. The mandrake acts, if thus considerately treated, as a kind of familiar spirit, 'Every piece of coin put to her overnight is found double in the morning'".

All this is similar to belief in the healing power of the unicorn's horn, and strange tales about impossible animals and the methods of catching them, which passed for truth in those credulous days. Belief in magic was, of course, universal; the mandrake was especially magical in nature, and its use in medicine was merely one instance out of many in which magic and superstition were introduced into therapeutics. (For further evidence see the entry "1431. Execution of Joan of Arc" below.)

Very occasionally rational attempts at pain relief were employed in the "Age of Superstition", but these events failed to influence mankind and played no part in the discovery of anaesthesia. The statements by John Arderne, Theodoric and others, must not be taken at their face value. The methods which they describe were merely amplifications of the tales by Pliny and Dioscorides, and depend on "authority", not on personal observation. In this regard, Arderne's *Treatise of Fistula in Ano, etc.*, although describing a method of pain relief (which would not have worked), also describes how his patients were restrained at operation.

c. 220–230.   Hua-T'o, Chinese surgeon.

According to the *Kou-kin-i-tong*, Hua-T'o successfully used a preparation called "mayo" in order to induce surgical anaesthesia. Unfortunately, the *Kou-kin-i-tong* is dated some thirteen or fourteen centuries after Hua-T'o, and cannot, therefore, be relied upon as evidence.

c. 250.   Issue of the *De Animalium Natura* of Claudius
        Ælianus.
c. 300–373.   St. Athanasius.
303.   Martyrdom of St. Cosmas and St. Damian.

The date of the birth of St. Athanasius is usually given as 296, but may have been as late as 326; the creed which bears his name is probably of the 5th century.

Saints Cosmas and Damian, who perished in the persecution of Diocletian, later became the patron saints of Medicine and Pharmacy respectively. They were held in special honour by the Confraternity of Surgeons in Paris, and are remembered in the name of the College of St. Côme.

318.   Arian controversy begins.
325.   The first great Church Council, held at Nicaea.
330.   Constantine removes the seat of government from Rome to Byzantium, renamed Constantinople.
335.   The closure of the temples in Constantinople by order of Constantine. Among those closed were the Asklepieia.
361–363.   Julian the Apostate, Emperor of Byzantium, tries to re-establish the pagan religion.
395.   St. Augustine (354–430) becomes Bishop of Hippo in North Africa.
c. 400.   Issue of the *Herbal* of Apuleius (Lucius Apuleius Barbarus).

Ælianus (c. 250), in his *De Animalium Natura*, had been the first to apply Josephus' story of the use of a dog to uproot the Baaras to the mandrake. Apuleius copied this account and referred to the mandrake in a manner which remains fairly constant in future medical works. His *Herbal* was frequently re-issued and translated into many languages.

410.   Alaric the Visi-Goth sacks Rome.
431.   Deposition of Nestorius, Patriarch of Constantinople, starts the Nestorian schism. The Nestorians carried the Greek classical works to Asia, where they were later translated into Arabic, and filtered back into Europe, as described above.
449.   The Saxons settle in Britain.
452.   Attila the Hun.
493.   Theodoric the Ostro-Goth tries to establish a civilized kingdom in Italy.
c. 502–565. Aëtius of Amida, the first Christian physician of note. Mandrake is mentioned in his *Tetrabiblion*.
c. 570–636. Isidorus, Bishop of Seville. He mentions the pre-operative use of mandragora wine.
622.   Muhammad (born 571) flees from Mecca to Medina (the Hajira, or flight, from which the Moslem calendar is dated). Since the Moslem calendar is lunar, not solar, conversion of dates to the European calendars is not easy.

625–690. Paul of Ægina, the last Byzantine surgeon of note.
634. St. Aidan.
644. Moslem conquest of Egypt.
661. The Umayyad Caliphate begins; Damascus now the capital of the Arab world.
672–735. The Venerable Bede, first English historian.
705–718. The Moslems conquer North Africa, Sicily and Spain.
732. Charles Martel defeats the Arabs at the Battle of Tours.
750. The 'Abbasid Caliphate begins; Baghdad becomes the capital of the Eastern Arab Empire.
756. Establishment of the Umayyad Western Caliphate at Gordova.
776. Jābir ibn Hayyān.

During the reign of Harūn ar-Rasheed at Baghdad, Jābir ibn Hayyān flourished in the town of al-Kūfah; his name is given in some modern works on anaesthetics as "Djafar Yeber", and he was known to the ancients as "Geberus". He was the "Father of Alchemy", and began the search for the mystical substance which would transmute base metals into gold. He is the reputed author of many treatises, some of which were translated into Latin. In one of these translations there is an interpolated passage, absent from the Arabic original, describing the manufacture of "oleum vitreoli" (sulphuric acid). This led to the belief at the end of the 19th century that Jābir was the discoverer of "oleum vitreoli dulce" (ethyl ether). (See Appendix A for further discussion.)

800. Charlemagne, King of the Franks, rules from the Elbe to the Ebro.
850–923. Rhazes.

Abu-Bakr Muhammad ibn Zakariya, known from his place of birth, as Rhazes, was probably the greatest and most original of all the Moslem physicians, and he was also one of the most prolific as an author. He was the first to distinguish between measles and smallpox.

c. 850. Compilation of the Bamburg *Antidotarium*.

The *Antidotarium* contains an account of the "spongia somnifera", made by steeping a sponge in a decoction of many herbs, including mandrake. Inhalation of the fumes from the sponge was said to produce unconsciousness. A similar recipe is found in the Codex of the Abbey of Monte Cassino, which had been founded by St. Benedict in 529. Since the drugs used were not volatile, the prescription could have been of little use : perhaps it never was used.

855.   The Northmen begin to settle in France and England.
871–901. Alfred the Great.
962.   Otho the German becomes Roman Emperor of the West.
980–1037. Avicenna.

Avicenna (Ibn Sina) was the most illustrious Arab physician after Rhazes. His *Canon of Medicine* was mainly a recapitulation of Galenic writings, and was in great demand up to the time of the renaissance in medicine. He repeats the usual nonsense about mandragora, omitting the dog. However, he thought poppy extract to be a better sedative. His contemporary, Haly Abbas ('Ali ibn al-Abbas), who died in 994, was the author of *al-Kitab al-Maliki* (the *Liber Regius* of Europeans) and of the *Thesaurus of Medicine*. His greatest contribution to medicine was the proof that, in the act of parturition, the child does not come out by its own efforts, but is pushed out by the muscular contractions of the uterus. Slightly later, Albucasis (Abu al-Qasim), who flourished *c.* 1050, wrote *The Method* which was to become the standard text-book of surgery.

1001.   Moslem conquest of Northern Hindustan.
c. 1050. Compilation of the *Lacnunga*.

This Saxon Leechbook, compiled by a monk shortly before the Norman Conquest, contains a host of incantations and charms for the treatment of disease. Among much that is purely superstitious, there are a few rational ideas, one of which is that chilling a part by the application of cold water deadens the pain of opening an abscess. This seems to be the first recorded use of refrigeration anaesthesia.

Figure 3. Asklepiades of Bithynia (124–56 B.C.), who was the first to describe the operation of tracheotomy. From a bust in the Capitoline Museum, Rome.

Figure 4. A reconstruction of the Asklepieion at Cos (4th cent. B.C.).

Figure 5. Mandrakes, from the Codex Neapolitanus (early 7th cent. A.D.).

1066.   William the Conqueror defeats Harold at the Battle of Hastings.
1095.   Peter the Hermit preaches the Crusade.
1098–1179. "St." Hildegarde of Bingen.
1098.   The capture of Jerusalem by the Crusaders.
1126–98 Averroës.
1135–1204. Maimonides.

"St." Hildegarde, in her book, De Plantis, described the mandrake at considerable length. "Being formed", she says, "of the moistened earth wherewith Adam was created", it has magical properties.

Averroës (ibn Rushd) was one of the great physicians of the Western Caliphate and did much to aid the spread of Aristotelian ideas from Arabia to Europe. He knew that smallpox conferred immunity from future attacks. His work as a physician was, however, eclipsed by his reputation as a philosopher.

Maimonides (Moshe ben Maimon) was court physician to Saladin (Salahud-Dìn) and pre-eminent among Jewish medical men of all ages. Like ibn Rushd, he was even more respected as a philosopher than as a physician.

1137.   Foundation of St. Bartholomew's Hospital in London by Rahere.
c. 1140. Nicolaus Salernitanus revives the "spongia somnifera" in his Antidotarium.
1162.   The first use of heraldry in England (the Great Seal of Henry II).
1170.   The murder of Thomas à Becket at the Altar of Canterbury Cathedral.
1187.   Jerusalem falls to the Moslems. The diminishing Frankish kingdom survives for a further century.
1200.   Charter delivered to the University of Oxford.
1205–96. Theodoric Borgognoni.

The Cyrurgia of Theodoric describes a method of surgery which approaches to the aseptic. His description of the "spongia somnifera" is very well known and is quoted in all histories of anaesthesia. Ugone di Lucca (Hugo of Lucca),

D   47

his teacher, and, perhaps, father, died in 1252. The description of the "mandrake broth" is presumably derived from the *Antidotarium* of Nicolaus Salernitanus.

1214–94 Roger Bacon.
1214. At the Battle of Bouvines, King John loses all his French possessions.
1215. Magna Carta sealed by King John at Runnymede.
1216. St. Francis of Assisi and St. Dominic found orders of friars; they meet.
1227–74 St. Thomas Aquinas.
1234–1315. Raymond Lull or Lully.
1256–1326. Mondino.

Lully is said to have described a substance which he called "oleum vitreoli dulce", but Keys (op. cit.) could find no evidence of this on searching his works (see Appendix A).

Mondino became professor of anatomy at Bologna in 1306. He carried out his first public dissection of the human body in 1315, and this occasion marks the revival of interest in anatomy.

1265–1321. Dante.
c. 1285. Invention of spectacles made of glass.
1295. First session of the complete English parliament.
c. 1298–1368. Guy de Chaulliac.
1307–c. 1390. John Arderne.

Guy de Chaulliac was probably the greatest of the medieval European surgeons. His *Chirurgia Magna*, first issued in 1363, continued to be much used until the end of the 16th century; in it he mentions the "spongia somnifera" of Theodoric, but he does not indicate that he himself advocated its use. He disapproved of the pre-operative use of opium, since some who had had it had gone mad and consequently died.

John Arderne was the English counterpart of Guy. From about the time of the Black Death, when his wife died, he practised at Newark, but he removed to London in 1370. He issued two important treatises, that *On Fistula in Ano, Haemorrhoids and Clysters* appearing in 1376. In it, there is a description of an ointment compounded of mandrake and many other herbs for producing surgical anaesthesia. Needless to say, such a prescription would have been valueless. D'Arcy Power, in the introduction to the 1922 edition of Arderne's *De Arte Phisicali et de Cirurgia*, writes, "His [Arderne's] medical treatment was essentially that of the Saxon leeches, treatment by spells, herbs and nasty or innocuous substances. In such matters he had no critical faculty but believed what he was told regardless of its source". This, of course, is typical of the medieval period, and accounts for all the mandragora broths, ointments and sponges mentioned by various authors. As a surgeon, he was of great repute, and the first treatise above-mentioned describes, for the first time, the operation for fistula in ano still in use today.

1309.	Removal of the Papal seat to Avignon.
1314.	The Battle of Bannockburn.
1315.	The Swiss secure their independence, a factor of great importance in the latter establishment of uncensored printing presses in Basle.
1328–1400.	Chaucer.

The works of Chaucer contain a number of references to narcotic drugs, but there is no evidence that he had had any first-hand knowledge of them. As an educated and travelled man, he would, of course, be familiar with the accepted views on the mandrake and opium, and his imagination was certainly equal to the task of inventing even more effective potions.

1340.	Edward III claims the French crown.
1346.	The Battle of Crécy; the first use of guns in war.
1349.	The Black Death ravages England.

The epidemic of bubonic plague which spread across Europe in 1347–49, and which is known as the Black Death, had, of course, important social effects. In addition, it opened men's eyes to the importance of *infection* as a cause of disease, and led to the establishment of quarantine stations at strategic points. The conception of the spread of disease by infection was the greatest step forward taken in the Period of Superstition.

1364.   Foundation of the Hanseatic League.
1412.   Foundation of the University of St. Andrews.
1415.   The Battle of Agincourt.
1431.   Execution of Joan of Arc.

The trial of Joan of Arc for witchcraft and heresy included a series of examinations, at one of which she was accused of possessing a mandrake. She denied this, and said that she knew mandrakes were dangerous and evil things to keep. The important point is that both she and her assessors (judges) believed that mandrakes were evil and magical. At about this time, there appeared an engraving by Jasper Isaacs showing witches preparing for their Sabbat: a mandrake is shown in the foreground. Later, about 1600, Franken used this picture as the basis for his painting of a similar subject; he again depicted the mandrake.

1453.   Constantinople falls to the Turks.
1454.   Gutenberg prints from movable type.

Printing had been known to the Chinese many centuries earlier, but the discovery was stultified by the multiplicity of Chinese "characters". Gutenberg's invention depended for its acceptance on the previous introduction of paper-making into Europe, which seems to have begun in Italy in about 1270. The knowledge of paper-making had been carried by Moslems from China to Europe, and paper was manufactured in Moorish Spain for some considerable time before the craft spread to Christian Europe.

E. THE RENAISSANCE (1454–1754).

The great cultural revival which we call the Renaissance cannot be dated accurately. Perhaps its first stirrings can be seen in the writings of Roger Bacon in the middle of the 13th century; certainly the spirit of the Renaissance began to move in literature long before the introduction of printing. The year 1454, however, is a suitable date to choose as the time when the Renaissance began to permeate the lives of all who lived within the bounds of European civilization. The next three hundred years saw the great artistic and scientific advances which overthrew the old Aristotelian and Galenic systems, while the ever-extending areas of commerce and colonization spread the new thought throughout the world, infusing in exchange new ideas, new drugs and new customs into the polity of Western Europe.

As we have seen, the preceding 1250 years had been a period of stagnation: with the budding of the Renaissance, the dead leaves of scholasticism and authority fell away, and man turned from dusty and inaccurate manuscripts to seek the truth in the shining face of nature; no longer did "authority" obscure the truth; observation and experiment, search and research, became of greater and greater importance, and soon yielded undreamed-of treasures.

With all this, the art of printing had much to do. Soon the works of Dante and Boccaccio, medieval in date but modern in spirit, were available for all to read; later the printing presses were working on scientific and medical publications, and books on these subjects appeared at a price far less than that of the manuscript versions. Naturally, the buyers were, at first, the poorer and less literate class, which led to the publication of books especially written for this market. Thus, the first medical book to be printed was the *De Re Medicina* of Celsus, chosen more for the purity of its Latin than for its scientific content, but later medical printed books were of the "Handy Home Doctor" type, written by indigent doctors, like William Bullein, whose *Bulwark of Defence* was written while he was in prison, in the hope of earning a few shillings. Such books were antiquated in spirit and inaccurate in body; they do not reflect the medical science of the time, but that of the earlier period. Naturally, they were despised and criticized by the medical profession who, until the issue of original printed works towards the middle of the 16th century, preferred their manuscripts. However, criticism of unworthy books led to the criticism of all books, printed and manuscript alike, so that the decay of "authority" proceeded with greater rapidity.

Meanwhile the Reformation of Religion was playing its part. The authority of the Pope became weakened, like that of Aristotle and Galen, by observation and by interest in the Scriptures. In all countries, the dominion of the Church became less pervading, and, in some, the Pope's rule was completely cast off. Thus, the way was made clear for scientific investigations which the Church had previously interdicted. The divorce of Henry VIII from Catherine of Aragon, the final strain which broke the link between England and the Pope, was thus of great importance in the history of Science, for it laid the foundation on which Britain's scientific supremacy was to be built.

The weakening of all authority led to the growth of democracy; the history of the 16th and 17th centuries records rebellion after rebellion which lessened everywhere the power of kings and brought down the feudal system. Thus when, in 1563, Mary Queen of Scots reproached John Knox with interfering in her affairs, saying: "What have ye to do with my marriage, or what are ye within this Commonwealth?", the Reformer replied, "A subject born within the same, Madam, and albeit I neither be Earl, Lord nor Baron within it, yet has God made me (how abject that ever I be in your eyes) a profitable member within the same". As has been said, modern democracy was born in that answer.

By the beginning of the 16th century, the Renaissance in

Art was well advanced. Leonardo da Vinci, in the interest of painting, had made many beautiful and accurate anatomical drawings; although these were not then published, they greatly influenced the anatomists to whom he showed them. The discovery of the elliptical arch is another example of the blend of science and art which was to have far-reaching effects.

Paracelsus, whom Osler called "The Luther of Medicine", was the first to throw off publicly the restraint of "authority". When he was appointed Professor of Chemistry and Medicine at Basle in 1526, he began his course of lectures by burning the works of Aristotle, and he further advanced the cause of freedom by delivering his lectures in German, instead of the customary Latin.

The early years of the 16th century are packed with important events, from among which we may select the foundation of the Royal College of Physicians of London (1518), the Incorporation of the Company of Barber-Surgeons, later the Royal College of Surgeons of England (1540), the issue of the first book on Physiology since Galen, the *De Naturali Parte Medicinae* of Fernel (1542), the publication of the first modern book on anatomy, the *De Humani Corporis Fabrica* of Vesalius (1543), the posthumous issue of the epoch-making *De Revolutionibus Orbium Coelestium* of Copernicus (1543), and the eponymous naming of syphilis from the poem by Fracastoro (1530).

The overthrow of the classical philosophers in the 16th and 17th centuries created a vacuum which the philosophers of the 17th and 18th centuries strove to fill. In this they were aided by the remarkable achievements in science during the early years of the 17th century. Giordano Bruno, the first to remove the fixed stars from a sphere and to place the boundaries of the universe at an infinite distance, came to the stake in 1600; his influence on scientific thought was great. In the same year Gilbert initiated the study of magnetism by the publication of his *De Magnete*: he introduced the term "electricity" and announced a connexion between electricity and magnetism. In 1601, Kepler, the real founder of modern astronomy, succeeded Tycho Brahe as astronomer to the Emperor Rudolf II. Galileo had made the Aristotelian system shake by his experiments with falling bodies at Pisa in 1591, and he brought it finally to the ground in 1604 by demonstrating that a new star had appeared in Serpentuarius, for the Aristotelian system demanded that the heavens be unchangeable.

Galileo, however, did more than this, for he enunciated the view that "science is measurement", thus stimulating, for example, Santorio to invent a clinical thermometer and to carry out his famous weighing experiments, by which he proved the existence of "insensible perspiration". A further extension of Galileo's fundamental idea by the mathematical genius of Newton led to the publication of the *Principia* in 1687, under the imprimatur of Samuel Pepys, at that time president of the Royal Society.

The discovery of the circulation of the blood, published to the world in the *De Motu Cordis* of William Harvey in 1628, laid the foundation of modern physiology and medicine, but further developments were delayed by the Civil War in England (1642–49) and by the unrest during the early years of Cromwell's Protectorate. In the latter years of his rule, the Invisible College, later to become the Royal Society, began its work, while the microscopical investigations of Malpighi and Leeuwenhoek, the researches of Boyle in chemistry and of Boyle and Mayow on air arose from the need for new theories and explanations of the activities of Nature.

Thus, attempts were made by the so-called iatrophysicists to explain the animal body on a mechanical basis, and foremost among workers in this field were Descartes, who first suggested the idea of the nervous reflex, and Borelli, who investigated muscles. Others, the iatrochemists, tried to find answers to the problems of animal economy in the newborn science of chemistry: of these, the most important were Sylvius, who had a clinical laboratory and who propounded a doctrine of acids and alkalis and explained digestion on the basis of fermentation, and de Réaumur, who carried out ingenious experiments on the gastric secretions of birds.

All, however, was not progress: one of the greatest setbacks to scientific advance was the explanation of combustion by postulating the mythical Phlogiston. This theory was propounded by Stahl, a leader of the Vitalist Group, which opposed itself to the Iatrophysicists and Iatrochemists mentioned above.

The 18th century was principally one of consolidation and classification of scientific and medical knowledge, but, within our period, we should mention the work of von Haller, who enunciated the principle of the irritability of muscular, and the sensitivity of nervous, tissues, and of Boerhaave, who instituted clinical teaching; since the time of Galen, medicine had always been learnt from books and not from observation of the patient. Boerhaave also founded the study of pathology, following such of his patients as died to the postmortem room, and comparing symptoms with lesions. Teaching was improving, and new centres were being opened, foremost of which was the Medical School of the University of Edinburgh, founded by Pitcairne in 1685. Meanwhile, in Britain, the voluntary hospital system was coming into being with the opening of infirmaries, not only in London, but also in the provinces.

Great as were the artistic, cultural and scientific advances of the period under review, the behaviour of "civilized" man left much to be desired. Lunatics were housed and treated in a manner which to us is unbelievably cruel, felons were punished in a most barbarous fashion, debtors were imprisoned in revolting circumstances, and vivisection was practised by men of great renown with a barbaric indifference to the suffering of animals. The pastimes most popular with all classes were brutal: bull-baiting, bear-baiting and cock-fighting. Add to this the almost inconceivable filth and squalor of the towns, with no sanitation, no drainage or cleaning of the streets, the household ordure and garbage rotting in the cellars and thoroughfares to form a stinking slush often more than a foot deep. There was an absence of police, of street lighting, and of a proper water supply; and all, even the rich, swarmed with fleas and lice, and almost never bathed. It is obvious that these were not the conditions in which humanity and human self-respect could flourish. The flower, Humanity, was not yet in bud: its fruit was later to be the desire to reduce suffering and, from this, in turn, grew anaesthesia.

The most important incidents which bear directly upon anaesthesia during this period are the discovery of di-ethyl ether (c. 1540), the rediscovery of local analgesia by the application of cold (1595 and c. 1646), and the experiments on the intravenous administration of drugs and blood undertaken by the Invisible College and its successor, the Royal Society. The idea of anaesthesia, however, was so foreign to the notions of the time that analgesia by refrigeration was soon forgotten, to be rediscovered a couple of centuries later.

1454.   Gutenberg prints from movable type.
1452–1519.   Leonardo da Vinci.
1455.   The first battle of St. Albans opens the Wars of the Roses.
1471–1528.   Albrecht Dürer, painter and engraver.
1475–1564.   Michael Angelo Buonarroti, sculptor and painter.

Leonardo da Vinci, painter, sculptor, architect and engineer, was the first of a remarkable galaxy of great artists whose work ushered in the period under discussion. Leonardo was one of the most original thinkers the world has ever seen: his art was little influenced by the antique, but was founded upon patient observation, an attitude of mind which was to become characteristic of scientists and without which the Renaissance could never have existed. In order to draw the human body more faithfully, he practised anatomy, and his drawings of the heart and other organs, although not published for nearly 300 years, influenced anatomists and others to whom he showed them. Among these was Dürer, who was particularly receptive to the ideas of Leonardo.

1476.　　Caxton erects the first printing press in England (Westminster).

William Caxton (1422–91) printed the first book in English at Bruges in 1475; the first book printed in England, *The Dictes or Sayinges of the Philosophres*, appeared in 1477.

1485.　　The Battle of Bosworth : the death of Richard III and the accession of Henry VII ended the Wars of the Roses. The period of good government which followed in England provided suitable conditions for the growth of the "New Learning".
1492.　　Ferdinand and Isabella, uniting the Spanish kingdoms, drive the Moors out of Spain; they help Columbus.
1493.　　Discovery of the North American continent by Columbus.
1495–1553.　François Rabelais, priest and physician, author of *Gargantua et Pantagruel*.
1497.　　Vasco da Gama of Portugal sails round the Cape to India.
1498.　　Columbus discovers the South American continent.

The New World had been discovered by Christopher Columbus, but the lands were named after Vespucci. Amerigo Vespucci, a Florentine, later a naturalized Spaniard, explored the coast of Venezuela in 1499; his distorted accounts of his voyage led to a misapprehension of the parts played by the two explorers, and so Vespucci's name was adopted in preference to that of the actual discoverer.

1498.　　Savonarola tries to reform religion in Florence and is burnt.
1503.　　The League of Cambrai is made against Venice, then at the height of her power.
1506.　　St. Peter's at Rome begun by Pope Paul III.
1509–47　Henry VIII, born 1491.
1513.　　The Battle of Flodden.

57

1516.   Publication of the *De Orbe Novo* of Peter Matyr Angherius (1459–1525).

The discovery of America, and the other voyages of exploration, widened the ideas of man concerning the world around him, and the new plants and herbs which were brought back showed him that even Aristotle had not known all that Nature had to teach. The *De Orbe Novo* contains the first account of the South American arrow-poison, curare.

1517.   Martin Luther nails his *Theses* on the church door at Wittenberg.

1518.   Foundation of the Royal College of Physicians of London. Thomas Linacre (1460–1524), the founder, was a champion of the "New Learning".

1519.   Charles V, King of Spain, Archduke of Austria and Duke of Burgundy, becomes Holy Roman Emperor.

1520.   The "Field of the Cloth of Gold", a conference in the Pas de Calais between Francis I of France and Henry VIII of England.

1521.   South America conquered by the Spaniards; Cortes in Mexico.

1526.   Paracelsus becomes Professor of Chemistry and Medicine at Basle.

Paracelsus (which is the Latin form of his surname, von Hohenheim) was born in 1493. His appointment to the chair of Medicine at Basle was a reflexion of Swiss independence, for he was already in disfavour with the orthodox churchmen. However, his arrogance and ill-behaviour, coupled with his lack of respect for Galen and Aristotle, lost him his job in 1528. His writings, which are many, are mystical and obscure. In the *Paradoxa*, published in 1605, he describes the action of oleum vitreoli dulce (di-ethyl ether) on chickens, and states that "it quiets all suffering and relieves all pain" (see Appendix A). Paracelsus is also credited, on no very good evidence, with the invention of laudanum (tincture of opium). Although not strictly a champion of the "New Learning", his defiance to the authority of the ancients, and his dependence upon experience did much to further the Renaissance in medical thought, and Osler has called him the "Luther of Medicine". He died in 1541.

1529.   At the Diet of Spires, Luther's followers appear as "Protestants".

1530.   Publication of the poem, *Syphilis sive Morbus Gallicus*, by Girolamo Fracastoro (1478–1553).

In the early years of the 16th century, syphilis spread across Europe with appalling rapidity and under various names. The name "syphilis" became attached to it as a result of Fracastoro's poem, which described the fate of a swine-herd of that name who was struck with the disease after he had incurred the wrath of the gods. Fracastoro was a man of wide learning; he had qualified in medicine at Padua and, in 1546, he published his *De Contagione et Contagiosis Morbis*, in which he described a theory of disease based on the existence of living organisms carried in the air or transmitted from person to person. He also contributed to the understanding of astronomy, geology and the nature of fossils.

1532.   Henry VIII, unable to obtain the Pope's consent to a divorce, makes himself head of the Church of England and, thereafter, annuls his marriage to Catherine of Aragon.

1534.   Ignatius Loyola, the Spaniard, forms the Society of Jesus.

1535.   Appearance of Coverdale's Bible, with a title-page designed by Holbein.

1539.   Henry VIII orders the dissolution of the monasteries.

c. 1540. Synthesis of di-ethyl ether.

The method of synthesis is described by Valerius Cordus in his *De Artificiosis Extractionibus Liber*, published in 1561. Cordus (1515–44) seems to have written this description in about 1540, about the same time that Paracelsus was writing his *Paradoxa* (see under 1526 and Appendix A). Since Cordus apparently worked with Paracelsus, there is now no means of deciding on the relative responsibility of these two men for this important discovery.

1541.   Calvin established as religious dictator at Geneva.
1542.   Publication of the *Tractado contra el Mal Serpentino* of Rodrigo de Isla (1462–1542).
1542.   Publication of the *De Naturali Parte Medicinae* of Jean François Fernel (1497–1558).
1542.   Publication of the *Commentaries on the History of Plants* of Leonhard Fuchs (1501–66).

"Mal serpentino" is another name for syphilis. De Isla states that, as a physician at Barcelona in 1493, he treated some of Columbus's sailors for this disease, and the *Tractado* is the strongest evidence for the American origin of syphilis. However, since Columbus did not return from his expedition until 1496, it is doubtful how much reliance is to be placed on de Isla's account.

Fernel was physician to Henri II of France and Professor of Medicine at Paris. His *De Naturali Parte Medicinae* was later published as a part of his *Medicina* (1554), its name being then changed to *Physiologia*, a word which has been current ever since. This was the first book on physiology since Galen. Fernel also wrote on syphilis, which he believed to be contracted by sexual intercourse, without supernatural interference.

The work of Fuchs was magnificently illustrated and marks a considerable advance in the subject of Materia Medica. The plant "fuchsia" is named after him.

1543.   Publication of the *De Revolutionibus Orbium Coelestium* of Nicholas Koppernik (Copernicus) (1473–1543).
1543.   Publication of the *De Humani Corporis Fabrica* of Andreas Vesalius (1514–64).

These two great works appearing in the same year emphasize the tremendous development in the first century of the scientific renaissance. Copernicus, the Polish mathematician, showed that the sun was the centre of the planetary universe. The work was completed in 1530, but Copernicus delayed publication until he knew that he was dying, from fear of persecution by the Church.

Vesalius (i.e., from Wesel), the founder of modern anatomy, studied medicine at Louvain and Paris. In 1537, he became the first of a long line of distinguished occupants of the chair of anatomy at Padua (e.g., Colombo, Falloppio, Fabrizi), and, in 1538, he published his *Tabulae Anatomicae Sex*, a book which was strongly Galenic in outlook, describing, for example, the five-lobed liver. However, in 1543, there appeared the magnificent *Fabrica*, illustrated with engravings by Jakob van Calcar from drawings of Vesalius' own dissections, and printed by Oporinus of Basle. This book marked a new era; many of its plates have never been equalled either in beauty or accuracy. From this time, anatomy became purely observational, and the way was cleared for the discovery of the circulation of the blood.

1551.   Gabriele Falloppio (Fallopius) (1523–62) becomes Professor of Anatomy at Padua.
1553.   Michael Servetus goes to the stake.

Servetus (1509–33), theologian and physician, studied medicine at Paris and was a fellow-student of Vesalius there. He interested himself in the movement of the blood, because he believed it to be the seat of the soul. He was burnt at Geneva by the Calvinists as a heretic, and was equally accused of heresy by the Roman Catholics. His last book, *Christianismi Restitutio*, was burnt with him. This work contains a description of the pulmonary or lesser circulation, which he had discovered, but, because very few copies of the book survived (only three are now known), his part in elucidating the circulation of the blood was unknown until a much later date.

1556.   Georg Bauer (Agricola), physician, mathematician and mineralogist, called the "Father of Mineralogy", publishes his *De Re Metallica*.
1558–1603.   Queen Elizabeth I.
1559.   Realdo Colombo of Padua publishes his *De Re Anatomica*, in which the pulmonary circulation is described.

1561.   Publication of Valerius Cordus's *Annotations on Dios-corides*, in which there are many notable additions to the subject of Materia Medica. The synthesis of ether is also described in a section of this work (see under 1540 and Appendix A).

1562.   Publication of the *Cinq Livres de Chirurgie* of Ambroise Paré (1510–90).

Paré was surgeon to three French kings, Henri II, Charles IX and Henri III, and, although he was a Huguenot, he was protected by the second of these during the Massacre of St. Bartholemew (1572). The greatest surgeon of his day, he substituted the ligature for searing with a hot iron as a means of stopping haemorrhage, and he also devised some ingenious artificial limbs. He disapproved of mandragora, but described a method of local analgesia by compression of nerves.

1562.   Publication of William Bullein's *Bulwarke of Defence against all Sickness, Sornes and Woundes that dooe Daily Assaulte Mankinde.*

Bullein's book has been cited as an authority for the use of mandragora as an anaesthetic, but it is merely a popular and debased version of the typical medieval herbal, issued for the semi-literate, and it is not to be considered as a physician's text.

1563.   John Knox (*c.* 1514–1572), in an interview with Mary Queen of Scots, enunciates the principle of modern democracy, that all members of the state have a right to a say in the conduct of public affairs.

1564–1616. Shakespeare. The plays contain several references to mandragora and to other narcotic drugs, but do not show any real knowledge of their use.

1569.   Publication of the *Natural Magic* of Giambattista della Porta (1543–1615).

Della Porta, physicist and inventor of the camera obscura, was not a medical man. However, he described a preparation of mandrake and other herbs, by which means, he said, sleep could be induced. He did not suggest using this preparation

B. RAYMVNDVS LVLLIVS PHILOSOPHVS.
Doctrinam Pandit Raymidus Lullius omnem, Cui Deus
infudit scibile quicquid erat. ex Vetustissimo prototypo
authentico. I. mittannour. Moncornet ex.

Figure 6. Raymond Lully (1234–1314), who may have been the first
to prepare "oleum vitrioli dulce" (ether). From an old print in the
author's possession.

Figure 7. Paracelsus (1493–1541), the discoverer of ether.

during surgical operations, and there is no evidence that it was ever used at all. It was simply an elaboration of the spongia somnifera of the medieval age.

1569.   William Chamberlen, a Huguenot, settles in England. He and his descendents kept until 1728 the family secret of the obstetric forceps which he had invented, and practised until that date with great success as man-midwives.

1572.   The death of John Knox; the Massacre of St. Bartholomew.

1577.   Frampton's *Joyfull Newes Out of the Newe Founde Worlde*, a translation of Nicolas Monardes' *Dos Libros* (1574), gives the first account in English of curare, and also mentions the coca plant.

1578.   Dodoens' *Herbal* mentions the mandrake in the usual way; a mention is also made of the pain-relieving qualities of opium, but it is not suggested for use during surgical operations.

1579.   Du Bartas (1544–90), French poet and soldier, publishes his poem, *La Sepmaine*, which describes the events in the first chapters of Genesis.

La Sepmaine was translated into English by Sylvester (1563–1618), whose translation of the account of the birth of Eve has often been quoted. Some have believed that this can be taken as evidence of the use of some sort of anaesthesia for surgical operations at this time, but an examination of the poem shows that it contains nothing more than is explicable by imagination and some knowledge of what the medievalists had written.

1581.   The United States of Holland declare themselves independent of Spain.

1582.   The Gregorian Calendar supersedes the Julian Calendar in Western Europe. This style of reckoning was not introduced into Scotland until 1600, or into England until 1752, by which latter date, there was a discrepancy of eleven days.

1587.   *An Herbal for the Bible*, by Lemnius, translated into English by T. Newton, describes the soporific action of the mandrake in connexion with Genesis xxx, 14–17.

1588.   The repulse of the Spanish Armada by the English.
1588.   De Acosta, after mountaineering in Peru, draws attention to mountain sickness and reports that air above 14,000 feet is not adapted to respiration.
1589.   Appearance of the first complete edition of della Porta's *Magiae Naturalis* (see under 1569). It contains a description of the combination of lenses which form a telescope or microscope.
1591.   Eufame Macalyean burnt at the stake at Edinburgh. According to some recent authors, she was executed for attempting to relieve the pains of childbirth, but she was in fact convicted of witchcraft (see Appendix B).
1595.   Sir Walter Raleigh (1552–1618) discovers Guiana.
1595.   Publication of Costaeus' *De Igniis Medicinae Praesidiis.*

Raleigh gives a very highly coloured account of the use of curare by the South American Indians and of its effects. Some modern writers have stated that he actually brought some of the drug to Europe, but this is untrue.

Costaeus, in his book, mentions (extremely briefly) the use of snow or ice for producing analgesia for surgery. This seems to be the first mention of refrigeration anaesthesia since the *Lacnunga* of 1050.

c. 1600.   Valverdi advocates analgesia by nerve compression (?).
1600.   Appearance of the *De Magnete* of William Gilbert (1540–1603).
1600.   Giordano Bruno burnt at the stake.
1601.   Kepler (1571–1630) succeeds Tycho Brahé as astronomer to the Holy Roman Emperor.
1603.   James VI of Scotland becomes James I of England.
1604.   Galileo Galilei (1564–1642) sees a new star in Serpentuarius.

Dr. William Gilbert, physician to Queen Elizabeth I and President of the Royal College of Physicians of London, described the magnetic properties of the Earth, and showed that magnetism and electricity are allied. He introduced the word "electricity" which appears for the first time in his book.

New ideas about astronomy brought the philosophy of the ancients, typified by Aristotle, to the ground in ruins, but the

Church fought hard to suppress such "heretical" notions. William Gilbert in Protestant England was safe; not so Giordano Bruno (1548–1600) in Italy. His conception of the universe placed the stars far outside the sphere demanded by Aristotle, and his idea of infinite distances led to his execution for heresy.

Galileo, safe as long as he remained in the Venetian territories (which included Padua), demonstrated that the "nova" which appeared in the constellation of Serpentuarius was a proof of the errors of Aristotle. His support for the Copernican theory in 1632, which he had shown to be correct with the aid of the telescope which he had constructed in 1624, led to his condemnation by the Inquisition as soon as he left the safety of Padua for the dangers of Rome. There is no foundation for the story that his recantation, made in the beautiful gothic church of Santa Maria sopra Minerva at Rome, was followed by the traditional phrase, "Eppur, si muove" ("But it does move").

1605.   Publication of Paracelsus' *Opera Medico-Chemica sive Paradoxa* (see under 1526 and 1540).
1607–69.   Rembrandt.
1608–74.   Milton.
1614.   Appearance of the *De Medicina Statica Aphorismi* of Santorio (1561–1636).

A friend of Galileo, Santorio (Sanctorius) was stimulated by the latter's pronouncement that "Science is measurement". His book contains the well-known picture of himself seated in the balance by which he proved the existence of "insensible perspiration".

1614.   Logarithms described by Napier.
1615.   Andreas Libavius mentions the idea of blood transfusion, but there is no reason to believe that he made any experiments in this direction.
1618.   Beginning of the Thirty Years War, which exhausted Germany and Spain.
1620.   Publication of the *Novum Organum* of Francis Bacon.

Francis Bacon, Viscount St. Albans, showed that knowledge is derived from experience, not from authority, and he described inductive reasoning, which he wished to see applied to the sciences. His death was due to pneumonia following a cold caught while experimenting on stuffing a chicken with snow in the hope of preserving the meat.

1623. The *De Lactibus* of Aselli (1581–1626) gives the first description of the lacteals, discovered by him when dissecting a dog. This work is the first to contain anatomical illustrations in colour.

1624–74. Thomas Sydenham. He wrote much, and concentrated on the natural history of disease : his ideas mark the beginning of a new outlook in medicine.

1625. In his *De Thorace*. Hoffman states that the Assyrians had produced unconsciousness during the operation of circumcision by compression of the vessels in the neck : there does not seem to be any foundation for this story.

1628. Publication of the *Exercitatio Anatomica de Motu Cordis et Sanguinis in Animalibus* of William Harvey (1578–1657).

Harvey had already expressed his ideas on the circulation of the blood as early as 1616 in his lectures at the Royal College of Physicians of London, but he waited until further experiments provided complete proof before publication. Harvey had studied under Fabricius ab Aquapendente at Padua, and the latter's work on the valves of the veins formed an important link in the chain of proof of the circulation of the blood. The *De Motu Cordis* (as it is usually called) is one of the most important books in the whole history of medicine, for it laid the foundation for modern physiology and medicine.

1637. Opening of the Académie Française in Paris.

1637–86. Jan Swammerdam, microscopist. His chief work, *Het Bijbel der Natuur*, was published by Boerhaave in 1737.

1640. Parkinson's *Paradisus in Sole* (Park-in-Sun!) advocates mandragora wine as pre-operative medication.

1642.   Death of Cardinal Richelieu, who had united and organized France for the crown.

1642.   Lausitz, an Austrian, amuses himself by inebriating dogs by the intravenous administration of wine.

1643.   Torricelli's barometer.

1646.   Severino, visited in Naples by Thomas Bartholin (see under 1661), is using refrigeration with snow or ice as an analgesic for lithotomy.

1648.   Van Helmont (1577–1644), who invented the term "gas", describes "gas sylvestre" (carbon dioxide) in his *Ortus Medicinae*.

1649.   Execution of King Charles I.

1649.   Francis Potter (1594–1678) discusses blood transfusion.

Aubrey writes in his *Brief Lives*, "At the Epiphany, 1649, when I was at his house he [Potter] then told me his notion of curing diseases, etc., by Transfusion of Blood out of one man into another, and that the hint came into his head reflecting on Ovid's story of Medea and Jason, and that this was a matter of ten years before that time. About a year later, he and I went to try the experiment, but 'twas on a hen, and the creature too little and our tools not good. I then sent him a Surgeon's Lancet. Anno 1652, I received a letter from him concerning the subject, which many years since I shewed, and was read and entered in the books of the Royal Society, for Dr. Lower would have arrogated the invention to himself, and now one R. Griffiths, Dr. of Physic, of Richmond, is publishing a book of the transfusion of blood. Mr. Meredith Lloyd tells me that Libavius speaks of the Transfusion of Blood, which I dare swear Mr. F. Potter never saw in his life".

1656.   Admiral Blake shows an English fleet in the Mediterranean.

1656.   (Sir) Christopher Wren (1632–1723), later Savilian Professor of Astronomy at Oxford, experiments with the intravenous administration of drugs to animals.

1656.   Giovanni Borelli becomes Professor of Mathematics at Pisa.

1658.   François de le Boë (Sylvius) becomes Professor of Medicine at Leyden.

Borelli, whose *De Motu Animalium* appeared in 1681, believed that physiology was only a branch of physics, and, treating the question of muscular movement as a mathematical problem, he achieved considerable results. He may be regarded as the leader of the so-called Iatrophysicists, who were in opposition to the Iatrochemists; the latter believed that the processes of life were essentially chemical in nature. Sylvius was the foremost of the Iatrochemists.

1658–95.	Purcell.
1660.	The Hon. Robert Boyle (1627–91), son of the Earl of Cork, publishes his *The Spring and the Weight of the Air*, in which Boyle's Law is stated.
1660.	The Restoration.
1660.	Wecker describes a compound of opium, mandrake, hemlock and henbane which will send a man to sleep simply by smelling it: none of these substances is volatile.
1661.	Marcello Malpighi (1628–94) describes the capillaries in the lungs of the frog. Harvey, who had postu ated the existence of the capillaries, had died four years before the publication of the *De Pulmonibus Obs rvationes Anatomicae*.
1661.	Publication of the *De Nivis Usu Medico* of Thomas Bartholinus (1616–80).

Bartholinus devotes a whole chapter to refrigeration analgesia, which he had seen Severino use (see under 1646). The Latin text is very corrupt, but it is evident that Osler was wrong in thinking that Severino advocated the use of refrigeration in cases of impending gangrene; in fact, he warned against its use.

1664.	Daniel Major of Kiel publishes his *Prodromus a se Inventae Chirurgiae Infusoriae*.
1665.	Richard Lower (1631–91) performs the first authenticated transfusion of blood from one animal to another.

Major, like others before him, had administered opium and other drugs intravenously to dogs. Lower actually transfused blood from one dog to another; his experiment is recorded at length in the *Journal Book of the Royal Society* (which had been incorporated in 1662). In 1669, Lower published his *Tractatus de Corde*, one of the classics of medical literature.

1666.   Appearance of Greatrakes' *Brief Account*.

Valentine Greatrakes, known as the Irish Stroker, seems to have been a bone-setter rather than a hypnotist, but he does appear to have been a precursor of Mesmer. His work was curative rather than anaesthetic. His pamphlet is whimsically entitled, "A Brief Account of Mr. Valentine Greatrakes and divers of the Strange Cases by him lately performed, written by himself in a letter addressed to the Hon. Robert Boyle, to which is annexed the testimonials of several Eminent and Worthy Persons of the Chief Matters of Fact therin Related".

1667.   Hooke's experiment on the function of the lungs.

Robert Hooke (1635–1702) performed his classical experiment in order to test Galen's theory that the function of the lungs was to cool the heart by continual fanning. First, Hooke showed that a dog could be kept alive by inflation of the lungs after the thorax had been opened, and, secondly, that actual movement of the lungs was not necessary to life, for, when the lungs were punctured, life could be maintained by forcing a steady stream of air through the lungs. Hooke was Curator to the Royal Society and he was also a pioneer microscopist. His *Micrographia* (1665) is the first work in which the word "cell" is used in the description of tissues.

1667.   First Latin edition of *Clysmatica Nova sive Ratio qua in venam sectam medicamenta immiti possint* of J. S. Elsholtz.

The first German edition of the *Clysmatica Nova* had appeared in 1665, but was unillustrated. The 1667 edition contains the first illustration ever made of blood transfusion.

The book describes the experiments of Lower and Boyle in England and of Major in Kiel and Denis in Paris. The latter was the first person to transfuse blood from an animal into a man (1667), an experiment which Lower also performed at about this time.

1674.   John Mayow's *Tractatus Quinque*.

The *Tractatus Quinque*, an expansion of the *Tractatus Duo* of 1671, deals with respiration, muscular activity and rickets. Mayow showed that a substance occupying about one-fifth of the volume of common air was necessary both for life and for combustion. He named this substance, which he made no attempt to isolate, the Spiritus Nitro-aereus. He may thus be considered as the discoverer of oxygen. Curiously, Mayow's book attracted little attention and was unknown to Priestley and Scheele when they isolated oxygen a century later.

1676.   Anton van Leeuwenhoek (1632–1723), petty official of Delft, and a pioneer in microscopy, observes bacteria, but is, of course, ignorant of their nature.

1678.   Publication of the *Philosophiae Naturalis Principia Mathematica* of (Sir) Isaac Newton (1642–1727), in which the effects of gravity on the heavenly bodies are described.

1679.   The *De Ortu et Occasu Transfusionis Sanguinis* of Mercklin contains the second illustration of blood transfusion, which the author, however, considered too dangerous for use.

1680.   Boyle synthesizes ether (Fulton, *Anaesthesiology*, 1947, **8**, 465).

1681.   The *De Motu Animalium* of Giovanni Alfonso Borelli (1608–79).

1683.   Sobieski the Pole saves Vienna from the Turks.

1685–1754.   J. S. Bach.

1685.   Foundation of the Medical School in Edinburgh University by Archibald Pitcairne (1652–1713).

1688–1744.   Pope.

1689.   William of Orange, King of England, is the chief opponent to a powerful France under Louis XIV. The Bill of Rights.

1690.   Dr. John Locke (1632–1704) issues his *Essay on Human Understanding*.

1693.   The *Armamentarium Chirurgicum* of Scultetus contains a somewhat fanciful illustration of blood transfusion.

1694–1778. Voltaire (François Marie Arouet).

1697–1763. William Smellie, a great pioneer in obstetrics and teacher of William Hunter.

1704.   The capture of Gibraltar makes England a Mediterranean power.

1704.   Newton synthesizes ether (Fulton, *Anaesthesiology*, 1947, **8**, 465).

1705.   Purmann's textbook of surgery describes and illustrates (very badly) blood transfusion.

1707.   Sir John Floyer issues his *Physician's Pulse-Watch*.

In this work, Floyer described a watch which would run for exactly 60 seconds, thus allowing accurate pulse rates to be counted. Even at this date, the construction of a watch with a seconds hand was impracticable, and, although Santorio had attempted to measure pulse rates by means of a pendulum, Floyer's invention made pulse counting possible for physicians for the first time. It was not, however, until the 19th century, when seconds hands became common features on watches, that counting the pulse became a regular feature of a medical examination.

1707.   Act of Union of England and Scotland.

1709.   Hermann Boerhaave becomes Professor of Medicine at Leyden.

1709.   Peter the Great of Russia defeats Charles XII of Sweden at Pultowa.

1709–84. Dr. Samuel Johnson.

1718.   J. B. Quistorp, in his *De Anaesthesia*, uses the word "anaesthesia" almost in its modern sense, and speaks learnedly of its derivation. He does not, however, mention surgical anaesthesia.

1720.   Alexander Monro primus (1697–1767), a pupil of Boerhaave, becomes Professor of Anatomy at Edinburgh. He, his son and his grandson held the chair in succession until 1846.

1720.   The South Sea Bubble.

1721–42. Walpole is Prime Minister.

1724.   Guy's Hospital opened a week after the death of its founder, Thomas Guy, publisher and merchant.

1730.   W. G. Frobenius publishes *An Account of a Spiritus Vini Æthereus* in the Philosophical Transactions of the Royal Society. This is an account of the "oleum vitreoli dulce" which has subsequently been known as Ether.

1731.   Georg Ernst Stahl (1660–1734) propounds the Phlogiston Theory of Combustion in his *Experimenta et Observationes Chemicae*.

1733.   Death of Augustus, King of Poland.

Meisser describes (*Skizzen*, 1782) how "Augustus, king of Poland and elector of Saxony (Augustus II, otherwise Frederick Augustus I) (1670–1733) suffered from a wound in his foot which threatened to mortify. . . . During sleep, induced by a certain potion surreptitiously administered, his favourite surgeon cut off the decaying parts". The whole incident (transferred by Ellis, *Ancient Anodynes*, 1946, to Stanislas Poniatowski) is apocryphal, except that Augustus died as a result of his wound.

1736.   Albrecht von Haller (1708–77), one of the world's great geniuses, becomes Professor of Medicine at Göttingen.

1743 (?). *An Account of the Extraordinary Fluid called Æther*, by Matthew Turner.

Turner described the history and manufacture of ether, and added directions for its use in headache: "In stubborn cases it will likewise be serviceable to snuff a little of the æther up the nostrils"; an heroic measure which hardly entitles him to a place as an originator of pain-relief by the inhalation of the vapour of ether.

1748.   Pomet, in *A Complete History of Drugs*, states that mandragora "was formerly esteemed to have a strong narcotic quality . . . but it is now never used".

1752.   Réné de Réaumur (1658–1757) describes gastric digestion in his *Sur la Digestion des Oiseaux*.

1752.   The Gregorian Calendar is introduced into England, September 2 being succeeded by September 14 (see under 1582).

1753.   Publication of the *De Somno; de Medicamento Somni-feris et de Natura Hominis in Somno* of L. C. Fabri, an early contribution to works on narcotic drugs, and of *A Treatise on Opium* by George Young.

1753.   Publication of *A Treatise of the Scurvy* by James Lind (1716–94), in which the use of lemon juice is shown to be of value in preventing the disease.

1753.   Publication of the *Species Plantorum* of Karl von Linné (Linnaeus, 1717–83), when the use of specific names in a binomial system is first employed.

F. The Pre-Anaesthetic Era (1754–1846)

This period of just under a century saw tremendous changes in the organization of the polity of Western Europe, and in the habits and manner of thought of the people, so that, at the end of this period, we unmistakably enter upon a scene familiar to us in almost every particular. The preceding three centuries had seen the marshalling of the forces which, now prepared, were to sweep away the last remnants of medievalism, and found a system of life bound, not upon agriculture and feudalism, but upon science, industry and democracy.

The loss of the American Colonies and the outbreak of the French Revolution practically coincided. The Napoleonic Wars which followed excluded British trade from the Continent of Europe, but the result was only to make Britain stronger and more resourceful. The conquest of India and Canada and the colonization of Australia led to an extension of trade, the more so because Britain had been forced to concentrate on naval rather than land forces. The prosperity which came in the wake of trade was necessarily unevenly distributed, but all classes benefited to some extent, and this was reflected in a tremendous increase in population which rose from about 8,000,000 in England and Wales in 1754 to about 17,000,000 in 1846. Meanwhile, the flow of people to the towns as a result of the increasing mechanization of industry brought about the Industrial Revolution. Similar changes, of course, occurred elsewhere, but Britain's grip on the seas and Napoleon's on the land, delayed the develop- ment of the Continental countries, so that Britain's pre-emin- ence was assured, while the invention of the steam-engine and its adaptation to locomotives and steamships revolution- ized transport and greatly influenced both mental and mater- ial growth.

Liberalizing influences were everywhere at work, not only in politics, but in Art and Religion as well. It is no accident that the final extinction of the Holy Roman Empire occurred only fifteen years after John Wesley's death. In literature, the work of Samuel Johnson, Kant, Goethe, Burns, Scott, Wordsworth, Byron and Shelley falls within this period; in art, Constable and Turner, in music, Mozart, Haydn and Beet- hoven; while public consciousness of the importance of art was revealed by the opening of the British Museum and the Royal Academy of Arts. The culminating political event was the passing of the Reform Bill in 1832.

In science, the work of such men as Priestley, Lavoisier, Cavendish, Galvani and Volta laid the foundation for the achievements of Thompson (Count Rumford), Humphry Davy and Michael Faraday, and the work of all these was united by close bonds with political, economic, religious and medical thought. In medicine, the power of diagnosis was greatly assisted by the discovery of percussion by Auenbrug- ger and of stethoscopy by Laennec, while the study of disease was advanced by John Hunter with his interest in compara- tive and morbid anatomy, and by Cullen who greatly in- fluenced medicine, not only in Edinburgh, but also on the American Continent. Obstetrics were revolutionized by Wil- liam Smellie and William Hunter; James Lind had opened the door to the study of vitamins; physiology was advanced by Sir Charles Bell's discovery of the separate sensory and motor functions of the posterior and anterior nerve roots; and surgical skill reached a great height in the hands of Liston.

74

However, for its immediate results, the most important therapeutic discovery of the period was the introduction of vaccination by Edward Jenner. The mortality from smallpox was enormous, and the publication of Jenner's *Inquiry into the Causes and Effects of Variolae Vaccinae* in 1798 disclosed a safe way to save countless lives. So important was the discovery deemed that Parliament voted Jenner a reward of £10,000, later supplemented by a further £20,000. Among all the benefactors of mankind, Jenner's name must stand high on the list.

Until the War of Independence, medicine on the North American Continent was mainly a pale shadow of British medicine, but with political separation came scientific and medical independence: the Medical School at Philadelphia was founded in 1765, and others followed, the Harvard Medical School being opened in 1783. Greatly influenced by the Edinburgh school, American medicine quickly grew to full stature and began to break new ground, particularly, for example, when in 1809 Ephraim McDowell successfully removed an ovarian tumour weighing 22½ lb., this being almost the first time in which the peritoneal cavity had been invaded by the surgeon. Knowledge of the physiology of digestion was much advanced by the work (1825–33) of Beaumont on his patient, Alexis St. Martin, who was suffering from a gastric fistula caused by a gunshot wound; and in 1843 appeared an essay *On the Contagiousness of Puerperal Fever* by the doctor and man of letters, Oliver Wendell Holmes.

Of considerable importance in the development of both psychology and anaesthesia was the work of Franz Anton Mesmer (1734–1815). At first working with magnets, and later using the "animal magnetism" which, he believed, flowed from his own body, Mesmer developed a system of therapy, first in Vienna and later in Paris, which had many adherents. In 1784, a commission appointed by Louis XVI, which comprised such famous men as Dr. Guillotin, Lavoisier, Bailly and Benjamin Franklin, reported that no evidence of "animal magnetism" was to be found and that Mesmer's results were entirely due to imagination. Mesmer's treatment consisted of bringing his patients into hysterical convulsions; it was a follower of his, de Puységur, who discovered hypnotic somnambulism, otherwise the mesmeric trance.

Paradoxically, the discoveries of the century under review had destroyed the confidence of the public in its doctors, and the doctors in themselves. The old humoral theory of disease had been swept away, and there was nothing to replace it. In the face of disease, the doctors, knowing their ignorance of the cause, were helpless, and there arose, both within and without the field of orthodox medicine, theorists and quacks who attempted to reduce all therapy to simple terms, such as John Brown of Edinburgh, whose theory was that all diseases were sthenic (i.e., caused by over excitation) or asthenic (i.e., caused by under excitation). The former were to be treated with opiates and the latter by stimulants. Such theories led nowhere and merely weakened the power of the profession by promoting feuds and discords among its members, each championing his own futile system, claiming successes which were often exaggerated for his own method, and denying success to his rivals.

With all the great changes in way of life during this period, an even greater change in the habit of thought was taking place; the idea of humanity was beginning to blossom and bear fruit. It may be that the carnage of the Napoleonic Wars and the frightful conditions in the towns which accompanied the Industrial Revolution caused a change in men's hearts. However that may be, the change disclosed itself in many ways, such as the abolition of the Slave Trade (1807), the founding of the Humane Society, the passing of Acts against bull-baiting, bear-baiting and cock-fighting, and the great reduction in the number of crimes for which capital punishment could be inflicted. Meanwhile, conditions were improved in lunatic asylums and prisons, and the great and rewarding advances in Public Health were set on foot by Chadwick and Southwood Smith. In the field of medical teaching, the passing of the Anatomy (Warburton's) Act and the licensing of schools of medicine in Britain brought about a great improvement in the standard of teaching and released the teachers from co-operation with body-snatchers.

It was only to be expected that this humane interest in the welfare of others which characterized the early years of the 19th century would soon extend itself to surgery, and that a demand for surgical anaesthesia would soon be felt; accordingly, we find that efforts in this direction were made by an increasing number of people at this time. Thus, in 1807, Baron Larrey rediscovered refrigeration anaesthesia, when he noticed that soldiers who had lain some time in the snow felt no pain during amputation; in 1821, Récamier used hypnotism during cauterization; in 1829, Cloquet successfully amputated a breast while the patient was in a mesmeric trance; in 1832, Wardrop employed bleeding to syncope for a surgical operation; and in the early 1840's, Esdaile in India and Elliotson in London were advocating and practising hypnotism during surgical operations.

It is not to be thought that all these advances occurred easily or without opposition. Every advance was opposed, often with violence, whether in the field of politics or of medicine. Thus, Elliotson was rewarded for his efforts to produce painless surgery by being branded as a quack and driven from his teaching post at University College Hospital.

In 1754, the year in which the pre-anaesthetic era may be said to have begun, Joseph Black announced the discovery of carbon dioxide, and also laid the foundation of the atomic theory by showing that a given weight of calcium carbonate always yielded a definite quantity of carbon dioxide, which could, in turn, be united with calcium hydroxide to form the original quantity of calcium carbonate. In 1772, Joseph Priestley discovered nitrous oxide, and a few years later both he and Scheele announced the isolation of oxygen (dephlogisticated air).

The work of Black, Priestley, Lavoisier and Laplace brought gases very much to the notice of the public. Early in 1799, Dr. Thomas Beddoes opened the Pneumatic Medical Institution at Bristol, with the young Humphry Davy as superintendent. Davy had already experimented with nitrous oxide, and, in 1800, he published his suggestion that nitrous oxide might be used with advantage during surgical operations. The advice fell on deaf ears.

In 1824, Hickman published *A Letter on Suspended Animation*, in which he advocated anaesthesia with carbon dioxide and, in 1828, he applied, through King Charles X, to the Royal Academy of Medicine of France. Hickman's proposal received no support, which was probably as well, since his method of anaesthesia was indubitably dangerous.

As early as 1795, Richard Pearson was advocating the inhalation of ether in the treatment of phthisis, and in the succeeding years both ether and nitrous oxide were inhaled from time to time on account of their intoxicating effects, especially in the U.S.A. These experiences led to the use of both ether and nitrous oxide as anaesthetics, first in 1842, when Clarke gave ether to a patient while Elijah Pope extracted a tooth, and when Crawford W. Long used ether on several occasions for minor surgery. Neither Clarke nor Long published his experiences. In 1844, Horace Wells used nitrous oxide for dentistry, but a demonstration arranged at the Massachusetts General Hospital proved unconvincing. It was left to a former partner of Wells, one William Thomas Green Morton, to demonstrate anaesthesia with ether, which he did at the hospital where Wells had failed, and, from that day, October 16, 1846, the "deepest furrow of the wrinkled brow of agony has been smoothed for ever".

1749–1832. Goethe.
1754.   Joseph Black submits a thesis, *De Magnesia Alba*, for his M.D.

Figure 8. A South American Indian using a blow-pipe with darts
poisoned with curare.
From a picture in the Ethnographical Museum, Gothenburg.

Figure 9. An amputation of the leg, from Johann von Gersdorff's "Feldtbuch der Wundartzney", 1517.

In his thesis, Black announced the discovery and isolation of carbon dioxide ("fixed air"), and, by establishing a quantitative basis for chemistry, he paved the way for the atomic theory. His paper was first published in 1756, and appeared in book form in 1777 and 1782.

1754.   Benjamin Pugh describes an "air-pipe" for the resuscitation of the newly born. It was made of a wire spring, 10 inches long, covered with thin, soft leather, and was to be introduced into the infant's mouth digitally as far as the larynx.

1755.   John Hunter (1728–93) conducts experiments on artificial respiration.

From the very outset of this period, there is an obvious increase in interest in the problem of respiration. John Hunter, one of the most original of medical thinkers, was quick to carry out investigations into the function of the lungs. Working with dogs, he used a double-acting bellows, one chamber of which filled the lungs with fresh air, while the other exhausted the lungs and discharged the "mephitic air" into the atmosphere. The bellows became popular for resuscitation of the apparently dead.

Hunter's contributions to surgery, dentistry and medicine were outstanding; his name is intimately associated with the Royal College of Surgeons of England.

1756–63.   The Seven Years War: Frederick of Prussia beats France in Europe; and Britain wins India and North America.

1756–91.   Mozart.

1757.   Pitt in power. The Battle of Plassey.

1759.   Quebec, Minden.

1759.   The British Museum opened.

1759–96.   Robert Burns.

1761.   Giovanni Battista Morgagni (1682–1771) publishes his *De Sedibus et Causis Morborum*, which has earned him the title of the Father of Pathology; it was translated into English in 1769.

1761.　Leopold Auenbrugger (1722–1809) publishes his *Inventum Novum*, in which Percussion is described, and the various differences in sound caused by hydrothorax, enlargement of the heart, etc., are pointed out. No notice of the invention was taken until Corvisart republished the *Inventum Novum* in 1808.

1763.　James Boswell becomes the faithful follower of the "Great Cham", Dr. Samuel Johnson (1709–83).

1765.　Foundation of the Medical School of Philadelphia.

1766.　Cavendish (1731–1810) discovers hydrogen.

1768.　Foundation of the Royal Academy of Art. The inventions of Watt, Arkwright and others begin the era of manufacturing industry.

1770–1850.　Wordsworth.

1770–1827.　Beethoven.

1771–1832.　Sir Walter Scott.

1772.　Prussia, Austria and Russia begin dividing Poland.

1772.　Discovery of nitrous oxide by Joseph Priestley (1733–1804).

The exact date of the discovery of nitrous oxide, which Priestley named "dephlogisticated nitrous air", is not recorded, but the experiments which he described are related to 1772 or, at latest, the early part of 1773, (vide *Experiments and Observation on Different Kinds of Air*, 2nd edition, 1775). He first produced oxygen ("dephlogisticated air") in 1771, but left his investigation of this gas unfinished until 1774–75. Meanwhile, Scheele also discovered oxygen independently in 1772, publishing his discovery in 1777 (*Chemische Abhandlung von der Luft und dem Feuer*, Upsala). Priestley discovered other gases, notably nitric oxide and methane. He was a Unitarian minister and a friend of Benjamin Franklin; he held pronounced liberal opinions, and was sympathetic to the French revolutionaries. He received much encouragement and protection from Lord Shelburne, but in 1794 he felt it advisable to emigrate to America on account of the hostility of the "rascal multitude".

1773.　Foundation of the Medical Society of London.

1773.　Publication of *A Collection of Authentic Cases Proving the Practicability of Recovering Persons Visibly Dead by Drowning, Suffocation, etc.* by Alexander Johnson.

In this book, Johnson gave a short account of a "Society for the Recovery of Drowned Persons", founded in Amsterdam in 1767, and he succeeded in focusing public attention on the practicability of resuscitative measures.

1774.   Foundation of the Humane Society (later, the Royal Humane Society).

1774.   William Hunter (1718–83) publishes *The Anatomy of the Gravid Uterus*.

William Hunter, elder brother of the great John Hunter, was himself a great anatomist and obstetrician. The illustrations in his *Anatomy of the Gravid Uterus* have never been equalled either in accuracy or in artistic merit. William Hunter's name is associated with the Museum which he bequeathed to the University of Glasgow.

1775–1861.   Turner, landscape painter.

1776.   The Abbé Fontana publishes a work on nitrous oxide and oxygen.

Later, in 1779, Fontana also described a method of carbon dioxide absorption using "quick-lime water", which receives mention by Ingen-Housz in that year. The Abbé also contributed substantially to the understanding of South American arrow-poisons.

1776.   William Cullen (1710–90) publishes the first volume of his *First Lines on the Practice of Physick*.

Cullen, whose interest in the natural history of disease was great, was one of the foremost teachers at Edinburgh. His interests were wide; in 1755, he had conducted experiments on the freezing of small animals as a method of producing suspended animation, and now (1776) he recommended the inflation of the lungs of drowned or suffocated persons by means of a bellows.

1777.   Publication of *Expériences sur la Respiration des Animaux* by Antoine-Laurent Lavoisier (1743–94).

Lavoisier was the first to observe the true nature of oxidation, and he realized that air that had been breathed resembled air which had been used for the oxidation of metals, with the addition of carbon dioxide. He renamed Priestley's "dephlogisticated air" "oxygène", because he thought it to be a constituent of all acids. He was executed by the Revolutionaries as an enemy to France ("The Republic has no need for scientists").

1778.   John Brown (c. 1736–88), originator of the Brunonian system of disease and therapy, publishes his *Elementa Medicinae*.

1779.   Publication of *A Medical Commentary on Fixed Air* by Matthew Dobson, the first book on the medical uses of carbon dioxide and carbonates.

1779.   John Ingen-Housz discovers ethylene, and publishes the first edition of his *Experiments upon Vegetables*.

Ingen-Housz proved that green plants utilize carbon dioxide and give off oxygen in sunlight: he was the first to appreciate that breathing is necessary for all living organisms, and that the carbon in plants comes from the air, not the soil. At the end of the preface to the *Experiments*, he wrote, "When this book was entirely printed, and nothing but the latter end of the preface unfinished, I was informed by my friend the Abbé Fontana, that he discovered a few days ago a new method of procuring to a sick person the benefit of breathing any quantity of dephlogisticated air at a cheap rate". He goes on to describe the use of a solution of quick-lime for this purpose, one of the earliest accounts of carbon dioxide absorption ever published. Scheele had also used "milk of lime" for absorbing "fixed air" from the atmosphere in which he kept bees alive by means of his "fire-air" (oxygen). Priestley was unable to confirm the results of Ingen-Housz and Scheele.

1779.   Publication of the *Mémoire sur la Découverte du Magnétisme Animal* by Franz Anton Mesmer (1734–1815).

1780.   Issue of the *Observations sur le Magnétisme Animal* by d'Eslon.

Born near Lake Constance, Mesmer qualified in medicine in 1766, and practised at first in Vienna, where he was friendly with Mozart. His mystical outlook and the quackish nature of his claims caused him to remove to Paris, where his method of treatment soon became popular. "Mesmerism" consisted of causing hysterical convulsions: the somnambulistic trance, later to be used as a form of surgical anaesthesia, was the discovery of one of Mesmer's pupils, de Puységur. In 1784, a commission of distinguished persons, including the celebrated Dr. Guillotin, Benjamin Franklin and Lavoisier, appointed for the purpose by Louis XVI, reported that there was no scientific basis for Mesmer's claims and that his results were due to imagination. The scientific basis of Mesmerism was to be established by James Braid (See under 1843).

D'Eslon was Docteur-Régent de la Faculté de Médecine of Paris and was Mesmer's most devoted pupil and admirer.

1780.	François Chaussier of Dijon (1746–1804) advocates a special mask and bag of chamois leather for performing artificial respiration on new-born babies. He advises the use of oxygen.
1781.	Appearance of Immanuel Kant's (1724–1810) great work, *The Critique of Pure Reason*.
1781.	Henry Cavendish (1731–1810), who had prepared hydrogen in 1766, demonstrates that the combustion of hydrogen and oxygen produces water.
1783.	Britain acknowledges the independence of the United States of America.
1783.	Publication of the *Traité sur le Vénin de la Vipère et sur les Poisons Américains* by the Abbé Fontana.
1783.	Von Schreber issues his *Über das Pfeilgift der Amerikaner in Guiana*.

Fontana showed by his experiments that curare affected the irritability of muscles, without any direct action on the heart. Von Schreber's work was the first botanical account of the American arrow-poisons. He believed that the principal ingredient of "Woorara" (curare) was *Strychnos*.

1783.   De Gardanne issues his *Catéchisme sur les Morts Apparents dits Asphyxiés*, an early essay on the apparently dead.

1784.   Laplace (1749–1827) publishes his epoch-making *Théorie des Planètes*.

1784.   James Moore describes *A Method of Preventing or Diminishing Pain in Several Operations of Surgery*.

James Moore was the brother of Sir John Moore of Corunna fame. His method consisted of a sort of vice which could be screwed down on to a limb, thus compressing the main nerves. It was used at St. George's Hospital in London by John Hunter, but this revival of an idea of Paré's never became popular.

1785.   Introduction of the use of digitalis in the treatment of cardiac dropsy by William Withering (1741–99).

1786.   Desgranges of Lyons describes a pump for artificial respiration.

1788.   The colonization of Australia begins.

1788–1824.   Lord Byron.

1788.   Edmund Goodwyn earns the gold medal of the Humane Society with his book, *The Connexion of Life with Respiration*, while Charles Kite of Gravesend wins the silver medal with his Essay on the *Recovery of the Apparently Dead*.

Goodwyn advocated the inflation of the lungs of drowned persons with the aid of Nooth's pump, which later became popular; he also advised oxygen in preference to common air, as did Kite also. Kite (d.1811) described the first endotracheal tube ("an instrument to pass beyond the glottis"), and mentioned the introduction of the tube through the nose, writing, "the crooked tube bent like a male catheter, recommended by Dr. Munro, and mentioned by Mr. Portal, Mr. le Cat, and others, is to be . . . introduced through the mouth or one nostril into the glottis, when, on blowing through the mouthpiece, or applying the bellows the lungs will be dilated". The reference to Dr. Munro cannot be identified, but it may be to Alexander Munro primus of Edinburgh, who apparently advocated the inflation of the lungs by artificial means as a method of resuscitation. Claude-Nicolas le Cat (1742–68) expressed a desire to see a tube designed which could be passed through the glottis to assist in artificial respiration (See Appendix C). Kite's *Essay* is also notable for the observation that the diaphragm can be stimulated by "throwing a strong galvanic current" across the chest.

1789.   Hans Courtois of Tournai invents a double pump for the ventilation of the lungs through a tracheotomy cannula.

1789.   Benjamin Rush (1746–1813) is appointed Professor of Physics at Pennsylvania.

Rush, one of those systematists who thought to simplify the theory of disease and, consequently, treatment, was easily the most famous American physician of the period.

1791.   Haydn (1732–1809) visits England, where he is acclaimed.

1791.   Luigi Galvani (1737–98). Professor of Surgery and Anatomy at Bologna, publishes his *De Viribus Electricitatis in Motu Musculari Commentarius*, in which he showed that electricity could be generated in animal tissues.

1792.   James Curry publishes his *Popular Observations on Apparent Death and Drowning*.

Curry, who qualified at Edinburgh in 1784, became a physician at Guy's Hospital. He had already designed an endotracheal tube (1791), similar to Kite's, and he now described additional instruments which also seem to be based on those which Kite had described. (He is not to be confused with James Currie, the celebrated hydrotherapist and editor of the works of Robert Burns).

1794.   The *Zoonomia* of Erasmus Darwin (1731–1802).

Erasmus Darwin, the grandfather of Charles Darwin, suggested blood transfusion for the treatment of "nervous and putrid" fevers. His offer to transfuse a person suffering from "an entirely impervious throat" is interesting for the ingenuity of the method proposed (See Keynes, *Blood Transfusion*, Bristol, John Wright, 1949, p. 19).

1794–95. Publication of the two editions of Beddoes and Watt's *Considerations on the Medicinal Use of Factitious Airs.*

Thomas Beddoes (1754–1808), a Shropshire man, received his M.D. at Oxford in 1786. A friend of Lavoisier, he was forced to resign his post at Oxford on account of his liberal political opinions. He established the "Pneumatic Institute" at Clifton for the treatment of diseases by the inhalation of gases, the first superintendent being the youthful Humphry Davy. The apparatus for the Institute was constructed by James Watt, the perfector of the steam engine. The second edition of Beddoes and Watt's monograph contained a letter on the inhalation of ether by Richard Pearson of Birmingham, who, the same year, published a tract, *A Short Account of the Nature and Properties of Different Kinds of Airs*, in which his ideas are given in greater detail. Pearson states that he had frequent opportunities for administering ether by inhalation to persons suffering from consumption, and that it relieved the dyspnoea and promoted expectoration.

1795. The British take Cape Colony from the Dutch.
1797. Jacques Garnerin makes a parachute descent of about 3,300 feet from a balloon.
1798. The Battle of the Nile.
1798. Edward Jenner (1749–1823) describes vaccination against smallpox.

Jenner will always be remembered as one of the world's greatest benefactors. At this date, smallpox was one of the most dreaded diseases of mankind. Jenner's *Inquiry into the Causes and Effects of the Variolae Vaccinae* not only saved countless lives, but opened the door to the study of immunity.

1800.   The union of Great Britain and Ireland.
1800.   Fine of Geneva describes a leather endotracheal tube.
1800.   Benjamin Thompson, Count Rumford (1793–1814), founds the Royal Institute of Great Britain.

Humphry Davy soon became a professor in the Royal Institute, as did Thomas Young (propounder of a theory of colour vision and instrumental in the decipherment of Egyptian hieroglyphics) and Michael Faraday. Although he was an American, Thompson was knighted by King George IV, became a Fellow of the Royal Society and was appointed a Count of the Holy Roman Empire.

In this same year, (Sir) Humphry Davy (1778–1829), still Superintendent of Beddoes Medical Pneumatic Institute, issued his *Researches Chemical and Philosophical, chiefly concerning Nitrous Oxide . . . and its Respiration*, which contains the remark, "As nitrous oxide in its extensive operation appears capable of destroying physical pain, it may probably be used with advantage during surgical operations in which no great effusion of blood takes place". Davy deserves great credit for inhaling nitrous oxide in spite of the pronouncement by the celebrated Latham Mitchill that this gas was the dreaded "contagium" or cause of disease. For full details of Davy's work on nitrous oxide, see Cartwright's *English Pioneers of Anaesthesia* (Bristol, John Wright, 1952).

According to Keys (*History of Surgical Anaesthesia*, New York, Schuman, 1905, p. 105), William Allen, also in 1800, in the presence of Sir Astley Cooper and others, demonstrated the results of the inhalation of nitrous oxide, noting especially the loss of sensation to pain. This incident is taken from a history of Guy's Hospital written in 1892, and seems to lack all contemporary evidence.

1803.   The Battle of Assaye.
1804.   Napoleon Bonaparte becomes Emperor of the French.
1805.   The Battle of Trafalgar.
1805.   Dr. John Warren of Massachusetts uses the inhalation of ether in the treatment of phthisis.

1806.   The Holy Roman Empire declared to be ended.
1806.   The Royal Humane Society authorizes special instruments for resuscitation. Somewhat similar to those designed by Kite, they include a silver endotracheal catheter.
1806.   Friedrich Sertürner (1743–1841) announces the isolation of morphine (*J. Pharmac.*, Leipzig).

The isolation of morphine, at first called morphium, was not only important in its own right, but, being the first alkaloid to be obtained in a pure state, it initiated the search for the active principles of many other medicinal plants, which could thereafter be given in definite dosage.

1807.   Abolition of the Slave Trade by Great Britain.
1807.   François Chaussier designs an endotracheal tube with a flange of sponge intended to secure an air-tight fit at the glottis.
1807.   Von Humboldt and Bonpland describe the manufacture of curare (*Voyage aux Régions Equinoxiales du Nouveau Continent*).
1807.   Count Maxime de Puységur publishes his book, *Du Magnétisme Animal*, in which reference is made to "somnambulism", the hypnotic trance which de Puységur had discovered.
1807.   The Battle of Preuss-Eylau.

It was after this battle, fought in the cold of a Polish winter, that Baron Dominique-Jean Larrey (1766–1842) rediscovered the analgesic action of cold, last noticed by Bartholin in 1661. Larrey is notable also as the inventor of the "Flying Ambulance", which was designed to collect wounded from the field of battle; he was also a pioneer in the use of intragastric feeding. Napoleon on St. Helena remembered Larrey and made a bequest to him.

1808.   The Peninsular War.
1808.   William P. C. Barton, a pupil of Benjamin Rush, publishes his *Dissertation on the Chymical Properties and Exhilerating Effects of Nitrous Oxide Gas*.
1809–47.   Mendelssohn.
1809–49.   Chopin.
1809.   William Allen and W. H. Pepys deliver a paper, *On Respiration*, at the Royal Society.

Allen and Pepys showed that the only change which occurs to air on respiration is the substitution of carbon dioxide for a portion of the oxygen; that, when pure oxygen is breathed, nitrogen is excreted by the lungs; and that the lungs do not completely collapse on expiration, as had hitherto been believed, but still contain more than 100 cubic inches of air.

1809.   Ephraim McDowell (1771–1830) performs the first successful ovariotomy.

The operation took 25 minutes, and the tumour weighed 22½ lb.; the patient survived for a further 33 years, dying at the age of 78. McDowell subsequently performed seven more ovariotomies, with only one death. Although intra-abdominal surgery had occasionally been undertaken before, nearly always unsuccessfully, McDowell's fearless interventions may really be taken as the starting point of abdominal surgery.

1811.   Sir Benjamin Brodie (1783–1862) delivers a paper on curare at the Royal Society.

Brodie showed that, in curarized animals, artificial respiration is capable of supporting life until the effects of the drug wear off. In his experiments, he performed tracheotomy, cannulated the trachea, and inflated the lungs with bellows.

Subsequently, Brodie opposed the introduction of ether anaesthesia : having killed some guinea-pigs by causing them to inhale ether, he pronounced anaesthesia to be dangerous.

1815.   The Battle of Waterloo.
1815.   The Apothecaries Act lays the basis for medical teaching in England. It was not, however, until 1828 that hospital attendance became obligatory for the student.
1815.   Nysten (*Dictionary of Medical Science*) speaks of the inhalation of ether for mitigating the pains of colic as being familiarly known.

1816. Réné Laennec (1781–1826) invents the stethoscope; the majority of the words used in describing the sounds heard on stethoscopy, such as râles, pectoriloquy, aegophony and bronchophony, are to be found in his *De l'Auscultation Médiate*.

It is possible that ether was used as an anaesthetic in Edinburgh at about this time, but, in the absence of contemporary evidence, the incident described in the *Edinburgh Medical and Surgical Journal* for April, 1847, must remain somewhat doubtful. It is there stated that a bone was removed from the throat of a woman "about thirty years ago", the operation having proved impossible without the assistance of the inhalation of ether (See a letter by Dr. Douglas Guthrie in the *Lancet*, 1947, **ii**, 921).

1818. James Blundell (d. 1877) read to the Medico-Chirurgical Society of London an account of the successful transfusion of 12–14 ounces of human blood.

Blundell reported a further six transfusions of human blood in 1824, and designed an ingenious apparatus (the "Impellor") for that operation. He also carried out a number of useful experiments on animals, proving that life might be saved after blood-loss by the infusion of comparatively small quantities of blood.

1818. An anonymous article on ether appears in the *Quarterly Journal of Science and Arts*.

This article has often been said to have been written by Michael Faraday, but there is no proof that he was, in fact, the author. The article states that "when the vapour of ether, mixed with common air, is inhaled, it produces effects very similar to those occasioned by nitrous oxide". A method of vapourizing ether by means of a bottle into the upper part of which a tube could be introduced for a variable distance is also herein described.

1819. Stockman in the U.S.A. demonstrated the exhilarating effects of nitrous oxide.

1819.   John Dalton reads a paper, subsequently published in the *Annals of Philosophy*, entitled *Memoir on Sulphuric Ether*. This is the classical paper on the chemistry and physical properties of ether.

1821.   Pierre Bretonneau (1778–1864) reads a paper before the Paris Académie de Médecine in which he asserts that "croup", "malignant angina" and "scorbutic gangrene of the gums" are a specific disease, for which he proposes the name "diphtheritis".

1821.   Récamier uses hypnotism as a surgical anaesthetic.

Joseph Claude Anselme Récamier (1774–1856), Professor of Medicine at the Collège de France, performed the first operation under intentional anaesthesia in modern times: the application of the cautery while the patient was under hypnosis. This epoch-making event appears to have been unnoticed by the historians of anaesthesia.

1823.   Thomas Wakley founds the *Lancet*.

From its first issue, the *Lancet* courageously attacked the corrupt management of hospitals and the inadequate requirements for the training of doctors. Wakley became the target for abuse, assault and libel actions, but he persisted in his policy until he had caused far-reaching reforms to be made.

1824.   Henry Hill Hickman (1800–30) writes his *Letter on Suspended Animation* to T. A. Knight, Esquire.

Hickman had already carried out the first experiments on surgical anaesthesia with carbon dioxide when he wrote his *Letter*, which was later modified and published. In 1828, he addressed a communication to King Charles X of France, requesting that his method of anaesthesia should be considered by the Académie de Médecine. A committee was formed, but it reported adversely; in a plenary session, Baron Larrey was the only person who commented favourably on Hickman's proposals.

1825.   François draws attention to a morphine-like substance present in lettuce at the time of seed-bearing.

1825. Waller and Doubleday, independently, employ blood transfusion in obstetric haemorrhage. Doubleday's patient, who received 14 oz. of blood, showed a striking improvement; Waller continued to use transfusion, and reported a successful case in 1859.

1825. Charles Waterton (1782–1865) publishes his *Wanderings in South America*, which contain an extensive and reasonably accurate account of curare.

1827. The Battle of Navarino secures the establishment of the Kingdom of Greece.

1827. Leroy shows that the use of bellows in artificial respiration may cause pulmonary damage; in the following year, he describes a spatula to aid in endotracheal intubation.

1827. Richard Bright (1789–1858), in his *Reports of Medical Cases*, shows the connexion between diseased kidneys and dropsy.

1827. Bousingault and Roulin prepare a partially purified extract of curare.

1828. The repeal of the Test Act.

1828. Cap (Lyons) describes an endotracheal tube and pump for resuscitation.

1829. William Wright in his *On the Varieties of Deafness*, shows that, in certain circumstances, carbon dioxide can act as a local anaesthetic.

1829. The French surgeon, Cloquet, performs a painless mastetomy with the aid of hypnotism.

1830. Opening of the Liverpool and Manchester Railway.

1831. Samuel Guthrie (1782–1848) of New York State discovers chloroform ("Guthrie's Sweet Whisky"). He is quickly followed by Eugène Soubeiran in France and Justus von Liebig in Germany; von Liebig also discovers chloral.

1831. The Reform Bill is passed. The Anatomy (Warburton's) Act institutes the licensing of medical schools, and also legislates for the supply of subjects for the teaching of anatomy, thus freeing the doctors from the activities of the "Body Snatchers".

1831. O'Shaughnessy of Newcastle upon Tyne shows that, in cholera, the fluids and salts in the blood are greatly reduced, with a corresponding increase of these substances in the excreta.

1832. During the epidemic of Asiatic cholera, Thomas Aitchison Latta of Leith, relying on O'Shaughnessy's observation, employs intravenous saline solution with great success in the treatment of severe cholera.

1832.   Wardrop advocates anaesthesia by bleeding to syncope.

1833.   Marshall Hall (1790–1857) demonstrates that the spinal cord is a chain of segments whose functional units are separate reflex arcs.

Marshall Hall's name is associated with the first modern method of artificial respiration, performed by rolling the prone patient to each side, which was an improvement on the earlier method of rolling the patient on a barrel.

1834.   J. B. A. Dumas (1800–84) discovers the chemical composition of, and gives its present name to, chloroform.

1835.   Robert James Graves (1797–1853) ("He fed fevers") describes exophthalmic goitre.

1836.   Lafargue injects a paste containing morphine under the skin with a blunt syringe, first making small incisions in order to insert the nozzle.

1837.   Liégard revives the method of local analgesia by compression of the limb.

1839.   Taylor and Washington in U.S.A. repeat Lafargue's method of injecting morphine (*vide* 1836).

1839.   The following is quoted from Clutterbuck's *Lectures on Bloodletting* (*vide* Clement, *Anesthesiology* (1953), **14**, 480): "In one of the great hospitals of the metropolis a case occurred lately where 128 ounces of blood were drawn at one time in order, by inducing syncope, to facilitate the reduction of a dislocation of the thigh. The patient lived a week afterwards, and then, as is said, died from inflammation of the vein punctured".

1839.   Edwin Chadwick (1800–90) succeeds in having a Sanitary Commission created.

1839   John Scoffern, in *Chemistry no Mystery, or a Lecturer's Bequest*, gives an account of nitrous oxide and its intoxicating effects. This is one of the few scientific books illustrated by Cruikshank ("Phiz") and contains a well-known frontispiece entitled "Laughing Gas".

1840.   Penny Postage introduced under Rowland Hill's scheme.

1840.   The "Health of Towns Association" founded by Southwood Smith (1788–1861).

1841.   Death of Sir Astley Cooper (*b.* 1768).

1841.   Robert Schomburgk, *On the Urari*, describes the plants used in making curare.

1842.   Robert H. Collyer, an immigrant to the U.S.A. from Jersey, extracts a tooth painlessly from Mrs. Allen of Philadelphia with anaesthesia achieved with alcohol. He had previously reduced a dislocated hip in an intoxicated negro without causing pain.

1842.   R. M. Glover of Newcastle upon Tyne describes (in his Harveian Prize Essay) the effect of chloroform and other halogenated substances when injected into the bloodstream of animals. He observed, among other effects, depression of the blood pressure and respiration.

1842.   In January, William E. Clarke, who had frequently participated in "Ether Frolics", in Rochester, N.Y., administered ether from a towel to a Miss Hobbie while one of her teeth was extracted by Elijah Pope. Neither Clarke nor Pope published an account.

1842.   In March, Crawford Williamson Long (1815–93) of Jefferson, Georgia, administered ether to a man called James Venable and excised a sebaceous cyst. Long carried out several operations under ether, but finally gave up its use. He published no account of his cases until after the demonstration of ether anaesthesia by Morton.

1842.   In October, W. Squire Ward of Wellow, near Ollerton, Nottinghamshire, painlessly amputed a leg of James Wombwell who had been hypnotized by W. Topham of the Middle Temple.

1843.   James Braid (1795–1860) publishes his *Neurypnology*, in which he shows that the "mesmeric influence" is entirely subjective, and that no fluid or other substance passes from the operator to the patient.

1843.   John Elliotson (1791–1868) issues his *Numerous Cases of Surgical Operations without Pain in the Mesmeric State*, in which he uses the word "anaesthesia", a word which he was to use again in the modern sense in his Harveian Oration of July 1846.

1843.   Oliver Wendell Holmes (1809–94), poet and man of letters, issues his essay *On the Contagiousness of Puerperal Fever*, in which he shows that the contagion of erysipelas and puerperal fever is the same and that the disease is frequently carried from one patient to another by the physicians.

1844.   F. Rynd of Dublin uses an ingenious trocar for injecting morphine subcutaneously in the treatment of tic douloureux. He did not publish an account until 1861.

Figure 10. Jean-Baptiste van Helmont (1577–1644), the discoverer of "gas sylvestre" (carbon dioxide). From an engraving in the Académie de Médecine, Paris.

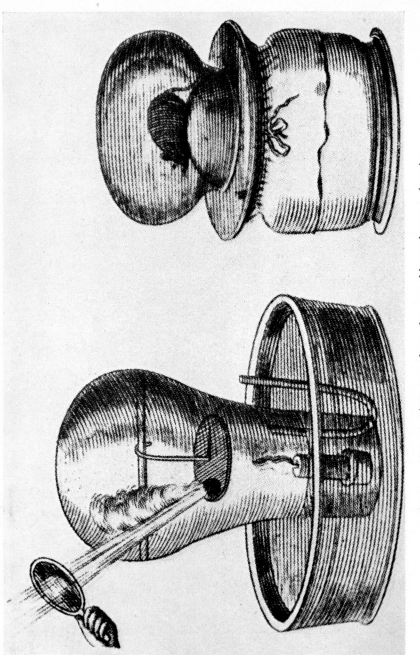

Figure 11. An experiment to show the resemblance between burning and breathing by John Mayow (1674).

1844.   E. E. Marcy of Hartford, Conn., "administered the vapour of rectified ether in my office to a young man . . . and after he had been rendered insensible to pain, cut from his hand an encysted tumour the size of an English walnut".

1844.   December 10: Horace Wells, a dentist of Hartford, Connecticut, attends a demonstration of Laughing Gas by Gardner Quinsy Colton.

Impressed by what he had seen, the following day Wells allowed Colton to administer the gas to him, while another dentist, Riggs, extracted one of Wells's teeth. Wells used nitrous oxide in some dozen cases with success, and then, later in December, obtained permission to demonstrate his method of anaesthesia at the Massachusetts General Hospital. The demonstration was a failure, and Wells abandoned the use of nitrous oxide.

1844.   Dr. E. R. Smilie of Boston claimed (in 1846) that he had rendered a certain John Johnson insensible to pain from the opening of an abscess in the neck by the use of an ethereal tincture of opium.

1845.   Erichsen advocates the use of oxygen in the resuscitation of drowned persons. Depaul modifies Chaussier's endotracheal tube (see under 1807), giving it a terminal, instead of a lateral eye.

1845.   George Wilson, Lecturer in Chemistry at Edinburgh, advocates the use of oxygen in resuscitation, describes the method of preparing this gas, and gives directions for constructing a sort of oxygen tent and its method of use. He also advocates the use of oxygen in diving bells and suggests the absorption of carbon dioxide by sulphate of soda and lime.

1846.   Repeal of the Corn Laws.

1846.   James Esdaile (1808–59) publishes his *Mesmerism in India and its Practical Application in Surgery and Medicine.*

Esdaile had performed his first major operation under hypnotism in 1845; he reported 261 cases in all, with a mortality of only 5.5 per cent, and a committee reported very favourably on his results.

1846.   March : Ducos recounts experiments on animals with ether, in which insensibility with recovery was noted. Like Glover (see under 1842), Ducos had failed to grasp the implications of his experiments.

1846.   September 30 : William Thomas Green Morton (1819-68) administers ether to Eben Frost for the extraction of a tooth.
          October 16 : Morton anaesthetizes Gilbert Abbott at the Massachusetts General Hospital, the surgeon being Dr. John C. Warren (1778-1856).

Abbott was suffering from a vascular tumour of the left side of the neck which was to have a ligature passed round it in order to reduce its blood supply. The ether was placed in a glass vessel, containing a sponge and having two orifices, one of which had a mouth-piece attached to it. The patient was asleep in four minutes, and the inhaler was then removed, the anaesthetic not being given during the operation. An incision about three inches in length was made over the tumour, a curved needle was then passed round it, and the ligature fastened. During most of the time, the patient showed no sign of sensation, but a short time before the end of the operation he moved his head, body and limbs, and began to mutter. On recovering consciousness, he declared that he had felt no pain, but only a scraping sensation. Dr. Warren expressed his satisfaction in the words, "Gentlemen, this is no humbug"; but Dr. Henry J. Bigelow, who was one of the numerous spectators, with a greater appreciation of the dignity which the occasion demanded, announced, "I have seen something today which will go round the world".

G.   MODERN PERIOD (since 1846).

It is no part of our duty to give here a complete account of the history of the world during the past century, but it is necessary to draw attention to certain trends in human activity which have a bearing on our subject. At the time of the discovery of anaesthesia, there was a galaxy of great men in the world of science and art: the names of Wordsworth, Heine, Carlyle, Macaulay, Victor Hugo, Mendelssohn, Chopin, Darwin, Thackeray, Dickens, Wagner, Emerson, Longfellow, Browning and Tennyson give lustre to the age; but it was not only in the *haut monde* of culture that developments were afoot. The year 1848 saw revolutions in almost every European country, and even in Britain, the Chartist riots caused disturbance and dismay. All this was the logical sequence to the idea of democracy, first enunciated in the modern sense by John Knox in 1563, and reaching its goal in universal franchise, which, for better or for worse, was only to be obtained by long and bitter struggles.

Meanwhile, the great manufacturing developments were leading to increased prosperity and to a huge increase in the population of the industrialized countries, and with this combination of population and prosperity came the itch for power. Thus were born the great wars of the last eighty years, and from them also the present political instability. The growth of democracy within states is now being paralleled by a similar attitude of the countries themselves: the expression of "nationalism", often exploited to the disadvantage of the country concerned, is now a commonplace, and, in this sense, the two World Wars may be regarded as the counterparts, at a different political level, of the revolts of 1848 and later. With complete "democracy" of nations has come "political instability" on a world scale, and in such fashion as to make one doubtful of the future. Yet the outlook is not all black: the barbarous peoples of the early 18th century developed humanity with industrial revolution, and, if a similar change occurs with the "democratization" of nations, as distinct from their individuals, then the future is bright indeed.

The developments of science in the last hundred years have been so obvious and so dramatic as to need no emphasis here. What is important, however, is the way in which medicine has learnt to make use of the most recent discoveries and inventions in other branches of science, and herein lies the main difference between the "Modern" period and the "Pre-Anaesthetic" age, when co-operation between medicine and science was negligible. The close association of all the branches of science is due to the great increase in means for the propagation of knowledge: the foundation of universities and schools of technology, the multiplication of learned societies and the publication of scientific journals.

The progress of medicine since the discovery of anaesthesia has been equally dramatic with that of the other sciences. At that date, there were only two specific curative drugs known: quinine for malaria, and ipecacuanha for amoebiasis; all other drugs were for symptomatic treatment only. Immunization, save for smallpox, was unknown; the germ-theory of disease was a forgotten philosophical concept; and antiseptics were not yet invented. The first great strides had, however, been taken in public health, and the study of statistics was beginning, but both these subjects had yet little influence. Medicine in 1846 was in the doldrums. The discovery of anaesthesia was a beacon-light which showed that further discoveries and inventions were possible, and that medicine was capable of advancing. Unfortunately, in the absence of a knowledge of the cause of infection, the discovery of anaesthesia led to a great increase in the amount of surgical interference with a correspondingly large mortality: in the years 1864–66, Lister at Glasgow performed 35 amputations with a mortality of 16 (45 per cent), and these figures were better than most; in some hospitals the mortality from this operation was well over 60 per cent. In 1867, Lister introduced his antiseptic technique; in the years 1867–70, he performed 40 amputations, with only 6 deaths (15 per cent). Antisepsis was not quickly adopted, and had many opponents who were gradually overwhelmed: from then onwards, surgical development was rapid, and the great era of the surgeon dawned. From 1880 to 1930, the surgeon was the hero of the medical world, but the developments in medicine in the last fifty years have lowered, by comparison, his prestige. Furthermore, the recent advances in anaesthesia and resuscitation have introduced a new type of surgery, meticulous and time-consuming, which lacks the dramatic brilliance of the earlier age, while the introduction of the National Health Service in Britain has also tended to level out the status of the specialties.

The first half-century of anaesthesia was largely occupied by the argument on the relative merits of chloroform and ether. It is surprising how few and how slow were the improvements before 1900, in spite of the immense impetus which was given to the subject by John Snow. It would seem as if his great book *On Chloroform and Other Anaesthetics* (1858) was either not read or was read with a closed intelligence.

Fifteen years before the end of the 19th century, local analgesia was discovered, but it was not until the beginning of the 20th century that it began to take its rightful place, a place from which it has declined somewhat with the development of safer methods of general anaesthesia in the last twelve years, in spite of the discovery of better agents, such as lignocaine.

The first quarter of the present century saw the gradual displacement of chloroform and the virtual supremacy of nitrous oxide used in conjunction with ether, but this advance has already given way to relaxant and other intravenous techniques, and the use of hypothermia and extracorporeal circulation has widened still further our horizons. It is fair to say that these more recent developments owe much to what is, perhaps, the most important advance in technique since the introduction of anaesthesia: namely endotracheal inhalation, developed by Rowbotham and Magill in 1917–20. The present combination of methods has made it possible for the surgeon to operate deliberately and definitively in every cavity of the body, and, so far from the prediction being correct, that the antibiotics would lead to the abolition of surgical intervention, the prospects for surgery are wider than they have ever been.

Against this background is to be set the introduction of the new drug, halothane. While it is not disputed that this drug may have some uses, it does not fit into the present trend of anaesthetic development, which is to produce narcosis, relaxation, and other desired phenomena, by separate drugs each with a specific action, rather than to return to the major use of agents with multiple effects. It therefore seems certain that, unless there be a great change in the line of evolution, it and similar drugs will play little part in the future of anaesthesia.

In retrospect, we can regard the last hundred years as being the age of the specialist, and, with the increase in scientific and medical knowledge, this specialism will increase. Thanks, however, to the means of propagating knowledge, each one, although he restrict his field more and more, is nevertheless better acquainted with other fields of work than has ever been the case in the past. It will therefore be seen that specialism is not merely a case of knowing more and more about less and less, but also of knowing more and more about everything. Fortunately, the human brain, unlike the electronic computing machine, has no upward limit to its capacity, and herein lies the challenge of the future.

The following chronology is not intended to be inclusive: it is merely meant as a series of signposts to the development of medicine over this period; in subsequent chapters the development of anaesthesia will be dealt with in detail.

1846.	October 16: Morton demonstrates ether anaesthesia at the Massachusetts General Hospital.
1846.	November 9: Bigelow reads a paper on etherization at the Boston Society of Medical Improvement. An account of this lecture was forwarded to Dr. Boott of Gower Street, London, some three weeks later.
1846.	November 12: Patent delivered to Morton and Jackson.

1846. December 19 : The first use of ether outside the United States of America. Dr. Boott wrote: " . . . a firmly fixed molar tooth was extracted in my study from Miss Lonsdale by Mr. Robinson . . . without the least sense of pain . . . the whole process of inhalation, extracting and waking was over in three minutes". Hooper's apparatus was used.

1846. December 21 : Liston, at University College Hospital, employs ether for (1) amputation of the leg and (2) avulsion of a toe-nail. Squire's apparatus was used.

1847. January 12 : At a meeting of the Académie de Médecine in Paris, Malgaigne described five anaesthetics which he had conducted personally.

1847. January 19 : James Young Simpson administers ether for the first time in midwifery.

1847. Semmelweiss (Vienna) introduces the use of an antiseptic (chloride of lime) for washing the hands before examining obstetric patients.

1847. Foundation of the American Medical Association.

1847. November 4 (?) : First use of chloroform by Simpson.

1848. January 24 : Death of Horace Wells by his own hand.

1848. January 28 : The first death under chloroform (Hannah Greener).

1848. Revolutionary movements in most European countries.

1849. John Snow, "On the Pathology and Mode of Communication of the Cholera". This paper in the *London Medical Gazette* demonstrated the waterborne nature of the disease. It was a triumph of deduction and is a milestone in the history of epidemiology.

1850. Von Helmholtz (1821–94) invents an ophthalmoscope. Three years previously he had read his epoch-making paper *On the Conservation of Energy*.

1850. William Detmold (New York) opens an abscess of the brain.

1851. The Great Exhibition in Hyde Park, London, was the first great demonstration of the progress of technology.

1852. Sir Richard Owen, while dissecting a rhinoceros, discovers the parathyroid glands.

1852. Louis Napoleon becomes Emperor of the French.

1853. Charles-Gabriel Pravaz (1791–1853), inventor of the galvanocautery, describes a glass syringe with tapered nozzle. This syringe was intended to be used with a special trocar for injecting ferric chloride into aneurysms, and thus to heal them by coagulation.

1853.   Alexander Wood (1817–84) of Edinburgh invents the hypodermic needle and adapts Pravaz's syringe for use with it.

1853.   At the birth of Prince Leopold, John Snow administers chloroform intermittently (in the manner later known as à la reine) to Queen Victoria. This event went a long way towards overcoming opposition on religious and moral grounds to the use of anaesthetics in midwifery.

1854.   The Crimea. Florence Nightingale (1820–1910), with thirty-eight nurses, took charge of the hospital at Scutari, where conditions were indescribably bad. Miss Nightingale had studied nursing at various places on the Continent and had become superintendent at the Hospital for Invalid Gentlewomen in London. She became a national heroine, and subsequently founded a school of nursing at St. Thomas's Hospital: her efforts led to a revolution in nursing and to the opening of this career to women of good class and education.

1854.   In the well-known Broad Street Pump episode, John Snow demonstrated the waterborne character of cholera. A public house close to the site of the pump (now Broadwick Street) has recently been named the "John Snow" in memory of this event. John Snow was a teetotaller.

1855.   Manuel Garcia, a Spaniard and teacher of singing in London, describes the laryngoscope.

1855.   Gaedicke extracts an alkaloid, erythroxyline, from the leaves of the coca plant.

1855.   Bessemer's steel process invented.

1857.   The Indian Mutiny.

1857.   John Snow again administers chloroform to Queen Victoria at the birth of Princess Beatrice.

1857.   Claude Bernard (1813–78) publishes his Leçons sur les Effets des Substances Toxiques, in which he demonstrates that curare acts at the myoneural junction. He had previously published papers on curare in 1850. Bernard made many discoveries, of which the most important are the glycogenetic function of the liver, the vaso-motor system (out of which grew his theory of maintenance of the milieu intérieur) and the digestive action of the pancreatic juice.

1858.   The laying of the Atlantic cable.

1858.   The death of John Snow at the moment of completing his book On Chloroform and Other Anaesthetics, which was seen through the press by his friend, (Sir) Benjamin W. Richardson.

1858. Passage of the Medical Act which established the General Medical Council in Great Britain.

1859. Charles Darwin (1809–82) publishes his *On the origin of the Species.* His *Descent of Man* followed in 1871.

1859. Niemann isolates cocaine (originally, cocaïne) from the leaves of *Erythroxylon coca.*

1860. China and Japan opened to European intercourse and trade.

1860. Joseph Wilson Swan of Newcastle upon Tyne makes the first carbon filament electric light.

1860. Ignaz Philipp Semmelweiss (1818–65) publishes his *Etiology, Concept and Prophylaxis of Puerperal Fever* at Budapest. His idea of contamination was hotly disputed, although, under his antiseptic routine, the mortality had fallen in his clinic from more than 12 per cent to less than 1 per cent.

1861. Cavour and Garibaldi free Italy from Austrian domination and unite the country as a kingdom.

1861. Paul Broca (1824–81) at Paris localizes the centre for speech in the third left frontal convolution of the brain.

1862. Joseph Clover describes an apparatus for administering chloroform in known percentage. The apparatus was identical with one described by John Snow in the *Lancet* in 1849.

1863. Hermann von Helmholtz (1821–94) publishes his *Die Lehre von den Tonempfindungen,* the classic work on the physiology of hearing.

1863. Louis Pasteur (1822–95) demonstrates that fermentation is caused by microscopic organisms. It was this work which stimulated Lister, who recognized the resemblance between fermentation and putrefaction, to adopt his antiseptic method.

1864. The Royal Medical and Chirurgical Society's Chloroform Committee's report emphasizes the depressant action of chloroform on the heart, and recommends the use of mixtures of chloroform and ether.

1865. End of the Civil War in the United States of America, quickly followed by the assassination of Abraham Lincoln. The war had lasted just over four years. Crawford W. Long, who had used ether anaesthesia in 1842, served as an anaesthetist with the Confederate forces, and W. T. G. Morton served in a similar capacity with the Federal troops.

1865.   Jean-Antoine Villemin (1827–92) shows that tuberculosis is infective and that the disease may be propagated by material from a granuloma: in other words, he anticipated Koch's "postulates" by 17 years.

1866.   The Battle of Sadowa leads to the formation of the North German Confederation under Prussia.

1866.   James Young Simpson created a Baronet.

1867.   The Second Reform Act confers household and lodger franchise in boroughs.

1867.   Bobbs of Indiana drains the gall-bladder.

1867.   Joseph Lister (1827–1912), Professor of Surgery at Glasgow, publishes an article On a New Method of Treating Compound Fracture, Abscess, etc. in which he describes the antiseptic method and attributes infection and putrefaction to airborne microbes.

1868.   Death of William T. G. Morton from apoplexy in New York.

1868.   Greene in the United States of America recommends the use of a pre-operative injection of morphine.

1868.   George Barth in England popularizes the use of cylinders for the storage of nitrous oxide under pressure.

1869.   Gustav Simon performs the first nephrectomy.

1869.   Friedrich Trendelenburg (1844–1924) designs a method of endotracheal administration of anaesthetics through a tracheostomy.

1869.   Suez Canal opened for traffic.

1870–71.   The Franco-Prussian War, followed by the Proclamation, at Versailles, of the foundation of the German Empire.

1872.   P. C. Oré of Bordeaux uses intravenous chloral hydrate as an anaesthetic.

1873.   Charles T. Jackson, claimant of the discovery of anaesthesia, becomes insane.

1873.   Sir William Gull (1816–90) describes myxoedema.

1875.   Leonhard Landois discovers that animal serum will haemolyze human blood.

1876.   Edoardo Porro of Pavia performs a successful Caesarean section with hysterectomy.

1876.   Johns Hopkins University founded.

1876.   Robert Koch (1843–1910) isolates the anthrax bacillus.

1876.   Bell invents the telephone.

1877.   Marc Nitze (1848–1906) invents the cystoscope.

1878.   The Afghan War.

1879.   The Zulu War.

1880.   Death of Charles T. Jackson.

1880. Various workers advocate the pre-anaesthetic use of atropine.

1880. Klikovitch of St. Petersburg advocates nitrous oxide in midwifery.

1880. Sir William Macewen describes peroral endotracheal intubation with a brass tube to facilitate the removal of a tumour of the base of the tongue.

1880. Advances in bacteriology include the isolation of staphylococci and streptococci (Pasteur) and of the typhoid bacillus (Eberth).

1880. (Sir) Joseph Swan at Newcastle upon Tyne gives the first large scale demonstration of electric lighting. Lord Armstrong's home, Cragside, at Rothbury, Northumberland, the first house to be designed to use electric light, is built Edison, who had worked independently, also developed an incandescent carbon-filament lamp, at about this time.

1881. Christian Albert Theodor Billroth (1829–94) of Vienna performs the first gastrectomy.

1881. Anton Wölfler (1850–1917) performs the first gastroenterostomy.

1881. Carlos Findlay of Cuba states that yellow fever is carried by the Culex (*Aedes aegypti*) mosquito.

1881. Pasteur demonstrates the prophylaxis of sheep against anthrax.

1881. Charles L. A. Laveran (1845–1922), while serving with the French Army in Algeria, discovers the parasite of malaria.

1882. Koch discovers the tubercle bacillus.

1882. Carl Langenbuch (Berlin) performs the first cholecystectomy.

1882. The British occupy Egypt.

1884. September 15: Carl Koller, at the Ophthalmological Congress at Heidelberg, demonstrates the analgesic action of cocaine in the eye.

1885. James Leonard Corning of New York performs spinal anaesthesia (accidentally) on a dog.

1885. William Stewart Halsted (1852–1922), then at New York, performs the first regional anaesthetic by injection of cocaine into a nerve trunk.

1885. (Sir) Frederic Hewitt constructs the first practical apparatus for nitrous oxide and oxygen.

1885. Pasteur saves Joseph Meister, an Alsatian boy of 9, who had been bitten by a rabid dog.

1886. Von Bergman introduces steam sterilization; this was the beginning of the aseptic era in surgery.

1887.   T. G. Morton of Philadelphia, son of the discoverer of anaesthesia, performs the first appendicectomy for acute appendicitis.

1887.   Taylor of Birmingham attempts to suture a perforated peptic ulcer.

1888–89.   Hyderabad Chloroform Commissions.

1889.   Foundation of Johns Hopkins Hospital.

1889.   Infectious diseases made notifiable in Britain.

1890.   Halsted, now at Baltimore, introduces rubber gloves for the benefit of his theatre sister, who ultimately became his wife.

1891.   Essex Wynter in England and Heinrich Quincke (the discoverer of angioneurotic oedema) in Germany describe lumbar puncture.

1891.   George Murray of Newcastle upon Tyne treats myxoedema with thyroid extract.

1892.   Carl Ludwig Schleich demonstrates local infiltration with a dilute solution of cocaine.

1892.   Heusner performs the first successful suture of a perforated peptic ulcer.

1893.   Foundation of the Johns Hopkins Medical School. The staff of the school was composed of many eminent men, chief among whom were Welch, Osler, Kelly and Halsted.

1893.   Foundation of the Society of Anaesthetists of London.

1894.   Alfred Kirstein invents a direct laryngoscope.

1894.   Ethyl chloride first used (accidentally) as a general anaesthetic.

1895.   Wireless telegraphy introduced by Marconi.

1895.   Nobel prizes instituted.

1895.   Wilhelm Conrad Röntgen (1845–1923) of Würzburg discovers X-rays.

1896.   Widal and Siccard introduce the agglutination test for typhoid fever.

1896.   Louis Rehn of Frankfurt performs the first operation on the heart, successfully suturing a stab wound and evacuating a haemopericardium.

1896.   Riva-Rocci introduces the mercury sphygmomanometer.

1897.   Joseph Lister elevated to the peerage with the title of Baron Lister of Lyme Regis. He was the first medical man to be raised to the English peerage.

1898.   Gustav Killian of Freiburg performs bronchoscopy.

1898.   Pierre and Marie Curie discover radium.

1898.　August Bier (1861–1949) performs spinal anaesthesia on man.

1899.　Korff introduces "twilight sleep" with morphine and hyoscine.

1900.　Karl Landsteiner of Vienna discovers human blood groups.

1901.　Sicard and Cathelin perform sacral epidural analgesia.

1902.　Charles Richet (1850–1935) of Paris discovers the phenomenon of anaphylaxis.

1902.　Ernest Henry Starling (1866–1927) of London discovers hormones.

1903.　Emil Fischer (1852–1919) and von Mering synthesize barbitone.

1903.　Einthoven invents the string galvanometer.

1904.　Ferdinand Sauerbruch (1875–1951) introduces a pressure cabinet to facilitate surgery in the open thorax.

1904.　Report of the Chloroform Committee of the British Medical Association which recommended the use of Vernon Harcourt's apparatus, designed to deliver not more than 2 per cent of chloroform vapour in air.

1905.　Heinrich F. W. Braun (1862–1934) introduces procaine, which had been first prepared by Alfred Einhorn in 1899.

1905.　Fritz Schaudinn (1871–1906) discovers the *Spirochaeta pallida*, later renamed *Treponema pallidum*.

1905.　Nikolai Korotkoff (b. 1876) introduces the auscultatory method of measuring the blood pressure.

1907.　Florence Nightingale becomes a member of the Order of Merit.

1907.　Barthélemy and Dufour describe the endotracheal insufflation method of administering anaesthetics.

1908.　Friedrich Trendelenburg (1844–1924) develops his operation of pulmonary embolectomy, but has no successful results.

1909.　Meltzer and Auer use endotracheal insufflation on animals, and Elsberg uses it in man.

1910.　Paul Ehrlich (1854–1915) and S. Hata (1873–1938) describe salvarsan ("606") in the therapy of syphilis. This was the first occasion on which chemists succeeded in producing a drug which had a predetermined action.

1911.　A. Goodman Levy and T. Lewis publish their epoch-making paper, *Heart Irregularities Resulting from the Inhalation of low Percentages of Chloroform Vapour, and their Relationship to Ventricular Fibrillation*, which explained the mechanism of "primary cardiac failure" under chloroform. This work largely stultified the report of a British Medical Association Committee, which appeared the same year.

1912. Hartwell and Hoguet stress the importance of restoring to the patient fluid lost by vomiting.

1912. Casimir Funk (b. 1884) demonstrates the cause of beriberi; he proposed the term "vitamines" for certain nutritional elements : because the discovery of the chemical formulae of some of these showed them not to be amines, the name has since been changed to "vitamins".

1912. Death of Lord Lister.

1912. Formation of a National Health Insurance scheme in Britain.

1912. (Sir) Robert Kelly popularizes endotracheal insufflation anaesthesia in England.

1914. Théodore Tuffier (1857–1929) performs the first successful valvotomy for valvular disease of the heart. Doyen of Lyons had unsuccessfully attempted a similar operation in the previous year.

1915. Dennis Jackson describes an anaesthetic apparatus which employed rebreathing with absorption of carbon dioxide.

1915. Franz Torek of New York successfully performs oesophagectomy.

1917. H. E. G. Boyle's first anaesthetic apparatus, inspired by earlier American machines.

1920. E. S. Rowbotham describes endotracheal inhalation anaesthesia. In the following year, he and I. W. Magill reported on nearly 3,000 cases.

1923. Haden and Orr demonstrate the importance of restoring chloride lost by vomiting.

1924. R. M. Waters introduced a practical apparatus for the absorption of carbon dioxide from anaesthetic atmospheres.

1924. Kirschner performs the first successful pulmonary embolectomy.

1929. Fleming discovers the bacteriostatic effect of penicillin in vitro.

1929. Hans Berger of Jena introduces electroencephalography.

1930. R. M. Waters introduces cyclopropane anaesthesia.

1931. Nissen performs the first successful pneumonectomy. Gluck in 1881 had already demonstrated on animals the possibility of this operation; in 1895 Macewen had removed a necrotic lung piecemeal; and in 1911

Kümmell had attempted pneumonectomy unsuccessfully.

1932. Weese and Scharpff develop Evipan (hexobarbitone).

1932. Leake and Chen introduce di-vinyl ether.

1933. Wangensteen introduces the aspiration treatment of intestinal obstruction.

1934. J. S. Lundy introduces thiopentone.

1934. R. J. Minnitt introduces an apparatus, suitable for use by midwives, for administering an analgesic concentration of nitrous oxide and air.

1935. Gerhard Domagk introduces prontosil, the first of the "sulpha" group of antibiotics.

1935. Striker experiments with trichloroethylene as an anaesthetic.

1935. King in London elucidates the structural formula of d-tubocurarine.

1938. Devine describes the synchronous abdominal and perineal operation for excision of the rectum.

1938. Crafoord constructs the "spiropulsator", the first practical positive pressure respirator for use in anaesthesia.

1940. Wiener and Landsteiner discover the rhesus factor in human blood.

1941. C. Langton Hewer introduces trichloroethylene.

1942. The isolation of adreno-cortico-trophic hormone. Cortisone had been isolated in 1936.

1942. H. R. Griffith and G. E. Johnson describe the use of curare in anaesthesia.

1942. F. M. Allen reports on refrigeration anaesthesia for amputation.

1942. R. A. Hingson and W. B. Edwards introduce continuous caudal analgesia in obstetrics.

1943. Florey introduces penicillin.

1948. Introduction of the National Health Service in Britain.

1948. Formation of a Faculty of Anaesthetists in the Royal College of Surgeons of England.

1952. Laborit and Huguenard introduce "hibernation".

1952. Cookson, Neptune and Bailey describe hypothermia in man.

1957. Halothane, developed by Imperial Chemical Industries, introduced into anaesthetic practice.

Chapter Two

ETHER

The discovery of di-ethyl ether has been attributed to Jābir ibn Hayyān, an Arabian philosopher who flourished in the eighth century and was a close friend of Ja'far al-Barmāki, the Wazīr to Harūn ar-Rashīd, immortalized in the *Thousand and One Nights*. Similarly, Raymond Lull or Lully, a Majorcan alchemist of the thirteenth century, has also been credited with the discovery, but there seems to be no evidence to substantiate these claims. The curious reader is referred to Appendix A for a fuller consideration of these persons.

The first unequivocal description of ether, under the name, "oleum vitrioli dulce" ("sweet oil of vitriol"), occurs in Conrad Gesner's edition of the works of Valerius Cordus, published in Strasburg in 1561 (*De artificiosis extractionibus*, Lib. 3, Cap. 12). A second, and more accurate, edition was prepared by Peter Condemberg ten years later. "Oil of vitriol" was the name of what we now call sulphuric acid; the "sweet oil" was obtained by the distillation of sulphuric acid and spirits of wine. Cordus advocated the internal use of ether in a dose of one to three drops in a moderate quantity of wine as a remedy for such diverse disorders as ulcer of the bladder and pneumonia.

In 1605, there appeared the first edition of Paracelsus' *Opera Medico-chemica sive paradoxa*. It contains an account of the action of ether on domestic fowls. "Of all the extracts of vitriol, this particular one is the most important, being

Figure 12. The second illustration of blood transfusion (Mercklin, 1679).

Figure 13. William Harvey (1578–1657) describing the circulation of the blood to King Charles I; Prince Charles sits at the table. From a painting in the Royal College of Physicians, London.

stable. Furthermore, it has an agreeable taste, so that even chickens take it gladly, and thereafter fall asleep for a long time, awakening unharmed. In view of the effect of this vitriol, I think it especially noteworthy that its use may be recommended for painful illnesses, and that it will mitigate the disagreeable complications of these."

Paracelsus had died in 1541, and Cordus three years later, the works of both appearing posthumously. It is generally believed that ether was discovered about 1540, at which time Cordus and Paracelsus seem to have been together. It is, therefore, impossible to apportion the credit for the discovery between them.

Ether was occasionally synthesized during the next two centuries; thus, the Hon. Robert Boyle describes the process in his *Experiments and notes about the producibleness of chymicall principles* (1680); and Sir Isaac Newton also mentions it in his *Optics* (1704). It was not, however, until the German chemist, Froben (Frobenius), wrote *An account of a spiritus vini æthereus* in the *Philosophical Transactions* of the Royal Society in 1730, that the "sweet oil of vitriol" became well known or acquired its present name. The place of ether in medical treatment became established in 1743, probably because in that year there was published *An account of the extraordinary medicinal fluid, called æther*, by M(atthew) Turner, Surgeon in Liverpool, who recommended the administration of two teaspoonfuls of ether in wine for various complaints, and also for headache, of which he writes, "In stubborn cases, it will likewise be serviceable to snuff a little of the ether up the nostrils, either alone or mixed with equal parts of lavender water, Hungary water or Brandy, or it may be convenient to apply a bit of linen rag, wetted with æther, up the nostrils". In 1795, Richard Pearson published his *Short account of the nature and properties of different kinds of airs*, in which he stated that he had found that the inhalation of the vapour of ether by patients with phthisis was very beneficial; "It abates the hectic heat, relieves and often removes the dyspnoea, and promotes and often improves the expectoration". By 1805, Dr. John Warren of Boston, Massachusetts, father of Dr. John Collins Warren, had adopted Pearson's treatment for phthisis; and Nysten's *Dictionary of Medical Sciences* (1815) speaks of the inhalation of ether as familiarly known for mitigating the pains of colic.

The stupefying effects of nitrous oxide had been described in 1800 by Humphry Davy. In 1818, the *Journal of Science and the Arts*, published by the Royal Institution, contained the following anonymous statement, "When the vapour of ether mixed with common air is inhaled, it produces effects very similar to those occasioned by nitrous oxide. . . . It is necessary to use caution in making experiments of this kind. By the imprudent inspiration of ether a gentleman was thrown into a very lethargic state, which continued with occasional periods of intermission for more than thirty hours, and a great depression of spirits; for many days the pulse was so much lowered that considerable fears were entertained for his life". A method of vaporization of ether by means of a bottle, into the upper part of which a tube could be introduced for a variable distance, was also described. In 1819, there appeared, in the *Annals of Philosophy*, a *Memoire on sulphuric ether*, by John Dalton, and this is the classical description of the chemical and physical properties of ether.

Christison, in the second edition of his work, *On Poisons* (1836) related the case of a young man who had been rendered completely insensible by the vapour of ether, but such occasional accidents did not deter people from indulging in the inhalation of ether, which was by now well known, especially in the United States of America, as an intoxicant, and so-called "ether frolics" became popular in that country. From 1839 to 1841, William E. Clarke of Rochester,

New York, then a student, and later a physician in Chicago, held a number of such parties, and it has been said, on what authority is unknown, that W. T. G. Morton was one of his guests on these occasions. Emboldened by his experience, Clarke, in January 1842, at Rochester, administered ether on a towel to a Miss Hobbie, and one of her teeth was then painlessly extracted by a dentist named Elijah Pope. Neither Clarke nor Pope published an account of the transaction, which seems to have been the first occasion on which anaesthesia with ether was undertaken, for we may discount the note in the *Edinburgh Medical and Surgical Journal* of April 1847, which refers to a case of ether anaesthesia "thirty years" before.

During an "ether frolic" at Anderson, South Carolina, in 1839, a youth named Wilhite forced a Negro boy to inhale ether until he became insensible. Wilhite is believed to have given an account of this experience to Dr. Crawford Williamson Long of Jefferson, Georgia, already accustomed to such diversions, who, in March 1842, persuaded a patient, from whose neck he was about to remove a tumour, to inhale ether until insensible. The operation was performed without pain and recovery was uneventful. The event was recorded by Long in his ledger: "James Venable, 1842. Ether and excising tumour, $2.00." Two similar operations were subsequently performed on Venable, and Long also used ether on three other patients in the following two years, after which he gave up its use, nor did he publish any account of his discovery until after the first public administration of ether by Morton.

According to the report of a select committee of the American House of Representatives in 1852, "Late in the autumn of 1844", Dr. E. E. Marcy of Hartford, Connecticut, as appears from his own affidavit and that of F. C. Goodrich of Hartford, suggested to Dr. Wells to substitute sulphuric ether for nitrous oxide, and informed him of its known effects and how to make it. Marcy "administered the vapour of rectified sulphuric ether in my [his] office to a young man . . . and, after he had been rendered insensible to pain, cut from his hand an encysted tumour of about the size of an English walnut". A slight doubt is cast upon this statement by the fact that it was not until December 10, 1844, that Horace Wells became interested in nitrous oxide; however, the story is probably otherwise true. A Dr. E. R. Smilie of Boston also asserted to the same committee "that he had employed successfully an etherial [sic] tincture of opium to subdue pain under the knife. He states that he applied this tincture by inhalation in the Spring of 1844; that he opened a serious abscess on the neck of the late Mr. John Johnson, while he was rendered unconscious of pain from the operation by this tincture." This story has little appearance of truth.

The committee further stated that in March, 1846, there appeared, in the *Paris Medical Gazette*, "an account of remarkable experiments performed by M. Ducos, by ether, on animals, exhibiting most of the phenomena since wisnessed in the human body".

In July 1847, when the "ether controversy" between Morton and Jackson was developing, Morton presented, through M. Arago, a *memoire* to the Academy of Arts and Sciences at Paris. This account is probably substantially correct. He stated that, in the summer of 1844, being then in dental practice and also studying medicine under Dr. Charles T. Jackson of Boston, he discussed with the latter the problem of destroying the nerve of a tooth. Jackson told him that, some years before, he had successfully extracted a tooth after applying ether topically, and he provided Morton with a bottle of the liquid. Morton used it by direct application. Jackson, on one occasion, saw Morton use it unsuccessfully in this way, but made no suggestion that he should get the patient to inhale the vapour. Later, however, Jackson did tell him what was then known concerning the inhalation of ether, and Morton, reading the subject up, came to the conclusion that there was nothing dangerous in the method. He became ill, and, while in the country convalescing, experimented unsuccessfully with some ether, locally obtained, on animals and birds.

In the winter of 1844–45, Morton assisted Horace Wells in the unsuccessful demonstration of nitrous oxide at the Massachusetts General Hospital. Morton's interest in ether was re-awakened in the Spring of 1846 when one of his dental students, Thomas R. Spear, told him of his experiences at "ether frolics". Morton then administered ether to his dog, a water spaniel, "inserting his head in a jar having sulphuric ether at the bottom. This was done in the presence of two persons at my house at West Needham, where I reside during the summer months. After breathing the vapour for some time, the dog completely wilted in my hands. I then removed the jar. In about three minutes he aroused, yelled loudly, and sprung some ten feet into a pond of water." In August, Morton inhaled ether himself from a handkerchief, and also gave it, without success, to his two students, Spear and Leavitt.

Late in September 1846, Morton had the idea that the results might be more successful if he administered the vapour from a gas-bag. Accordingly, he went to borrow a bag from Jackson whom he asked if it were possible to give ether vapour in order to relieve pain. Jackson said that it was, spoke of "ether frolics", advised him to use Burnett's ether, since this was the purest, and also gave him a flask and glass tube, considering this better than a gas bag. Morton now tried again the effect of ether on himself, with complete success.

On September 30, in the evening, a man called Eben Frost "came in, suffering great pain and wishing to have a tooth extracted. He was afraid of the operation, and asked if he could be mesmerized. I told him I had something better, and, saturating my handkerchief, gave it to him to inhale. He became unconscious almost immediately. It was dark, and Dr. Hayden (a dentist) held the lamp, while I extracted a firmly rooted bicuspid tooth. There was not much alteration in the pulse, and no relaxation of the muscles. He recovered in a minute, and knew nothing of what had been done to him."

Morton next called on Jackson, told him what he had done, and asked for a certificate to the effect that it was harmless; this Jackson refused to give. Morton also obtained permission to demonstrate his discovery at the Massachusetts General Hospital; meanwhile, he used ether several times in his surgery, but not very successfully. One child, who vomited, was pronounced by a physician to have been poisoned, and the patient's friends threatened legal proceedings.

On the morning of October 16, 1846, Morton obtained a glass inhaler from an instrument maker called Chamberlain, and used this on the patient, Gilbert Abbott, with that success which has since become so famous, and which proved the efficacy of ether as a reliever of pain during surgical operations. Morton subsequently administered ether at the hospital and elsewhere on frequent occasions.

On October 23, 1846, Jackson called on Morton and, having heard that a patent was being taken out, asked for payment for his share in the discovery. Eventually, Morton allocated a 10 per cent share in the patent to Jackson, which would seem to have been a generous award. Morton's account is corroborated at a number of points by the evidence of his patients and colleagues and is probably reasonably accurate.

The subsequent efforts of Jackson to obtain the full credit for the discovery need not detain us here: it is sufficient to record that his pertinacity in this direction led to the defeat of Morton's claims in the United States Senate so that the discoverer, whose patent had been tacitly ignored by the government, never received any financial reward.

News of Morton's successful demonstration soon spread across the Atlantic; H. J. Bigelow's letter, written on November 28, 1846, reached Boott in London in three weeks. The latter immediately sent a communication to the *Lancet* and wrote to Robert Liston, then Professor of Clinical Surgery in the University of London. On December 19, under Boott's direction, his neice, Miss Lonsdale, had a tooth extracted by a Mr. Robinson. Ether was administered by means of an apparatus made by Hooper. Boott wrote again to the *Lancet*, describing the procedure, "the whole process of inhalation, extracting and waking was over in three minutes," he said.

On December 21, 1847, Liston, at University College Hospital, performed two operations under ether anaesthesia, an amputation through the thigh, and an avulsion of the toenail. The apparatus employed, which was similar to Hooper's, was designed by an instrument maker called Squire, who probably administered the anaesthetics, and who subsequently developed a practice as an "etherizer". The success was such that the future of anaesthesia was assured.

On the same day, 19th December, as Boott and Robinson made their fruitful experiment, a surgeon named William Scott apparently operated on a patient under the influence of ether administered by Dr. Frazer at the Dumfries and Galloway Royal Hospital. Dr. Frazer had crossed the Atlantic in the same ship (the *Acadia*) which had carried Bigelow's letter to Boott.

Naturally, it was in London that the new idea flourished most in Europe, but the news spread: in December it had reached France; on the 24th de Lamballe had a successful anaesthetic at the Hôpital St. Louis, and on January 12, J. F. Malgaigne described five anaesthetics, given by himself, before the Académie de Médecine in Paris. He used to administer ether through a tube inserted into the nostril, and this technique won a certain popularity in France, but was soon displaced by Charrière's apparatus, which was an improved version of Hooper's and Squire's inhalers.

The successful use of ether anaesthesia for surgical operations stimulated James Y. Simpson, Professor of Midwifery in the University of Edinburgh, to employ this agent in obstetrics, and his first operation with this anaesthetic was successfully (so far as the mother was concerned) undertaken on January 19, 1847, and subsequently reported in the *Edinburgh Monthly Journal of Medical Science*. This use of anaesthetics, however, raised a storm of protest which was only slowly quelled, and it was some years before anaesthesia in midwifery became general. Since, by then, ether had been largely displaced by chloroform introduced by Simpson in November 1847, the account of the midwifery dispute properly appertains to the consideration of that agent. In France, anaesthesia for midwifery was reported by Dubois, on February 13, 1847; the first obstetrical anaesthetic in the United States of America was undertaken by Dr. N. C. Keep of Boston on April 7, 1847, and the second, an instrumental intervention, on May 5, Walter Channing being the surgeon.

Meanwhile anaesthesia was spreading throughout the world. Ether was popularized in Germany by Dieffenbach, then in his last year of life, whose inhaler was very similar to the glass globe used by Morton. The first scientific account of anaesthesia in Germany was published by von Siebold in the *Proceedings of the Royal Society of Sciences* (Goettingen) on May 8, 1847, but Heyfelder of Erlangen had begun the extensive use of ether anaesthesia as early as January 17, while Schuh of Vienna used anaesthesia on January 27, and Behrend of Berlin and Halla of Prague on February 6. The first anaesthetic in Sweden seems to have been given by E. G. Palmgren on February 9, and in Spain by de Argumosa y Obregon on February 14. By July 1847, Parker had used ether in China and, before this, the subject had been taken up on the South American continent.

At the same time, other methods of administering ether were sought. During 1847, no less than four people (Pirogoff, Roux, y'Yhedo and Duprey) experimented with the rectal administration of liquid ether, with or without the addition of water : Pirogoff reported eighty-one cases with two deaths.

However, the most important anaesthetic event of the year 1847 was undoubtedly the publication of John Snow's *On the Inhalation of the Vapour of Ether*. Snow's attraction to the subject of anaesthesia, brought about by Squire, was accidental, but his fertile brain was ready to respond to the stimulus, and the assiduity and eagerness with which he turned to the investigation of the new science are revealed in his writings : it is not too much to say that he was the first to understand and give clinical appreciation to the physical properties of ether vapour and its pharmacological effects. Among other things, his book contains a description of the stages of ether anaesthesia, an accepted classification which was to remain the basis of clinical anaesthesia with ether until it was modified by Guedel in 1920. Perhaps more important was Snow's influence on the design of apparatus; he was later (1858) to write :

> When the inhalation of ether was first commenced, the in-halers employed consisted generally of glass vases containing sponge, to afford a surface for the evaporation of the ether. Both glass and sponge being very indifferent conductors of caloric, the interior of the inhalers became much reduced in temperature, the evaporation of ether was very much checked, and the patient breathed air much colder than the freezing point of water, and containing very little of the vapour of ether. On this account, and through other defects in the in-halers, the patient was often very long in becoming insensible, and, in not a few cases, he did not become affected beyond a degree of excitement and inebriety.

In addition to facilitating the evaporation of the ether by maintaining it at a nearly constant temperature, Snow's inhaler was designed with tubes of a sufficient diameter to minimize the resistance to airflow.

The introduction of chloroform towards the end of 1847 led to the virtual abandonment of ether in many parts of the world. The North American continent, however, generally remained faithful to ether, and it was there that, in 1853, Squibb revolutionized the commercial manufacture of this highly inflammable substance. In 1866, B. W. Richardson invented his ether spray, at first intended to be used with a volatile hydrocarbon called rhigolene, for the production of local anaesthesia by freezing.

The defection from ether lasted in England until at least 1872, and, on the Continent, until almost the end of the century. The first advocate of a return to this peculiarly safe drug was J. W. Haward of St. George's Hospital, who read a paper on the subject before the Royal Medical and Chirurgical Society in October 1871; but the reintroduction of ether was really due to two men, B. J. Jeffries of Boston, Mass., and Joseph Clover. Jeffries visited England in 1872 and demonstrated the method at that time in use in America, "a towel rolled into a cone, with a napkin or sponge pushed to the top of the inside . . . to pour our ether on." His enthusiasm awakened a response among those who had already become seriously alarmed by the never-ceasing toll of death taken by chloroform, and, in spite of the technical difficulty of administering ether compared with chloroform, a considerable number of surgeons adopted this method. Clover set the seal on this decision by the introduction, in 1872, of his method of procuring the insensibility of the patient by means of nitrous oxide, and continuing the anaesthetic with ether, thus avoiding the unpleasant sensations which were inevitable with a slow ether induction. Clover's "Combined Gas-and-Ether Apparatus", which was received with a measure of enthusiasm, appeared in 1876, after much industrious experiment, and this was followed the next year by his "Portable Regulating Ether Inhaler", which, both in its original form and as modified by Hewitt (1901), was still in use sixty years later.

Parallel with the introduction of the nitrous oxide-ether sequence, the use of "open drop" ether was developed, particularly by Lawson Tait, who favoured "anhydrous methylated ether". This method was also used by Allis, who published an account of his mask in the *Philadelphia Medical Times* of 1874. It was not until 1907 that Bellamy Gardner introduced the frame-mask still used for this purpose. In 1876, Lawson Tait devised his warmed ether inhaler, the intention of which was to reduce the incidence of pulmonary complications. By means of a piston, liquid ether was pumped, one drachm at a time, into a glass vaporizing chamber immersed in water which was heated by a spirit lamp. The ether vapour was conducted to the patient by means of a rubber tube, four or five feet long, which Tait believed to be long enough to avoid the danger of an explosion from the ignition of the ether vapour by the flame of the spirit lamp. A somewhat similar apparatus was introduced by R. W. Carter in 1896. In this, the reservoir of a Junker's inhaler was warmed by burning "Japanese Tinder".

The revival of ether on the Continent began in 1877 with the work of Gustave Julliard of Geneva, who adopted a semi-open technique, but it was not until the late 1890's that the use of ether became general. In 1884, Mollière of Lyons resuscitated the rectal administration of ether, using, however, the technique of insufflation of the vapour instead of instillation of the liquid, as in the earlier methods.

By the beginning of the twentieth century, ether was firmly re-established and the famous nurse-anaesthetist, Alice Magaw, was able to report 14,000 cases in 1906, but the end was in sight. In 1910 W. D. Gatch developed an apparatus for the administration of nitrous oxide and ether simultaneously, also permitting the use of fractional re-breathing, of which he was a confirmed advocate. Teter, Gwathmey and others developed similar machines, and the use of a stream of nitrous oxide and oxygen to vaporize ether came into fairly general use at the time of World War I. The first Boyle machine, the outcome of a visit by H. E. G. Boyle to the United States of America, appeared in 1917, and his apparatus, with modifications, is now that which is most commonly used in this country.

The cost of the new machines was considerable and, in Britain at least, the general standard of anaesthesia did not develop rapidly in the inter-war period. Ether, administered by open drop or by means of the Clover Inhaler, continued to be used alongside the "nitrous oxide with minimal ether" technique, a method in which the word "minimal" was interpreted very broadly. In 1920 Arthur E. Guedel issued the revised description of the stages of anaesthesia, including the sub-division of the third stage into four planes, and emphasizing the respiratory changes occurring with increasing depth of ether anaesthesia.

The rectal route once again became popular with the introduction of the "colonic oil-ether" method of Gwathmey in 1913, and this continued to be used, in obstetrics at least, until about ten years ago.

Some other drugs, rather similar to di-ethyl ether, have been introduced from time to time. B. W. Richardson, for example, experimented with a great many, as did Lawson Taït. One interesting development was the "construction" of di-vinyl ether, suggested by Leake and Chen in 1930. The successful use of ethylene, a rather weak anaesthetic, gave rise to the idea that an ether composed by the conjunction of two molecules of ethylene would prove a satisfactory compound. The drug was, at last, manufactured after considerable difficulty, and, while it achieved some measure of success and is still employed, especially for children, its influence on the discovery of new plastics was probably of much greater importance than the part which it has played in anaesthesia. Krantz and his co-workers have also sponsored the introduction of various ethers in the last twenty years, chief of which is N-methyl propyl ether, but none has proved popular.

Since World War II, the introduction of the relaxants and the extended use of the surgical diathermy apparatus have militated strongly against the use of ether, and it is now unusual for this substance to be used as the sole, or even as the main, agent of anaesthesia. Nevertheless, ether is still an important tool in the hands of the anaesthetist, and it will long remain so. More than a hundred years of almost continuous use have led to the building up of a body of experience with ether which is probably greater than that of any other drug used by the medical practitioner. Because of this knowledge, and because of its inherent property of safety, the experienced anaesthetist will often make use of ether in cases in which the patient's physical condition gives rise to alarm, and, should some great emergency necessitate the use of a number of untrained, or only partly trained, anaesthetists to cope with a sudden influx of casualties, ether will again be used, as it was by the inexperienced Morton, and with equal safety and success.

Chapter Three

NITROUS OXIDE

Nitrous oxide was discovered by Joseph Priestley, whose pioneering experiments with gases have ensured him an honourable place in the history of science. He was the son of a cloth-dresser, and was born in London in 1733. After attending a Dissenting Academy at Daventry, he became a Unitarian minister, serving at Needham Market, Nantwich, Mill Hill (Leeds), Birmingham and Hackney. In 1794 he emigrated to America, where he died ten years later in his 71st year. Priestley wrote a number of religious works, and also dabbled in political affairs. His reply to Burke's *Reflections on the French Revolution* led to the burning of Priestley's house by the mob (1791). It was during his stay in Leeds that he became interested in the nature of air, and his discoveries earned him the Fellowship of the Royal Society, of the French Academy of Sciences, and of the St. Petersburg Academy. The assistance of the Earl of Shelburne, who fitted up a laboratory for Priestley at his house at Calne, enabled him to pursue his experiments for some time without interruption.

Throughout his life, Priestley was bedevilled by the Phlogiston Theory of Stahl, and he thus never came to understand the nature of the chemical reactions which he demonstrated. The discovery of nitrous oxide (dephlogisticated nitrous air) is described in Priestley's *Experiments and Observations on Different Kinds of Air* (1775); unfortunately the event is undated, but it ensued upon the discovery of nitric oxide (nitrous air), and is therefore to be related to the second half of 1772 or, at latest, early 1773.

Nitrous oxide remained a chemical curiosity until its further investigation was undertaken by Humphry Davy. This eminent scientist had been born at Penzance in 1778; in 1795 he was apprenticed there to a surgeon called Borlase. In 1798, he became superintendent of the Pneumatic Institute, opened in that year at Clifton, by Dr. Thomas Beddoes, whence he moved to the Royal Institution in 1801. He became a Baronet in 1818 and was elected President of the Royal Society two years later. He died in 1829, at the age of 55. Davy's interest in chemistry seems to have begun at Penzance in 1797, and it was there that his attention was drawn to nitrous oxide on reading an essay by Dr. S. Latham Mitchill of New York, in which nitrous oxide was denounced as the cause of febrile disorders. Davy prepared the gas, inhaled it, and, noticing its intoxicating effect, renamed it "Laughing Gas". This investigation was the direct cause of Davy's appointment to the Pneumatic Institute; while there, he pursued his researches with the gas, and, in 1800, published his findings in the important book, *Researches Chemical and Philosophical chiefly concerning Nitrous Oxide . . . and its respiration*, wherein he described the analgesic effect of nitrous oxide and suggested that it might be used during surgical operations "in which no great effusion of blood takes place".

Davy's advice fell on deaf ears, but the lay-public exhibited an increasing interest in "Laughing Gas", an interest which was catered for, especially in the United States of America, by itinerant chemists. The medical profession held aloof from the gas, and there is no evidence that it was used by Hickman or anyone else until 1844. The actual use of nitrous oxide as an anaesthetic occurred in the following way. An itinerant chemist, Gardner Quincy Colton, visited the town of Hartford, Connecticut, and, on December 10, 1844, demonstrated the intoxicating effects of "Laughing Gas". In the course of the demonstration, members of the audience were allowed to inhale the gas, and one of these, while still under the influence of it, knocked his shin against a bench with sufficient violence to draw blood. This incident was observed by a dentist, Horace Wells, who was also in the audience, and who noticed that, although the injury must have been extremely painful, the victim appeared to be completely oblivious to it; indeed, when Wells apprised him of it, he was at first incredulous. Wells immediately realized the significance of the incident and, on the following morning, he permitted Colton to administer nitrous oxide to him while another dentist, John M. Riggs, extracted one of Wells' teeth. Riggs has another claim to fame for, 32 years later, he was to introduce a treatment of pyorrhoea alveolaris which was so successful that the disease came to be known in the United States as "Riggs' Disease".

The experiment of December 11, 1844, was a complete success. Emboldened by it, Wells used nitrous oxide on about a dozen patients, and Riggs also made use of it, the latter on one occasion extracting six teeth at a sitting, without causing any suffering. Wells now communicated his discovery to the chief surgeon at the Massachusetts General Hospital, John Collins Warren (1778–1856), an old student of Astley Cooper and of Dupuytren. Warren's father, John Warren (1753–1815), had preceded his son as professor of surgery at Boston, and, it will be recalled, had advocated the use of the inhalation of ether in the treatment of phthisis. Somewhat reluctantly, John Collins Warren gave permission for Wells to address the students on his discovery and to demonstrate the anaesthetic effects of nitrous oxide on a volunteer. Unfortunately, the demonstration proved a fiasco: anaesthesia was insufficient, and the volunteer emitted a scream as the tooth was extracted. Wells left the hospital amid the jeers and boos of the students.

Figure 14. Joseph Black (1728–1799) lecturing; a caricature by John Kay.

Figure 15. Franz Anton Mesmer (1734–1815) treating patients in his salon at Paris. A group of patients sit round the *baquet*, a tub filled with "magnetised" water; Mesmer himself attends to a patient on the left, who has gone into hysterical convulsions.

Figure 16. Antoine-Laurent Lavoisier (1743–1794) conducts an experiment on the chemistry of respiration. From a sketch by his wife, who is shown seated at the right-hand side.

The subsequent career of the discoverer of anaesthesia with nitrous oxide was short and tragic. Giving up dental practice, it is said after a fatality, he followed various occupations, became interested in chloroform to such an extent as to become an addict, and finally, in 1848, he took his own life in the Tombs Prison at New York, whither he had been lodged following an act of an insane nature: at the behest of a chance acquaintance, he had thrown vitriol at a prostitute. The French Academy of Medicine belatedly acknowledged the importance of his contribution to the discovery of anaesthesia, but news of the award of a gold medal to him did not arrive in America until after his death.

The failure of Wells to demonstrate publicly the anaesthetic action of nitrous oxide led to the abandonment of its use. It had, however, one good result, for it caused W. T. G. Morton, who had been present at the fiasco, to turn his attention to more effective agents, and so to the discovery of the action of ether, the introduction of which obscured for a time the potentialities of the weaker drug.

One man alone seems to have retained his belief in the efficacy of nitrous oxide anaesthesia, and that man was Colton. It is true that both Bigelow and Nunneley gave the gas a trial in 1848: the former thought it inferior to ether, while the latter, who only experimented with it on animals, considered it to be so short acting as to be useless, and was worried by the cyanosis produced. Colton, however, remembered the success which he had had with Horace Wells and, continuing his career as a lecturer, frequently referred to that incident. In 1862, a lady who had attended one of Colton's demonstrations, asked him to administer the gas to her for the extraction of teeth. The dentist, Dunham by name, was so impressed that he began to use this agent in his own practice, and, a year later, Colton gave up his lecturing and, in association with Dr. J. H. Smith, opened the Colton

Dental Association in New York. Within a very short time, nitrous oxide became the accepted anaesthetic for dental extraction in the United States of America.

News of this development naturally came to Britain, and a few experiments were carried out, notably by Rymer at the National Dental Hospital. The results were encouraging, but little notice was taken, and the introduction of nitrous oxide anaesthesia to Britain was delayed.

One of Rymer's difficulties had been his inability to procure sufficient supplies of the gas. This problem was solved in America by A. W. Sprague of Boston, Mass., who devised an apparatus for the manufacture of nitrous oxide by heating ammonium nitrate, passing it through wash-bottles, and storing it in a small gasometer, from which the gas could be used direct or drawn off into bladders for use outside the dentist's home. The apparatus was costly, but easy to manage, and gave satisfactory results.

In 1867 Colton demonstrated his apparatus and method at Paris, where he so impressed an American dentist, T. W. Evans, that the latter came to England in the following year, bringing with him Sprague's apparatus: he gave a series of demonstrations at the National Dental Hospital and elsewhere. Evans succeeded in persuading several dentists, notably Alfred Coleman, to make use of the gas, but there was some opposition from B. W. Richardson, who believed nitrous oxide to be unsafe. Following his lead, it was proclaimed that anaesthesia resulted solely from asphyxia when this gas was used, a conclusion which was disproved almost at once by Sanderson and Murray at the Middlesex Hospital, who compared the action of nitrogen with that of nitrous oxide, and showed that, with the latter, consciousness was lost sooner and before cyanosis was pronounced. Later in 1868, the Odontological Society formed a Committee to examine the question, but its reports were disappointing. Meanwhile, Joseph Clover turned his attention to the new agent, and modified his chloroform apparatus (really, Snow's apparatus) for use with nitrous oxide.

The extending use of nitrous oxide in 1868 led to the need for some simpler method for its distribution. The difficulty was overcome by compression into cylinders, not at first under sufficient pressure to cause liquefaction. Cylinders of compressed air had been used as early as 1833 by the Vienna fire brigade, and in 1856, the Medical Pneumatic Apparatus Co. of London was offering nitrous oxide and other gases in this form, but without attracting much attention. Following the lead of the Editor of the *British Medical Journal*, Ernest Hart, both Coxeter's and Barth's were providing compressed nitrous oxide in 1869, and, almost at once, the gasometer was abandoned, and the gas was taken direct from the cylinder to the patient. The liquefied gas became available on the American market in 1873.

By the end of 1868, nitrous oxide anaesthesia was firmly established in dental practice throughout Europe and America, and already it had become the custom to prolong anaesthesia by permitting the patient to breathe a limited amount of air. Early in 1869, Professor E. Andrews of Chicago described the use of a mixture of nitrous oxide and oxygen, and similar experiments were also made in England. It was at this time that Alfred Coleman introduced the economical use of nitrous oxide by rebreathing, passing the exhaled gases through slaked lime; this was the first use of carbon dioxide absorption in anaesthesia, although the principle had been understood since the days of the Abbé Fontana.

In 1871, at the time of the reintroduction of ether into English anaesthetic practice, Clover described his nitrous oxide-ether sequence: he developed various types of apparatus for this purpose, all of which were extremely successful, and this method of anaesthesia continued to be much used for some sixty years.

At this time, when the clinical use of nitrous oxide was increasing, and when the anaesthetic action of the gas had already been proved by Sanderson and Murray, French physiologists again put forward the theory that anaesthesia with this agent was the result of asphyxia, and this remained the orthodox belief until the important work of Paul Bert, who showed that nitrous oxide was a true anaesthetic. In 1878, Bert, read a paper to the French Académie des Sciences on the harmlessness of prolonged anaesthesia with nitrous oxide. He said:

> "The fact that nitrous oxide must be administered pure indicates that, in order to be absorbed by the organism in sufficient quantity, the tension of the gas must be equal to one atmosphere. In order to achieve this at normal pressure, the gas must be in the proportion of 100 per cent. But let us suppose that the patient is placed in an apparatus where the pressure can be increased to two atmospheres; then one could submit him to the desired tension by making him inhale a mixture of 50 per cent nitrous oxide with 50 per cent air. Thus one could achieve anaesthesia while maintaining the normal quantity of oxygen in the blood; and it follows that the normal conditions of respiration would be preserved. This is what, in fact, has been done; but I must add that, up to the present, I have only experimented upon animals".

Bert's hypothesis was first tested in the following year. The pressure used was 920 mm Hg, an increase of rather more than 20 per cent of the normal; nitrous oxide and oxygen were given in the proportions of 85 and 15 per cent respectively. The result was so satisfactory that a mobile pressure chamber was constructed, but this failed to stand the test of time. Although the anaesthesia was excellent, the cost and complication of the apparatus caused it to be abandoned in the early 1880's. Bert's original hypothesis was, however, borne out by the work of Faulconer, Pender and Bickford in 1949 (*Anesthesiology*, **10**, 601).

About this time, the Russian obstetrician, S. Klikowitch, introduced nitrous oxide and oxygen as an analgesic in labour, a method which has found much favour in Scandinavia, and which led, indirectly, to the invention of a gas-air analgesia apparatus by Minnitt in 1934, self-administration of the gases being advocated by A. E. Guedel in 1912. Minnitt's apparatus had the advantage that it could be used by relatively untrained midwives. In 1883, Bert turned his attention also to the administration of nitrous oxide and oxygen mixtures at normal pressure, and similar work was done by a Viennese dentist, H. T. Hillischer, who, a few years later, produced an apparatus in which the percentage of nitrous oxide and oxygen could be regulated.

Meanwhile, other methods of prolonging nitrous oxide anaesthesia were being sought. Coxon in 1888 used a stream of gas directed into the patient's mouth during dental extractions; in 1898, Coleman described the nasal mask, a method of administration, however, which both he and Clover had used many years before and which is substantially the same as that employed today; in the same year, Hilliard described the use of a naso-pharyngeal tube for the administration of gas during dental procedures.

It was Hillischer's apparatus which stimulated Hewitt to construct a more easily regulated apparatus. Before 1893, Hewitt had designed an apparatus for administering nitrous oxide, employing a special stop-cock by which the patient could be made to rebreathe or not, as desired. His nitrous oxide-oxygen apparatus embodied this valve, and was provided with two reservoir bags, one for oxygen and one for nitrous oxide, which were to be kept equally distended by manipulation of the foot-keys controlling the cylinder outlets. The two reservoir bags were separated from the stopcock by a regulator which permitted a variable proportion of the gases to reach the patient by altering the sizes of the orifices. A modified regulator and stop-cock were described in 1897. Some fifty years later, R. R. Macintosh produced a somewhat similar apparatus, differing from Hewitt's in that, in order to equalize the pressures between the two bags, the oxygen reservoir was placed within the nitrous oxide bag.

Nevertheless, in spite of these developments, in 1901 Hewitt was still advocating the use of a gasometer filled with known quantities of nitrous oxide and oxygen for administering a constant mixture. The focus of development now shifted to the United States where anaesthetic apparatus underwent considerable improvement during the first two decades of the twentieth century. The first machine was designed by S. S. White; it appeared in 1899 and was essentially similar to Hewitt's apparatus. Three years later, C. K. Teter of Cleveland produced another machine along rather similar lines, but incorporating a device for warming the gases, and an ether vaporizer, a device in which he had been preceded by Coleman. In 1906, the Clark apparatus appeared, again incorporating a proportional regulator. This machine may be regarded as the direct ancestor of the first McKesson apparatus, which appeared in 1910, the brain-child of Elmer I. McKesson of Toledo, Ohio. This machine, which has undergone many modifications, was the first of the intermittent flow machines. McKesson introduced fractional rebreathing in the following year; his Nargraf apparatus appeared in 1930, and is still a popular machine in dental practice.

At the same time that McKesson was perfecting his mixing valve (1910), Boothby and Cotton opened the door for the modern continuous flow apparatus by employing a water sight-feed flow-meter. This was somewhat unwieldy, and was improved by J. T. Gwathmey in 1912. Boothby and Cotton also introduced the reducing valve into anaesthetic practice. Other apparatus was designed by Gatch, Heidbrink and Foregger soon afterwards.

American developments aroused the interest of H. E. G. Boyle in this country: his first apparatus was designed in

1917. After a continuous series of modifications, this apparatus is still the most popular machine in the British Isles. The Walton intermittent-flow machine was designed in 1925, while Magill's apparatus appeared three years later. This apparatus was fitted with Siebe Gorman dry flowmeters in 1931, and with rotameters in 1937. These latter had been used in industry for some years and their value to anaesthetists was realized by Magill and, soon after, by Mr. Salt of the Nuffield Department of Anaesthesia at Oxford; the use of rotameters by Neu of Vienna in his anaesthetic apparatus (1911) was an isolated event which failed to influence future development.

The gas ethylene is somewhat similar as an anaesthetic to nitrous oxide; although rather more potent, it has the disadvantage that it is inflammable. Its anaesthetic properties were first noticed by Luckhardt and Thompson in 1918, and it was introduced into clinical practice five years later, when it immediately became popular in the United States of America. It has not, however, achieved a similar popularity in this country.

This section must close on a sombre note. After the extensive use of nitrous oxide with remarkable success, especially for dentistry, for three-quarters of a century, the warning of the dangers of anoxia was first sounded by C. B. Courville (*Untoward Effects of Nitrous Oxide Anaesthesia*, California, 1939). Experience has proved the truth of Courville's contentions, and it is now fully realized that nitrous oxide anaesthesia must not be accompanied by reduction in oxygen intake. This has led to the supplementation of nitrous oxide for almost all procedures, a technique which reached its apogee after the introduction of the relaxants. The satisfactory results obtained by this combination led to an extension of its use to the treatment of tetanus, and, once again, a warning has been sounded, this time by H. C. A. Lassen and his associates (*Lancet*, 1956, **1**, 527), who have shown that prolonged anaesthesia with nitrous oxide may cause acute aplasia of bone-marrow. Nevertheless, nitrous oxide is still one of the most valuable anaesthetic agents we possess, and its future place in anaesthesia would seem to be assured for many years to come.

Chapter Four

CHLOROFORM AND DRUGS RELATED TO CHLOROFORM

CHLOROFORM

Chloroform was discovered in 1831 independently by three chemists. Priority is usually awarded to Samuel Guthrie (1782–1848) of Sackets Harbor, New York, who published an account in *The American Journal of Science and Arts*, in October, 1831. It appears (Pawling, *Dr. Samuel Guthrie*, Brewster Press, 1947) that the discovery was made in February of that year, and the article was submitted for publication in July. Eugène Soubeiran (1793–1858), the second independent discoverer, claimed priority for his paper, in the *Annales de Chemie et de Physique*, for October, 1831, but, owing to the second French Revolution, the issue was delayed until the beginning of 1832. The third discoverer, Justus von Liebig (1803–1873), published a note in the *Annalen der Physik* in November 1831. Of the three discoverers, Guthrie was the only one who used the modern method of manufacturing chloroform from alchohol and bleaching powder. He advocated his product, which he believed to be a form of "chloric ether", as an intoxicating beverage, and it came to be known as "Guthrie's Sweet Whisky". Chloric ether, otherwise known as Dutch Oil or Liquid of the Dutch Chemists, had been known since 1796: its composition is uncertain, but it was probably an unstable mixture of chlorinated hydrocarbons. Soubeiran gave the name "bichloric ether" to the substance which he produced and which he believed to have the formula CHCl; von Liebig called his preparation "chloride of carbon" and assessed its formula as C₄Cl₅.

The formula of chloroform was worked out by Jean-Baptiste Dumas in 1834. Ignorance at that time of the biatomic nature of the hydrogen molecule led him to express it as C₂HCl₃ and he bestowed upon it its name, thinking it to be a halogen derivative of the imaginary radical "formyl".

Chloroform was quickly introduced into medicine and became a standard constituent of the "cough-bottle". As early as 1831, Ives of New Haven used chloroform vapour for the treatment of a patient with dyspnoea, but this seems to have been an isolated event. The liquid was recommended for such diverse conditions as hysteria, neuralgia and cancer during the twelve years after its discovery.

In 1842, R. M. Glover, of Newcastle upon Tyne, injected various brominated and chlorinated compounds into the veins and arteries of dogs and rabbits. He noticed that chloroform produced coma, a lowering of the blood pressure, and irregularity of the action of the heart (*Edinburgh Medical Journal*, 1842, **58**, 353).

Animal experiments with chloroform were also carried out by M. J. P. Flourens (1794–1867) during February and March 1847; he recognized the anaesthetic action of the drug, but considered it too toxic for clinical use.

The story of the introduction of chloroform anaesthesia has often been told. It was a chemist, David Waldie of Liverpool, who had had much to do with the preparation of pure specimens of this substance, who first recommended its use as an anaesthetic to Professor (later Sir) James Young Simpson. The latter had introduced anaesthesia with ether into the practice of midwifery on January 19, 1847, but he was not altogether satisfied with this substance, particularly because of the objectionable smell which hung about his clothes after its administration. After meeting Waldie in October 1847, Simpson procured a specimen of chloroform from Messrs. Duncan, Flockhart & Co., and his assistant, Matthews Duncan, ascertained its narcotic properties by inhalation in the first day or two of November. On November 4, Professor Simpson, Drs. Keith and Duncan had dinner at Simpson's house, 32 Queen Street, Edinburgh, and after the meal they inhaled chloroform from tumblers, with devastating results. Unfortunately the date of the first administration of chloroform is not known, but, by November 8, it had already been used in midwifery and for several minor operations. Simpson's paper, *Account of a New Anaesthetic Agent as a Substitute for Sulphuric Ether in Surgery and Midwifery*, was read to the Medico-Chirurgical Society of Edinburgh, on November 10, and appeared in print on November 15; it was subsequently reprinted, with some additions, on numerous occasions.

The use of chloroform quickly spread to England: on November 20, "several operations were performed at St. Bartholomew's Hospital, upon patients rendered insensible to pain by the administration of chloroform. . . . The chloroform was administered by Mr. Tracy, by means of a thick flat piece of sponge . . . " (*Lancet*, 1847, **2**, 571). Within a short time, ether had been displaced from its position and chloroform had become the routine anaesthetic in Britain and elsewhere, although the former still retained its popularity in the Northern States of the U.S.A. Familiarity, of course, bred contempt, and, on January 28, 1848, the first death occurred during the inhalation of chloroform. This case was reported very extensively in the medical press of the time: it is surprising that it should have made such a stir, for there had already been at least three deaths during the inhalation of ether, one in France, one in Russia, and one in Alabama, but these had all received but scant notice. The deciding factor, was, probably, the fact that the victim of chloroform was a young, healthy girl undergoing a very trivial operation, an operation moreover which she had undergone safely a fortnight before under the influence of ether. Professor Simpson plunged into print in defence of chloroform, denying that it could have been the anaesthetic which had caused death, and asserting that this had been the result of the efforts at resuscitation undertaken by the two doctors present: they had poured brandy into her mouth.

Within the next four months, three more fatalities with chloroform anaesthesia were reported, two in the U.S.A. and one in France. These deaths led to a consideration of the manner of administering chloroform and had repercussions on the design of anaesthetic apparatus.

Originally, the apparatus for the administration of chloroform was very simple, a handkerchief, a towel or even, as John Snow wrote, "a piece of lint, *a worsted glove, a nightcap* or a sponge", and such simple methods continued to be used, especially in Scotland, until quite recent times. However, many inhalers were designed in England and on the Continent as chloroform became more widely used. Of these, the most important were Charrière's, an early and effective, but somewhat cumbersome machine, and Snow's, which incorporated a "wick" of blotting-paper and a non-rebreathing valve.

In 1849, Snow described another apparatus which "consisted of a hydrogen balloon holding upwards of two thousand cubic inches, which was provided with a tap, and attached to a face-piece, containing valves, by means of a short and wide tube. When used, a measured quantity of chloroform was put into the balloon, which was then inflated with air from a bellows; in this way the exact proportion of vapour in the air breathed by the patient was known . . . (Snow) found that 3 per cent by measure of vapour sufficed to induce insensibility in two minutes. . . . The expired air escaped by a valve, without returning into the balloon"

(*Lancet*, 1849, **1**, 588). This apparatus, the first quantitative apparatus to be invented, was modified by Clover, and is generally known by his name; a somewhat similar device was used by Hewitt at the close of the 19th century for administering nitrous oxide and oxygen in known proportions.

In spite of these developments, deaths under chloroform continued to occur, and considerable alarm began to be felt, but the number of fatalities was not so very great, considering the lack of understanding of the problems of anaesthesia; world literature revealed only 393 deaths during the first 34 years of chloroform anaesthesia, and about 10 per cent of these were post-operative, the form of anaesthesia apparently having little influence on the outcome. On the other hand, reported deaths from other anaesthetics during the same period amounted only to 48.

As a result of these continuing fatalities, there sprang up two schools of thought. The "clinical" school, headed by Sir James Y. Simpson and, after his death, by Joseph Lister, maintained that the simplest apparatus was the best and advocated administering chloroform on a handkerchief or towel. Since, they claimed, death only occurred either in light anaesthesia or from respiratory failure, the drug should be given in adequate amount and care should be taken to watch the respirations. On the other hand, the "scientific" school, led by John Snow, and, after his death, by Joseph Clover, maintained that death was frequently due to cessation of the heart's action, often induced by too high a concentration of chloroform in the inspired air. They advocated the use of quantitative and, therefore, less simple apparatus, and advised that a finger should be kept on the patient's pulse throughout administration.

Concern continued to be felt, and, in 1864, the Royal Medical and Chirurgical Society (now the Royal Society of Medicine) appointed a committee to enquire into the problem. The report of this committee described experiments which had been undertaken on animals, and concluded that concentrations of chloroform of 2–4 per cent in air were safe, but that higher concentrations were extremely liable to lead to death from "syncope". Such an outcome was rendered less likely in the animal if the vagus nerves were divided.

The introduction of nitrous oxide and the re-introduction of ether anaesthesia, already described, led to a reduction in the use of chloroform during the last 30 or so years of the 19th century. However, chloroform still continued to be used extensively, and the practice of administering atropine and/or morphine before the use of this drug seems to have developed in the 1880s.

In 1875, the British Medical Association appointed a committee, known as the Glasgow Committee, to enquire further into the problem of chloroform fatalities. This committee did not meet until 1877, and reported in 1880. The conclusion reached was that chloroform was much more injurious to the heart than ether, and a recommendation was made that ethidine dichloride should be used as a compromise, since it "stood intermediate whether as regards the time required, or the dose needed".

In 1889, the first Hyderabad "Commission", financed by the Nizam, and consisting of experiments undertaken by his Resident Surgeon, Edward Lawrie, reported that, after killing 128 fully grown dogs with chloroform, in no case did the heart become dangerously affected until after the breathing stopped. This forthright support for the "clinical" (Edinburgh) school, roused the "scientific" (London) opposition, and the *Lancet* took up the cudgels on the latter's behalf. The Nizam of Hyderabad offered a further sum of £1,000, and the *Lancet* sent (Sir) Thomas Lauder Brunton, a leading physiologist, to assist Lawrie in further experiments. This was the second Hyderabad "Commission". It reported in

1890, further reports being issued in 1891 and 1893; 588 animals had been used, and the results confirmed completely the report of the previous year, even the sceptical Brunton being convinced. The *Lancet*, however, refused to accept the situation, and the "opposition" remained unshaken in its views. In 1891, the British Medical Association elected another committee, which did not report until 10 years later. This committee requested the anaesthetists in Britain to record all their anaesthetics in 1892, and submit the records for examination; 25,920 records were considered. The report was disappointing and consisted of vague generalities, no definite conclusions being reached. In consequence, the British Medical Association appointed yet another committee in 1901; this was known as the Special Chloroform Committee. It reported in 1911; having concluded that the dosimetric administration of chloroform was the safest, and that no adverse effects upon the heart could be expected with concentrations of 2 per cent or less in air, the committee recommended the use of the Vernon Harcourt inhaler, which had first appeared in 1904.

It was also in the year 1911 that Goodman Levy "communicated a note to the Physiological Society describing a hitherto unrecognized form of sudden cardiac failure which occurred in cats under chloroform, and stating that he had, acting upon a suggestion made by Professor Cushny, looked for and found ventricular fibrillation in such cases. At the same time he showed that an exactly similar form of death could be reproduced by injecting small doses of adrenaline into the vein of a cat lightly anaesthetized with chloroform. These observations became the starting-point of a series of experiments elucidating the conditions under which ventricular fibrillation occurs, and showing that it happens only in light chloroform anaesthesia, never in full or deep anaesthesia" (Levy, A. G. *Chloroform Anaesthesia*, 1922, London: Bale and Danielsson, p. 96). The twofold dangers of chloroform death in either light or too profound anaesthesia, were thus explained.

As we have seen, Simpson had introduced ether anaesthesia into midwifery in January 1847. In November of that year, he turned to chloroform. The use of anaesthesia to mitigate the "curse of Eve" aroused strong objections among a class of religious folk, who, being men, could afford to be high-principled in such a matter. A Dr. Gream, for example, said that to use anaesthesia in midwifery was to "turn the lying-in chamber into a scene of drunken debauchery"; and many, both medical men and clergy, protested that this particular form of alleviation of distress was in direct opposition to the biblical authority, "In sorrow shalt thou bring forth children". Simpson, however, was equal to the occasion: he showed that the Hebrew root of the word, translated as "sorrow", really meant "struggle". Opposition to anaesthesia in midwifery was slow in subsiding. Queen Victoria herself did not dare to make use of it at the birth of Prince Arthur in 1850, although she made enquiries about it. It was not until the birth of Prince Leopold in 1853 that she allowed John Snow to administer chloroform to her; this he did intermittently, a method which then became known as "chloroform à la reine". The final seal of acceptance came when the Queen again accepted chloroform at the birth of Princess Beatrice in 1857.

Simpson was so imbued with the success of chloroform as an anaesthetic that he came to regard "chloroform" and "anaesthesia" as virtually synonymous; he would hear no argument against it, and he convinced himself that his own contribution to anaesthesia was of greater importance than the discovery of ether anaesthesia by Morton. Called upon to write an article on "Chloroform", for the *British Encyclopaedia*, he wrote it in such a way as to suggest that he was himself the discoverer of anaesthesia. This, and other public utterances, involved Simpson, at the end of his life, in an

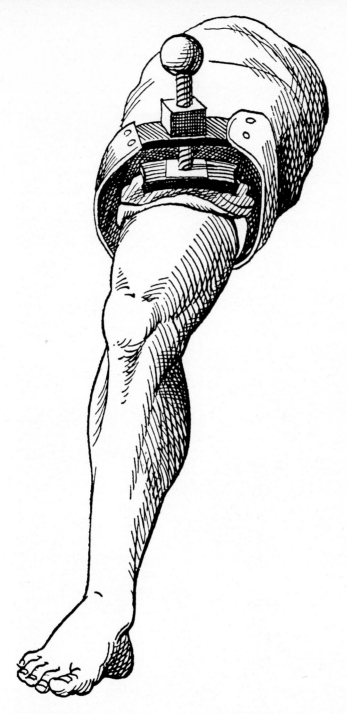

Figure 17. George Moore's clamp for compression analgesia (1784).

Figure 18. Gilray's cartoon of the pneumatic treatment of disease. Humphry Davy stands behind the desk, right centre.

acrimonious correspondence with Henry J. Bigelow, who had been present on the historic occasion at the Massachusetts General Hospital on October 16, 1846. Simpson was not without failings; he had many enemies, chief among whom was Professor Syme; and the story of how and why he assumed his second name, "Young", indicates his forceful, tactless behaviour; yet his friends loved and respected him, and, although chloroform has lost its position as the most important anaesthetic agent, nevertheless Simpson's contribution in the field of anaesthesia alone (and there were many other fields in which he made important advances) make his memory justly renowned.

Among many others who advocated and advanced the use of chloroform is John Snow, justly regarded as the foremost anaesthetist that the world has seen. His famous book *On Chloroform and other Anaesthetics* was his last achievement, and he was seized with his fatal illness on its completion (June 9, 1858); he died seven days later. Snow, unlike Simpson, recognized that chloroform was not without its dangers, but he accepted the risk and, as he said himself, he did not allow this to stand in the way of "its ready applicability". A. E. Sansom, a close friend of Snow, issued a handbook, *Chloroform: Its Action and Administration* in 1865; this work had considerable influence and helped to retain chloroform in its place of pre-eminence. The book is interesting in that it contains an account of artificial respiration performed by electrophrenic stimulation with both surface and buried electrodes.

From the time of the beginning of the first world war, the use of chloroform ostensibly diminished. Since the reintroduction of ether anaesthesia into Britain (1872), chloroform had continued to be used on the continent of Europe, and it was by no means displaced entirely in this country. Experience with war casualties showed the advantages of nitrous oxide, and since then there has appeared an attitude of mind which has made it seem almost reprehensible to use this agent; in some places, strictures by coroners after fatalities have influenced the profession against chloroform, an intrusion into the field of anaesthesia which is much to be deprecated. In spite of this, chloroform is still quite widely used, although the majority of its users tend to be reticent about their experiences. Dr. John Gillies found in 1948 that 97.5 per cent of Scottish general practitioners used chloroform in obstetrics, and that 80 per cent of specialist anaesthetists throughout Britain used it at least occasionally. The last important work on the subject was done by R. M. Waters and his associates. Published in 1951, *Chloroform: A Study After 100 Years*, detailed the results obtained in more than 1,100 clinical administrations, the anaesthetics being carefully monitored and recorded. They concluded that "chloroform does not deserve to be abandoned", but made certain apparently illogical reservations (see *Anaesthesia*, 1959, **14**, 130).

DRUGS RELATED TO CHLOROFORM

As we have seen, the term "chloric ether" was first applied to a substance, or, more probably, a mixture of unstable substances, otherwise known as Dutch Oil. Guthrie believed that he had discovered a new method of manufacturing chloric ether, and, for some considerable time, the terms "chloric ether" and "chloroform" were used rather indiscriminately. Thus, we find that Richard Formby of Liverpool suggested the use of "chloric ether" to Simpson in 1845 (Dundee, J. W., *Anaesthesia*, 1953, **8**, 218), and it was presumably Dutch Oil which was intended.

"Chloric ether" was also used in the Middlesex Hospital as early as 1847. Jacob Bell stated (*Pharmaceutical Journal*, 1846–47, **6**, 357) that it was "rather less powerful in its effects than sulphuric ether", suggesting that his preparation was not chloroform.

Simpson experimented with Dutch Oil (and also with acetone and nitric ether) in 1847, but found it to be insufficiently powerful. Thomas Nunneley of Leeds, however, in 1849, thought that it was a promising agent; "in a very young or feeble person, I should feel disposed to employ it in preference to chloroform", he wrote. Snow also investigated a number of compounds, including Dutch Oil, which he found to be slow in action, although he believed it to be very safe. He also experimented with ethidine dichloride (1:1–dichloroethane), a similar substance, which achieved some popularity and was eventually recommended by the Glasgow Committee of the British Medical Association. The committee also reported unfavourably on Dutch Oil, stating that it invariably caused convulsions before anaesthesia appeared. Evidently the various investigators were not using identical substances.

The 1864 Chloroform Committee advised the use of mixtures of chloroform and ether, with or without the addition of alcohol. The first move in this direction had been made by John Gabb, who, in 1848, suggested that it might "be desirable to add a little of the stimulating effect of ether to the directly sedative influence of chloroform" (*Lancet*, 1848, **1**, 521). Mixtures of chloroform and ether became popular in Southern Europe in the 1850s, the Vienna mixture, for example, consisting of one part of chloroform to six or eight parts of ether. The familiar A.C.E. mixture (alcohol, one part; chloroform, two parts, ether, three parts) was invented by George Harley, in about 1860. It had the advantage over simple mixtures of chloroform and ether that the addition of alcohol made an azeotropic mixture. The 1864 Committee was unable to decide between A.C.E. and a simple mixture of chloroform, one part, and ether, two parts; both retained their popularity well into the 20th century.

When, in February 1847, Flourens experimented with chloroform, he also tried ethyl chloride on animals, and found its action to be similar to that of ether. Ethyl chloride was also investigated by von Bibra and Harless during the same year, and F. Heyfelder used this agent in three patients. He thought it to be satisfactory, but stated that the volatility of the drug, its high price and difficulty of obtaining it pure, made it unsuitable for general use. In 1849, Nunneley tried ethyl bromide, and this drug obtained a measure of acceptance, being advocated by Silk as late as 1891. One of this latter agent's most famous advocates was the American surgeon, J. Marion Sims.

Meanwhile, ethyl chloride had been forgotten: the medical profession was reminded of it, however, by the description in 1890 by Redard of Geneva of the ethyl chloride spray still in use today. Redard advocated ethyl chloride as a local refrigeration anaesthetic, and it quickly became popular; by 1891 it was being used very successfully in dental surgery in London. In the following year, Wood and Cerna of Philadelphia investigated ethyl chloride as a general anaesthetic, but came to the conclusion that the "fugaciousness" of its action would interfere with its efficiency.

However, in 1894, H. Carlson of Gothenburg, and, in the following year, Thiesing of Hildesheim both accidentally produced general anaesthesia when using ethyl chloride for dental extractions. Thiesing experimented on animals with satisfactory results. Others began to use ethyl chloride under the name "Kelene", but its acceptance depended substantially on the work of Lotheissen of Innsbruck, who used it extensively from 1896. His first death was reported in 1899, the patient being shown at autopsy to have a seriously diseased heart. The death occurred immediately after administering a further dose of ethyl chloride, and it was from this mishap, and the accounts of several others, that the idea arose that it was dangerous to administer the substance other than by the "single shot" method.

In 1901, Rolland and Robinson of Bordeaux introduced

"Somnoform", a mixture of ethyl chloride, 60 parts; methyl chloride, 35 parts; and ethyl bromide, 5 parts; but this mixture only achieved a short-lived reputation.

Trichloroethylene had been discovered in 1864. Its anaesthetic action appears to have been first noticed by K. B. Lehmann of Würzburg, in 1911. He administered it to 8 cats, found induction to be unduly prolonged, and noticed the tachypnoea which is often caused by it. He also remarked on the formation of dichloroacetylene when the substance was heated in the presence of an alkali (Ostlere, G., *Anaesthesia*, 1953, **8**, 21). The use of trichloroethylene as a solvent in industry led to a number of cases of poisoning, the symptoms of which frequently included prolonged or permanent palsy of the trigeminal nerve: this suggested the use of trichloroethylene in trigeminal neuralgia, for which it was first given in 1915, by Oppenheim of Berlin.

In 1934, Jackson and Herzberg, both of Cincinnati, published experiments on animals, which showed that the drug had potentialities and was apparently fairly safe. Consequently, trichloroethylene was used clinically in 304 minor operations by Striker and his associates at Cincinnati; they published an account in 1935. In Britain, the drug was introduced in 1940 by Langton Hewer and C. F. Hadfield, at St. Bartholomew's Hospital, where it was used in the chloroform bottle of Boyle's apparatus as a supplement to nitrous oxide and oxygen anaesthesia. At first it seemed satisfactory when used in the closed circuit with soda lime, but the occurrence of several examples of poisoning with di-chloroacetylene (produced by decomposition) led to the embargo on its use with carbon dioxide absorption.

Halothane, developed by Imperial Chemical Industries, was introduced into clinical practice in a limited way in 1956. It is too soon to comment on this substance, but it has been accepted with very considerable enthusiasm, despite the fact that its properties seem to be remarkably similar to those of chloroform. Like di-vinyl ether, halothane is a "tailor-made" substance, "constructed" by chemists with the object of obtaining an anaesthetic having certain desirable qualities. Other fluorinated compounds have also been investigated and used clinically, but, so far, halothane appears to be the only one which is likely to become generally accepted.

It is to be hoped that chemists will continue their efforts to produce more anaesthetic agents which may be desirable for one or more reasons. Early investigators sought the "perfect" anaesthetic agent; the experience of the last century teaches us that this is a chimera: the "perfect" anaesthetic does not—indeed, cannot—exist, but the more agents with diverse actions which we possess, the better are we fitted to meet the demands of ever-extending surgical interventions with forms of anaesthesia which will further the requirements of the operator and decrease the risk and discomfort for the patient.

Chapter Five

ENDOTRACHEAL INTUBATION

Endotracheal anaesthesia, as we know it today, is the result of the work of E. S. Rowbotham and (Sir) Ivan Magill during the years 1917 to 1920, when they were working in Sir Harold Gillies' clinic for maxillo-facial injuries at Sidcup. They deserve to be remembered for having simplified and made universally practicable the technique of endotracheal anaesthesia, and for having so popularized their methods that they were adopted by anaesthetists throughout the world. Nevertheless, the roots of this technique go far into the past, and the work of Magill and Rowbotham had many precursors.

The operation of tracheotomy was first described by Asklepiades of Bithynia (1st century B.C.), who is remembered principally as an early leader of the Methodists, medical men who opposed the humoral theory of disease and the Hippocratic doctrines in general. The operation was revived by the great Cordovan physician, Avenzoar (Ibn Zuhr), who flourished in the twelfth century, but seems not to have been practised in Christian Europe until it was again described by Armand Trousseau (1801–67) in 1859. However, both Vesalius (1543) and Robert Hooke (1667) had shown the practicability of ventilating the lungs of animals through a cannula inserted through a tracheotomy opening, and this idea was to be taken up by John Snow in an experiment with chloroform on a rabbit (reported in 1858), and by Friedrich Trendelenburg for anaesthesia in man (1871).

The first efforts to introduce a tube into the trachea through the glottis were made by Charles Kite of Gravesend (1787), who designed a metal tube "shaped like a male-catheter" which could be introduced through either the nose or the mouth. In Kite's case, as with many subsequent workers, the tube was intended to overcome laryngeal and pharyngeal obstruction in cases of asphyxia, and also provided a convenient means of inflating the lungs by bellows or the mouth. Kite himself claimed no originality for the idea, but referred to the suggestions of "Mr. Portal, Mr. le Cat, Dr. Munro and others" (see Appendix C).

After Kite came Hans Courtois (1789), James Curry (1792) and Pierre-Joseph Desault (1744-95), all of whom worked on the same problem at about the same time, followed early in the nineteenth century by François Chaussier, whose catheter (1807) had a flange of sponge in order to procure an air-tight fit.

The problem of the introduction of the catheter was overcome in several steps. The earliest workers relied on their fingers or on "luck" for the insertion of their tubes. In 1827, J. J. J. Leroy d'Etoilles (born 1798) invented a spatula to aid intubation by direct vision, while the invention of the indirect laryngoscope by Manuel Garcia, a teacher of singing, in 1855 familiarized doctors with the anatomy of the pharynx. In 1889, Friedrich Voltolini described an operating tracheoscope which was illuminated by reflected light, and this was followed in 1895 by Alfred Kirstein's (1863-1922) method of direct laryngoscopy using an electric "autoscope", an idea which was extended to bronchoscopy three years later by Gustav Killian (1860-1921). In 1909, W. Hill introduced his slotted laryngoscope, and this was improved by Chevalier Jackson, who wrote the first book on endoscopy in 1907. In 1913, H. H. Janeway invented a laryngoscope with a curved blade, the glottis being exposed by pressing the beak into the vallecula. Magill's laryngoscope, first designed *c.* 1920, was frequently modified and copied, but, since 1943, it has been virtually displaced by the model designed by (Sir) Robert Macintosh, in which Janeway's curved blade has been restored and exaggerated.

Meanwhile, the problems of anaesthesia had been pressing, and, in 1878 (reported in 1880), Sir William Macewen (1848 –1924) of Glasgow employed endotracheal intubation with a brass tube for the administration of an anaesthetic during the extirpation of a tumour at the base of the tongue. But the efforts to find a satisfactory catheter for dealing with laryngeal obstruction and for artificial respiration had continued, culminating in 1885 in Joseph P. O'Dwyer's (1841– 98) modification of a tube designed by Eugène Bouchut (1818–91) in 1858. O'Dwyer's tube was quickly adapted for anaesthesia by Karel Maydl in 1893, by Théodore Tuffier two years later, and by Rudolph Matas in 1900. A tube of a different design was described by Franz Kuhn (1866–1929) in 1902: He employed one made of jointed metal or "gas-piping". Other early users of the endotracheal inhalation method of anaesthesia were J. Annandale, Professor of Surgery at Edinburgh, who advocated an elastic catheter in 1889, and Victor Eisenmenger, whose tube of 1893 was made of hard rubber and fitted with an inflatable cuff, a device first used by Trendelenburg in his tracheotomy cannula of 1871.

Although the inhalational type of endotracheal anaesthesia continued to be used by some workers (e.g., Dorrance, 1910; Morriston Davies, 1911; Hill, 1914; Mart, 1914), it was generally displaced as a result of the development of the insufflation technique, in which the anaesthetic vapours were blown continuously down a narrow endotracheal catheter, and were allowed to escape outside the tube through the glottis. This method had the advantage of minimizing respiratory movements owing to the reduction in dead-space, and it was the pious hope of its users that the up-rush of gases would prevent the entry of blood into the trachea during oral operations. The method was first used by Barthèlemy and Dufour in man in 1907, followed, in 1909, by C. A. Elsberg, and, for animal experiments, by Meltzer and Auer in the latter year. The technique was strongly supported by Sir Robert Kelly of Liverpool, whose anaesthetic apparatus came to be widely used in Great Britain, to the almost complete exclusion of the inhalational method.

When Rowbotham and Magill began their work in 1917, they also employed an insufflation technique, using a single endotracheal catheter and a naso-pharyngeal tube to allow the escape of the gases. It was soon realized that this would not prevent aspiration of blood from the pharynx into the bronchial tree, and they then devised a two-tube method, both tubes being inserted into the larynx, and a gauze tampon being placed in the pharynx to secure a seal. Later, the two tubes were fused and passed together, and, finally, a single-lumen tube was used, with reversion to the old inhalational technique. The tubes designed by Rowbotham and Magill were of stiff rubber, and it was found that, in inserting the naso-pharyngeal tube, the end sometimes slipped accidentally into the larynx. The frequency of this occurrence led Magill to develop his method of blind nasal intubation (1928). By 1921, these two workers were able to report nearly 3,000 cases of endotracheal anaesthesia. The familiar Magill tube received its cuff from A. E. Guedel and R. M. Waters in 1928.

Experimental endobronchial intubation began as early as 1871 with the work of S. Wolffberg on dogs, on which animals H. Head (1889), who used a cuffed tube, and B. Werigo (1892) also worked. Endobronchial intubation in man does not seem to have been carried out until J. W. Gale and R. M. Waters reported "one-lung" anaesthesia for chest surgery in 1931. P. Frenckner (1934) and, particularly, Magill (1935) furthered the technique, and the tubes designed by the latter became virtually standard in Britain. Bronchial occlusion, to prevent the spread of infection from one part of a lung to another during surgery was first undertaken by E. Archibald in 1935, but it was the "blocker" of V. C. Thompson (1943) which came to be popular. Finally, we may mention the double-lumen catheter of Bjork and Carlens (1950) which has been so valuable in estimating the capacity of either lung at will.

The discovery of endotracheal methods of anaesthesia has been gradual, and many workers have participated in the development; it eventually culminated in a success which has proved to be one of the most important and far-reaching in the whole story of anaesthesia.

Chapter Six

· MUSCLE-RELAXANTS

The publication, by H. R. Griffith and G. Enid Johnson, of an article, *The Use of Curare in General Anesthesia*, in *Anesthesiology* in July, 1942, marked a turning-point in the history of anaesthesia, and has been followed by advances and benefits which would have appeared impossible before that date. The break-through was the result of work by a number of persons, and we should especially notice, first, R. C. Gill, who, after a hazardous expedition to Guiana and the Amazon Valley, brought back to the United States in 1938 considerable quantities of crude curare; secondly, a reasonably pure and standardized extract of this curare was prepared in the laboratory of A. R. McIntyre of Nebraska; and, thirdly, this extract was developed on a commercial scale by Messrs. E. R. Squibb & Sons.

Yet, curare was not unknown to science, and a great deal of information had been gathered about this substance since the time when Europeans had first come in contact with the South American Indians, and had seen the fatal effects of their poisoned darts. The first to describe the action of South American arrow-poison was Peter Martyr Angerius, whose *De Orbe Novo* appeared between 1504 and 1516; thereafter, long accounts were given by travellers, including Sir John Hawkins and Sir Walter Raleigh. The first physician to mention the subject was Nicolas Monardes, whose *Dos Libros* appeared in 1565 and 1571 (republished together in 1574); they were translated into English by John Frampton under the title of *Joyfull Newes Out of the Newe Founde Worlde* (1577). Monardes advocated "Tabaco" as an antidote to the poison.

These early authors gave no name to the arrow-poison, and it is by no means certain that they all described the same substance. A name similar to "curare" was first used by Jorg Marggraff in 1648 (*Historia Rerum Naturalum Braziliæ*), and this term, of doubtful etymology and varying orthography, has at length become standardized.

The first samples of curare to reach Europe were brought by de la Condamine in 1745, and he also conducted the first experiments with the substance, some of which (on hens) were performed in the presence of van Swieten and Albinus at Leyden. Other experiments were also conducted by Brocklesby (*Phil. Trans. roy. Soc.*, 1747, **44**, 408), but the first to be carefully planned were undertaken in 1781 by the Abbé Fontana, who tried to elucidate the chemistry of curare, and who also experimented on animals. He showed that the fumes of curare were not poisonous, that the substance was inactive when taken by mouth, that neither salt nor sugar was an antidote (as had been believed by some previous authors), and that it did not affect the heart.

Early in the nineteenth century, as samples of curare became less rare, F. H. A. von Humboldt applied curare to the nerves of frogs and then stimulated them with galvanic current, but his results were inconclusive.

In 1811, Sir Benjamin Brodie and Edward Bancroft showed that curare killed by causing paralysis of the muscles of respiration, and that artificial respiration would preserve life. These experiments were confirmed and elaborated by Charles Waterton, who had himself brought specimens of curare back to England in 1812, and who also showed the value of artificial respiration (by means of a bellows attached to a cannula inserted through a tracheotomy) in dogs, oxen and donkeys, one of the latter being the famous animal named Wouralia. As a direct result of these experiments, Francis Sibley, a friend of Waterton, was led to employ curare in the treatment of equine tetanus; Brodie had already suggested its use for that disease in man.

During the years 1850 to 1864, Claude Bernard investigated the action of curare thoroughly, and showed by his simple experiment of ligating the leg of a frog before injecting curare (reported in his *Leçons sur les Effets des Substances Toxiques* of 1857) that the site of action could only be at the myo-neural junction.

It had been realized for a long time that the various samples of curare obtained for experiment varied considerably in their potency and effects. The situation was clarified by R. Boehm in a series of papers from 1886 to 1897. He found that, as a rule, the curare varied with the type of container in which the natives packed it, and that these containers varied with the regions from which the substance was obtained. He therefore classified curares into three groups: Calabash-(or Gourd-) curare, from which he obtained the alkaloid "curarine"; Pot-curare, which yielded "protocurarine"; and Tube curare, which contained "tubocurarine". The actual chemical formulae of these alkaloids exercised chemists for years, but were finally elucidated by H. King of London in 1935. The plants used in the manufacture of arrow-poison by the South American Indians themselves vary and are numerous. For a long time, it seemed that the most important was *Strychnos toxifera*, but the work of Wintersteiner and Dutcher (1943) has shown that *Chondrodendron tomentosum* gives the best yield of *d*-tubocurarine.

As we have seen, Brodie, writing to Flourens in 1811, suggested the use of curare in the treatment of tetanus, but this idea was not taken up until 1858, when L. A. Sayres of New York applied the drug locally to the wound in a case of lock-jaw: the patient died. The first successful use of curare in tetanus was reported by (Sir) Thomas Spencer

MUSCLE-RELAXANTS

Wells in the following year (*Proc. roy. Med. and Chir. Soc.,* 1859, **3**, 142). By 1863, at least twelve cases had been reported with nine deaths. Curare continued to be used from time to time, not only for tetanus, but for epilepsy, hydrophobia and chorea as well, but results were unsatisfactory, partly owing to the difficulty of dealing with accidental overdosage, and partly because of the unstandardized samples employed. Some stimulus to its use resulted from Boehm's papers (A. Hoche used "curarine" in 1894) and, much later, from the work of King, which encouraged Leslie Cole and Ranyard West in this field.

In 1938, A. E. Bennett, acting on McIntyre's suggestion, introduced curare into shock therapy, in order to prevent the injuries caused by severe convulsions, and it was the success of this form of treatment which led to the work of Griffith and Johnson in Montreal. The extensive use of curare in general anaesthesia throughout the world was delayed by the war, but, by 1946, the drug was being widely used, and great interest began to be taken in synthetic substances which might also cause neuro-muscular block. The first of these new "curares" was 3381RP, synthesized by Bovet (1946), who, in the following year, described the synthesis of gallamine triethiodide. In 1948, Barlow and Ing, and Paton and Zaimis, working independently, reported on the action of decamethonium.

This last drug set off a train of events of some importance. Paton and Zaimis had discovered that the action of decamethonium could be shortened by the administration of the closely related pentamethonium. It was soon found, however, that the latter substance produced a dramatic fall in blood-pressure, but this side-effect was turned to advantage by some workers (Armstrong Davison; Hale Enderby; Scurr), and the hypotension produced by drugs with a similar pharmacological action has now replaced that previously achieved by the "total" spinal analgesia of Griffiths and

Gillies as a means of reducing blood-loss during surgical operations; and a whole new field of medical therapy was opened when it was found that these drugs could be used in the treatment of hypertension.

In 1906, R. Hunt and R. M. de Taveau had prepared succinyl (di-)choline; in 1949, Bovet and Phillips, independently, discovered the muscle-relaxant properties of this drug, while, more recently, suxethonium (first used by Valdoni in 1949) and laudexium (reported by Bodmin, Morton and Wylie in 1952) have been used.

The introduction of the muscle-relaxants has wrought a revolution in anaesthesia, and the benefits and successes which have resulted have been innumerable. Above all, they have led to a clearer understanding of the process of respiration and the importance of adequate pulmonary ventilation in the minds of all anaesthetists, and they have familiarized the whole medical profession with the value of artificial respiration, and the potentialities of mechanical respirators. During the first hundred years of anaesthesia, muscular relaxation could only be achieved at the expense of inadequate respiratory exchange; now, the necessity of adequate ventilation, and the knowledge of how it is to be obtained, are part of the skill of all anaesthetists: the muscle-relaxants have taught anaesthetists how to use ether!

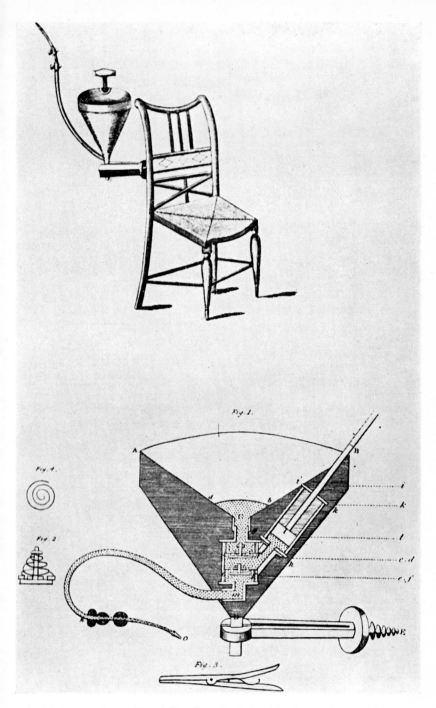

Figure 19. James Blundell's "Impellor" for blood transfusion (1824).

Figure 20. Henry Hill Hickman (1800–1830) conducting experiments
on the narcosis of animals with carbon dioxide. (From a water-colour
painting in the Wellcome Historical Museum, London.)

Chapter Seven

PREMEDICATION

The history of the introduction of premedication has received little attention, and is by no means straight-forward. The only person who has so far done it justice is Dr. William M. Shearer of Dundee, who has kindly permitted me to make use of the articles which he published recently (*Brit. J. Anaesth.*, 1960, **32**, 554 & 1961, **33**, 219).

The early use of morphine pre-operatively arose from the realization that chloroform, at that time almost the sole anaesthetic agent in use in Europe, was dangerous when used in large quantities. Thus, Nussbaum in 1864 gave morphine acetate (gr. 1) to a patient in order to reduce the amount of chloroform required. Soon after, J. Harley (1868) observed that atropine would reverse the bradycardia of chloroform, but he only used it during operation.

In 1869, Claude Bernard used morphine before chloroform in animal experiments, and his success led L. Labbé and E. Guyon in 1872 to use a similar premedication in man. This technique, however, was criticized by Demarquay, who had also employed it and considered it to be dangerous.

During the period 1870–90, the French physiologist, A. Dastre, who followed Bernard in his chair at the Sorbonne, conceived the idea of using both morphine and atropine as premedication in his experiments on dogs; the atropine was given in order to prevent the bradycardia of chloroform, and was given in large dosage. He also realized that morphine

L   159

and atropine, being in some sense antagonistic, overcame each other's disadvantages.

By 1880, E. A. Schäfer in England was preaching the importance of atropine pre-operatively in order to prevent death from vagal inhibition with chloroform, and P. Aubert of Lyons was following Dastre in the use of morphine and atropine, but using doses similar to those in use today. He, in his turn, was followed in England by P. Smith, who reported his success with this technique in 1891.

These pioneers were, however, voices crying in the wilderness, and, save in brain surgery, premedication was little used. In this last sphere, Sir Victor Horsley, as early as 1886, was insisting on the pre-operative use of morphine to reduce the quantity of chloroform required for long operations.

In 1900, von Schneiderlin introduced the combination of morphine and scopolamine (hyoscine) as an anaesthetic. Large doses were required, and, even then, it was often necessary to administer chloroform at times during the operation. With this in mind, von Dirk (1905) purposely reduced the dose of morphine and scopolamine, and used this combination as a true premedication, a method in which he was copied by H. Macnaughton-Jones (1908).

Meanwhile, in Australia, E. H. Embley had carried out experiments (1902) which seemed to prove that section of the vagi or premedication with atropine would prevent death from chloroform in dogs, and, during the first years of the century the use of pre-operative atropine became common.

However, in 1911, the British Medical Association's Chloroform Commission reported unfavourably, and ether, which had been struggling to make headway against its rival since 1872, rapidly became the anaesthetic of choice. At first, ether was used without any premedication, because the reasons for which drugs had been given before chloroform anaesthesia were not valid for ether; but the salivation and the violence of the "second stage" delirium soon led to a revival of the use of premedication. Thus, in 1911, Dudley Buxton, G. Brown and F. Rood were all advocating various pre-operative drugs, and C. L. Leipoldt, in an article in the *Lancet*, drew the attention of anaesthetists to the use of papaveretum, which had been prepared two years previously.

The first burst of enthusiasm for the new method, which seems to have been adopted in America soon afterwards, died down, and some opposition continued until after the first world war. It was in the 1920s that premedication came into general use, and it was then that the word itself was coined, being first used in print by F. H. McMechan in 1920.

During the 1930s, there was a vogue for using very heavy pre-operative sedation, which came to be known as "basal narcosis". The trend was stimulated by the introduction of bromethol and new barbiturates at about this time, but the responsibility cast upon the nursing staff by the administration of such potent drugs in the wards, and the risks entailed in the transport of unconscious patients to the operating theatre have led to the virtual disappearance of such heavy sedation, save in cases of severe thyrotoxicosis or abnormal anxiety.

Chapter Eight

REFRIGERATION ANAESTHESIA

The numbing effect of cold must have been apparent to many people in the distant past. The repeated failure to make use of this simple method of reducing the pain of surgical operations, even after the technique had been published, and the continued cycle of its rediscovery and neglect are perhaps the most powerful among the reasons for believing that, until the opening years of the nineteenth century, the idea of anaesthesia was not only absent from the public mind, but was positively antithetic to it. Appreciation of this fundamental notion is essential to a proper understanding of the evolution of anaesthesia and the development of the idea of humanity in the public conscience.

Bearing this in mind, and considering the danger which necessarily attended the use of unstandardized drugs, such as opium, it would not be surprising that the action of cold was the first anaesthetic agent to be described, nor that the discovery should come from a country remote from the essentially warm climates of the localities where the earliest civilizations flourished.

Yet snow and ice were known to Hippocrates, who, in his *Aphorisms*, recommends their use to check haemorrhage, and he was even aware of the analgesic action of cold, for he writes, "Swellings and pains in the joints, without ulceration, those of a gouty nature, and sprains are generally improved by a copious affusion of cold water, which reduces the swelling, and removes the pain; for a moderate degree of numbness removes pain". Nevertheless, Hippocrates no-where advocates cold as a surgical anaesthetic, and, even two thousand years later, the great William Harvey, who treated his own gout according to the method described in this Hippocratic aphorism, was equally uninterested in what, to us, seems its obvious application. In this connexion, it is interesting that Francis Adams, himself a surgeon and the learned translator of the works of Hippocrates, writing as late as 1849, comments on this aphorism, "that all the commentators hold that it [cold] acts, not by producing cold, but by rousing the vital heat of the part". Progress was indeed difficult when physiology was obscured by such curious notions.

There is no extant record prior to the year A.D. 1050 of any effective technique of surgical anaesthesia; the majority of the methods which had been described were purely magical in nature, and all would have been completely ineffective. It was about fifteen years before the Norman Conquest that an unknown Anglo-Saxon monk transmitted to writing the leechbook which Gratton and Singer published in 1952, and which they call the *Lacnunga*. As is to be expected at the height of the dark ages, this collection of recipes and invocations is largely superstitious in nature, but the allusion to cold as a surgical anaesthetic is unequivocal. The translation runs thus:

"Again, for eruptive rash. Let him sit in cold water until it be deadened; then draw him up. Then cut four scarifications around the pocks and let drip as long as he will".

As has been stated, this is the first description of a practicable anaesthetic, and it should be no small matter of pride that it was an Anglo-Saxon discovery. If the work of the Venerable Bede (*c.* 673–735), of Alcuin of York (735–804) and of Roger Bacon (*c.* 1214–*c.* 1294) be considered, it will be seen that the earliest stirrings of what was later to become the Renaissance are more intimately associated with

England than orthodox historians are usually prepared to admit.

Refrigeration anaesthesia was discovered only to be forgotten, and no further reference is made to it for more than five hundred years. In 1595, Johannes Costaeus (de Costa) published at Venice his *De Igneis Medicinæ Præsidiis*, in which there is a short reference to the use of cold water, snow or ice in relieving the pain of surgical incisions (Bk. 1, Cap. 31). Severino of Naples, the originator of comparative anatomy, actually employed this technique, which was seen by Thomas Bartholin, the celebrated anatomist and discoverer of Bartholin's glands, when he visited Italy in 1646. Fifteen years later, Bartholin published at Copenhagen his *De Nivis Usu Medico*, in which he devoted almost a whole chapter (Cap. XXII) to Severino's use of snow as an anaesthetic, but it does not appear that he used the method himself. Osler (*Bibliotheca Osleriana*, 1378h) thought that Bartholin had realized that cold could be used with benefit in vascular disease, but he was undoubtedly misled by the corrupt state of the text, which abounds in misprints. This is a translation of what Bartholin actually wrote:

"Before treating ulcers of the limbs by cauterization, the rubbing-in of snow produces insensitivity. Marco Aurelio Severino, my old teacher and friend, who is the foremost surgeon of our time, taught me this at the University of Naples. As a general rule, he put the snow in a capacious vessel . . . and applied it to the skin. He told us that, *if we were not afraid of gangrene*, we could apply it under narrow, parallel bandages; in a quarter of an hour, the nerves will be numbed, and it will be possible to make an incision at that point without causing pain. The surgeon can employ this method successfully even when opening up the area between the thighs, close to the perineal arch, for lithotomy. . . . When he wishes to conceal the nature of the treatment, in order to make the results seem more astonishing, the aforesaid

Severino dyes the snow with ground ultramarine or some other colouring matter".

From this it will be seen that Severino, far from advocating cold in the treatment of vascular disease, actually warned against its use in the case of impending gangrene.

Despite the reputation of such men as Severino and Bartholin, and the popularity of the latter's books, the resurrected art of refrigeration anaesthesia was again forgotten. Perhaps one reason for this was the advocacy of the method for cauterization; the application of a hot iron would quickly dispel the effects of cooling and destroy the analgesia.

Nevertheless, philosophers were already turning their attention to the use of snow for other purposes. In 1626, Francis Bacon, Viscount St. Albans, literally caught his death of cold while experimenting on the preservation of meat with snow. In 1755, William Cullen invented a sort of refrigerator with which he attempted to reduce small animals to a state of suspended animation, and, eleven years later, John Hunter tried, unsuccessfully, a similar experiment on some carp. James Boswell, Johnson's biographer, satirized these experiments in a witty paper, *On the New Freezing Discovery*, which appeared first in the *Publick Advertiser* of 1770, and was reprinted eleven years later in the *London Magazine*. By the 1790s, the use of cold packs and both the internal and external use of cold water began to be favoured in the treatment of febrile disorders. One of the foremost of these "hydrotherapists" was James Currie, whose *Medical Reports* appeared in 1797.

Refrigeration anaesthesia was discovered once more in 1807, when, after the battle of Preuss-Eylau, Napoleon's Surgeon-General, Baron Dominique-Jean Larrey, noticed that amputation could be painlessly performed on soldiers who had lain for some time in the snow. Although this observation seems to have had no direct practical results, the possibility of refrigeration anaesthesia was not again forgotten.

When the discovery of the anaesthetic action of ether had shown that surgical anaesthesia was a practical reality, refrigeration was again considered and eventually re-introduced. The credit for this must go to James Arnott (1797–1883), physician of Brighton. Between 1848 and 1867, Arnott published a long series of articles on this subject, the first of which was entitled *On Cold as a Means of Producing Local Insensibility*. (See an interesting and informative article by Marcus Bird in *Anaesthesia*, 1949, **4**, 10).

Arnott, however, did not restrict his advocacy of cold to anaesthesia. In 1852, he published a pamphlet *On the Internal Application of a Low Temperature in Asiatic Cholera*, an idea which foreshadowed the therapeutic use of hypothermia. It is to be noted, however, that Arnott applied the cold by making his patients drink considerable quantities of a saline solution, which had been reduced to a temperature of $26°$ F. ($-3.3°$ C.), and it is highly probable that his good results were, in part at least, due to the correction of the patient's depleted salt reserves.

In 1866, Benjamin Ward Richardson, the biographer of John Snow, stimulated by Arnott's successes in local anaesthesia, described his well-known spray. Originally intended to be used with a highly volatile hydrocarbon, called rhigolene, the spray soon came to be used with ether, which proved a satisfactory freezing agent. Richardson's ether spray became so popular that the term "freezing" has passed into the English language as a synonym for local anaesthesia.

The introduction of cocaine as a local anaesthetic in 1884 did not lead to the discontinuance of the use of the spray, which still remained popular for the opening of abscesses. The substitution of ethyl chloride for ether occurred when, in 1890, Redard developed the glass container with spring-loaded nozzle still in use for ethyl chloride today. The new agent proved peculiarly successful in dentistry, partly because the Redard spray could be directed with great accuracy, and partly, no doubt, because the patient inevitably inhaled a quantity of the vapour, and thus achieved a substantial degree of general analgesia. As a matter of fact, the accidental production of full general anaesthesia by Carlson of Gothenburg in two dental patients (1894) was one of the steps in the series of events which led to the introduction of ethyl chloride as a general anaesthetic by Lotheissen of Innsbruck in 1896.

With the advances in local anaesthetic drugs and techniques which were made towards the end of the nineteenth century and during the early part of the twentieth, local refrigeration anaesthesia was almost forgotten. However, in 1905, Simpson and Herring at Edinburgh (*J. Physiol.*, **32**, 305) experimented on the chilling of cats, and observed that, when the body temperature had fallen to about 25° C., the animals became insensible.

To move to a less scientific field, it is interesting that the use of cold as a therapeutic agent had spread to the sphere of Indian folk-lore. Gandhi (*Mahatma Gandhi*: *His Own Story*, ed. C. F. Andrews, London, 1930, p. 292) tells how, during World War I, an itinerant quacksalver treated his patients, including the Mahatma himself, by the application of ice all over the body.

In 1936, Smith and Fay (*J. Amer. med. Ass.*, 1939, **113**, 653) began the combined used of local and general hypothermia for the treatment of cancer. The rectal temperature of their heavily sedated patients was kept as low as 30 to 32° C. for up to five days. The cooling was achieved by exposure to a low room temperature.

In 1937, Frederick M. Allen began his work on local refrigeration for limb surgery, his first paper appearing in the *Transactions of the Association of American Physicians* (**52**, 189) in that year. A number of other papers followed, but he did not succeed in arousing much interest until, in April 1942, he read his important paper, *Refrigeration Anaesthesia* *for Limb Operations* before the American Society of Anesthetists, Inc., at New York (*Anesthesiology*, 1943, **4**, 12).

At this point, respect must be paid to those victims of the Nazi concentration camps who suffered and died from experiments in cooling which were conducted by men whose actions have tarnished the history not only of medicine, but of all humanity. The records of those inhuman trials were rightly destroyed, but the memory of them must not be permitted to fade, lest the bestial Hitlerian régime receive in due course as many coats of whitewash as has that of Napoleon.

To return to the field of science, other early workers in the field of refrigeration were Blalock, Alfred and Mason, who reported (*Arch. Surg.*, 1941, **42**, 1054) the beneficial effect of cold in the prevention and treatment of shock, and stated that "hypothermia, by lowering the rate of metabolism, reduces the tissue requirement for oxygen". In April 1942, Bancroft, Fuller and Ruggiero (*Ann. Surg.*, **115**, 621) were also advocating refrigeration for amputation in cases of diabetic gangrene. By the end of that year, such was the interest in the newly revived technique, that thermostatically controlled refrigerators were in use, thus avoiding not only the risk of wound contamination from dirty ice, but also the labour of cracking large quantities of it.

In 1946, Kanaar (*Curr. Res. Anesth.*, **25**, 177, 228) pointed out the value of prolonged cooling in the treatment of vascular injuries to the limbs. By that date, animal experiments were being undertaken at numerous centres and, in 1948, Eichna (*Arch. phys. Med.*, **29**, 687) and, in the following year, Lange and his co-workers (*Ann. intern. Med.*, **31**, 989) had both reported ventricular fibrillation at low body temperatures.

Surface cooling of the body by means of ice packs was advocated by Bigelow (*Ann. Surg.*, 1950, **132**, 849), while Delorme (*Lancet*, 1952, **2**, 914) introduced extracorporeal cooling by circulating the blood through a refrigerator system. This method was first applied to man in 1953. Meanwhile, Boerema had also begun work on extracorporeal refrigeration as early as 1950, but soon abandoned this method in favour of surface cooling.

It was at this stage that the method of "artificial hibernation", as it was at first called, was introduced by Laborit and Huguenard, who made use of certain phenothiazine derivatives, especially the then newly isolated chlorpromazine, in order to diminish the homeostatic response of patients to shock. Since the drugs employed caused marked peripheral vasodilatation, a fall in body temperature not infrequently occurred, but this was not an integral part of the technique. Indiscriminate use of the term "hibernation" led to some confusion, which was not lessened when the value of chlorpromazine in the production of surface cooling came to be recognized.

The use of phenothiazine derivatives, especially chlorpromazine and promazine, has been greatly extended. These drugs are now used frequently in the treatment of mental disorders, as premedication before general anaesthesia, and as sedatives during operations under local anaesthesia, especially in ophthalmic work, where sedation, low intra-ocular tension and blanching of the eye are combined, without loss of the patient's ability to co-operate. These drugs are also useful in the prevention and treatment of vomiting after anaesthesia, in the management of the intractable pain of inoperable cancer, and, because of the depressant effect upon spinal convulsions, in the treatment of tetanus.

The importance of hypothermia in modern anaesthesia derives from the desire of the surgeon to carry out more and more drastic and time-consuming operations on the heart, vascular system and brain. The success which has attended the introduction of the technique in permitting operations of this sort to be performed is an indication of the vast improvements in anaesthesia which have taken place during the past fifteen years, but it is also a success which could not have been achieved without the closest co-operation and mutual faith between the surgeon and the anaesthetist: it is, more than anything else, a sign that the anaesthetist has at last entered into his rightful place in the surgical team.

At the present time, animal experiments are being conducted in various centres on the problem of cooling the living animal to very low temperatures, even below 0°C. If these experiments should result in a technique by which the human body can be safely reduced to a state of true suspended animation, the boundaries of surgery will become virtually limitless. Nevertheless, caution must be exercised in the approach to such a nirvana; and one particular objection is now looming large indeed. During the last ten years, the duration of surgical operations has increased considerably. The technique of refrigeration is also time-consuming. A few years ago, the amount of surgical work, which could be done in a hospital, depended on the number of beds available; today, the number of operating theatres has become the limiting factor. The cost of new operating theatre blocks is great, and the expense of running an increasing number of them with a full complement of highly trained anaesthetists, surgeons and nursing staff may throw an excessive strain, not only on the Welfare State, but on the institutions of countries in which financial support comes directly from the pockets of the patients. Anaesthesia and surgery are approaching a cross-roads, and, so far as can be discerned at present, the sign-posts are inadequate.

Nevertheless, it begins to look as if John Hunter's hopes may one day be realized and that it will be possible to put a man to sleep for a hundred or a thousand years. Perhaps this may solve some of the problems of the conquest of space.

Chapter Nine

LOCAL ANALGESIA

The effects of cold, the first successful local analgesic ever recorded, have been dealt with in the previous section. The development of true local analgesia by drugs has, unlike most other developments in anaesthesia, been rapid, once the initial steps had been taken. However, hints of the possibility of such drugs go back a long way, and, in Homer's *Iliad* (Book II), we find that Patroclus, having cut an arrow out of the thigh of Eurypylos, "cast [on the wound] a bitter root . . . that took pain away and ended all his anguish, the wound began to dry, and the blood ceased".

Another early mention, probably apocryphal, is by Dioscorides (second century, A.D.), who speaks of the analgesic effect of the "Memphian stone". Some have thought that this was a form of marble which, on being moistened with vinegar, would generate carbon dioxide, and Sir James Y. Simpson was so impressed by this idea that, when he experimented with various gases (even hydrocyanic acid!) in 1848 to discover whether they had any local action, he tried repeatedly with carbon dioxide and even convinced himself of its efficacy.

Local analgesia by the compression of nerves was sometimes attempted during the centuries before anaesthesia, but failed for the same reason as did cold: the world was not yet prepared for pain relief. In this connexion, we may mention Paré (1562), Valverdi (c. 1600), James Moore (1784) and Liégard (1837).

171

Local analgesia as we know it today depended on two things: the discovery of a suitable drug, and the invention of a convenient syringe. The latter invention was due to Alexander Wood, who, in 1853, made a hollow needle, and combined it with the glass syringe of Pravaz, invented earlier in the same year.

The conquest of Peru by Pizarro in the years after 1530 brought to light the properties of a wonderful plant, whose leaves and roots were remarkably stimulating when chewed. The natives regarded this plant as divine, and, stressing its importance in their economy, called it, in their language, "khoka", meaning "the plant"; and this word was to be Europeanized as "coca". The first to write of it was Pedro Cieza de Leon, who mentioned it in 1532 and subsequently, and the first English account apepared in Frampton's *Joyfull Newes Out of the Newe Founde Worlde* (1577), quickly followed by a fuller description in *The Strange and Delectable History of the Discovery of Peru*, a translation of 1581 by T. Nichols from the Spanish of Augustin de Zarate (1555). Other writers made the plant familiar and, by the end of the eighteenth century, supplies of the dried leaves were frequently brought to Europe.

In 1855, Gaedicke succeeded in isolating an alkaloid, which he named "erythroxyline" from the leaves of this plant, known to botanists as *Erythroxyline coca* (Lamarck). Four years later, Albert Niemann repeated this extraction and simplified the process; he re-named the alkaloid "cocaïne". Interest in the new drug was quick, but not extensive. In 1862, Schraff demonstrated mydriasis in the eye of the rabbit, while, in 1874, Alexander Hughes Bennett (1848–1901) reported (in the *Edinburgh Medical Journal*) an analgesic effect on mucous membranes. It was later reported by Foy (*Anæsthetics, Ancient and Modern*, London, Baillière, 1889) that Charles Fauvel "the famous Paris laryngologist" had been using a solution of cocaïne for surface (topical) analgesia in the pharynx as early as 1869. In 1875, Coupart (*Tribune Médicale*) described the similar use of a strong alcoholic solution, and, in 1877, Saglia, from the same clinic, reiterated the value of cocaine in laryngology (*Gazette des Hôpitaux*); Coupart and Borderan again reported in 1880, while, according to Foy, "The experiments of Dr. Coupart were repeated and verified by Dr. Labordt, the well-known experimental physiologist, who, in addition, proved that cocaine possessed general anaesthetic properties". V. K. (von) Anrep (born 1852) had also suggested the possibility of local analgesia with cocaine in 1880.

The real stimulus to local analgesia, however, came from the demonstration of analgesia of the eye by Carl Koller (1857–1944) at the Congress of Ophthalmology at Heidelberg in 1884. The use of topical cocaine at once became popular, and a few bold spirits started to use solutions of the alkaloid by injection. Probably the earliest of these was H. J. Knapp (1831–1911) of New York. About the same time, in 1885, J. Leonard Corning (1855–1923) carried out the first spinal (or epidural; opinions vary) analgesia on a dog.

The use of strong solutions of cocaine, especially by injection, led to serious side-effects and even death, and, in 1887, J. B. Mattison of Brooklyn read a paper on *Cocaine Toxæmia*, in which he reported thirty cases of "cocaine convulsions", but, since no other drug was yet available, the use of cocaine continued, and infiltration techniques were developed by De Takàts (1890), Paul Reclus (1847–1914) in the same year, and, particularly, by Carl Ludwig Schleich (1859–1922), whose use of a dilute solution of cocaine (1894) became popular throughout Europe.

The search for new drugs was, however, stimulated by the obvious dangers of cocaine; the first success was with Tropacocaine, introduced by Giesel in 1891. This was followed by others, including Forneau's Stovaine (1901), and, still more successfully, procaine. This drug was first synthesized in 1899 by Alfred Einhorn, and was introduced into anaesthetic practice by Heinrich Braun (1862–1934) in 1905. A great many other drugs with local analgesic action have also been synthesized, but we may particularly notice Percaine (cinchocaine) (1931), later re-named Nupercaine, and Xylocaine (lignocaine), synthesized by N. Löfgren in 1943, and reported by him and B. Lundquist in 1946. This latter drug has proved even more successful than procaine, and it is unfortunate that its price is so much higher. A search has also been made for a long-acting drug, but without much success. Early use of oily solutions was disappointing, and Efocaine, introduced in 1952, causes neural degeneration.

It will be noticed that the termination "-caine" has been given to the names of most local analgesic drugs. This is, of course, etymologically accidental, being derived from the last syllable of "coca" plus the ending "-ine", originally pronounced di-syllabically. This use of a generic termination has led to many mistakes being made in prescribing; for instance, the similarity between "procaine" and the much more potent "Percaine" was responsible for several fatalities, and caused the manufacturers to change the proprietary name of the drug to "Nupercaine".

The development of true regional (conduction) analgesia, foreshadowed by W. S. Halsted (1852–1922) as early as 1885, when he injected cocaine into the mandibular nerve, is due to the work of Braun, who realized that the toxicity of local analgesic drugs was related to the rate of absorption, and therefore, in 1897, recommended the addition of adrenaline to the solution, and to George Washington Crile (1864–1943) and Harvey Cushing (1869–1939) who, also in 1897, demonstrated the possibilities of the technique, the former performing an amputation of the leg after blocking the sciatic and femoral nerves, and the latter repairing a hernia after regional block. Rudolph Matas (born 1860) worked on this subject for many years from 1898: in 1899, he used regional

Figure 22. Oliver Wendell Holmes (1809–1894), from a caricature by himself.

Figure 21. William Thomas Green Morton (1818–1868), the discoverer of anaesthesia.

DR H J BIGELOW   DR A A GOULD   DR J C WARREN   DR W T G MORTON   DR SAMUEL PARKMAN   DR GEORGE HAYWARD
DR J MASON WARREN   DR S D TOWNSEND

The First Public Demonstration of Surgical Anaesthesia
Boston, October 16, 1846.

Figure 23. The first public demonstration of anaesthesia, 16th October,

analgesia in a case of cancer which required the extirpation of both maxillae.

Spinal analgesia, perhaps performed by Corning on a dog in 1885, was given an impetus by the description of lumbar puncture by Essex Wynter in 1891 and, a few months later, by Heinrich Quincke. In 1893, von Ziemssen injected the lumbar spines of cadavers with methylene blue, and suggested the possibility of spinal analgesia, while, in 1898, A. Sicard used lumbar puncture for the introduction of serum in a case of tetanus. The first papers on spinal analgesia in man came from August Bier (1861–1949), and rather later, from Théodore Tuffier (1857–1929), both in 1891. The former had experimented on animals before himself submitting to spinal analgesia at the hands of an assistant. At first, spinal analgesia was only used for operations on the lower limbs, but, in 1899, Tuffier described the technique for operations on the lower abdomen, and spinal analgesia was gradually extended to higher levels of the body. The new method was placed on firm ground by Wayne Babcock in 1904. Others who described specific techniques or otherwise contributed to the understanding of the spread of analgesic solutions in the cerebro-spinal canal were Howard Jones (1930), W. Etherington Wilson (1934), N. C. Lake (1937) and R. R. Macintosh (1948), while the publication of the book *Spinal Anesthesia* by Louis H. Maxson in 1938 was another forward step. Continuous spinal analgesia, by means of a catheter inserted into the subdural space, was first used by H. P. Dean of the London Hospital in 1907, but it is associated particularly with the names of W. T. Lemmon (1940), E. B. Tuohy (1945) and J. G. Arrowood (1944). "Total" spinal analgesia, as a means of lowering the blood-pressure and thus reducing operative haemorrhage, was introduced by H. W. C. Griffiths and John Gillies in 1948. It is interesting to note that both Le Filliâtre (1902) and J. Jonesco (1909) had already given spinal analgesia to the level of loss of consciousness, and had, to some extent, foreshadowed the work of Griffiths and Gillies.

In 1901, Sicard and Cathelin described sacral epidural analgesia, while epidural analgesia at a higher level was used by Fidel Pagès in Spain in 1920. R. A. Hingson and W. B. Edwards adapted sacral epidural (caudal) analgesia to obstetrics with great success in 1942.

We have seen that Labordt apparently knew of the possibility of using cocaine as a general anaesthetic. In 1909, Bier described a method of intravenous local analgesia, in which a limb was isolated by tourniquet, and procaine solution was injected into the veins. J. L. Ransohoff (1910) in America and J. Goyanes (1912) in Madrid developed this technique into an intra-arterial method, in which, because of the rapid absorption of cocaine in the capillaries, no tourniquet was required. In 1935, R. Leriche and R. Fontaine described the beneficial effects of intravenous procaine in cases of arteritis obliterans, and other workers used the same technique for various complaints (Levy, 1937, for tinnitus aurium; Lundy, 1942, for the pruritis of jaundice). In 1940, E. A. Rovenstine and his colleagues noticed the action of intravenous procaine in preventing cardiac irregularities during thoracic surgery; and, soon after, Tovell (1942) recommended its use during the dressing of severe burns. Some advantage was claimed for the same technique by M. C. Peterson in the early treatment of poliomyelitis, and he and D. J. Graubard, in 1955, described the "procaine unit": the amount of procaine which the body can metabolize in a certain time (4mg./Kg./20 mins.). At about that time, general anaesthesia with intravenous procaine was used by a few workers, but the developments in pharmacology (particularly of the cortico-steroids), and the obvious dangers of over-dosage have led to the virtual abandonment of the intravenous administration of these drugs.

Local analgesia has played a great part in the painless

surgery of the twentieth century, and it may never be replaced for the performance of minor operations. However, the unpredictable and disastrous complications of spinal analgesia have long made themselves apparent, and it seems likely that, with the provision of competent anaesthetists to hospitals throughout the whole world, all forms of local analgesia for major surgery will give place to general anaesthesia.

Chapter Ten

OXYGEN AND HELIUM

OXYGEN

The first researches into the nature of air seem to have been made by J. B. van Helmont (1577–1644), who followed in the iatrochemical footsteps of Paracelsus and, like the latter, was imbued with *mystique*. It was van Helmont (1648) who invented the word "gas" (derived from the Greek word, "chaos"), and described a particular gas (gas sylvestre) which, in some regards, is to be identified with carbon dioxide, but the difficulty of comprehending van Helmont's writings obscured the value of his discovery, and he influenced later workers but little.

John Mayow (1643–79), concerning whose life but little is known, came very near to the discovery of the true role of oxygen in respiration; his *Tractatus quinque medico-physici* (1674) is regarded as one of the greatest of the English medical classics, but the researchers who followed (Black, Priestley and Lavoisier) were completely ignorant of his work. Mayow began with the premise that there was a "vital substance" present in air, and that this substance was essential for cumbustion. Since wet gunpowder will burn, Mayow postulated that this vital spirit was also present in nitre and he therefore named it the *spiritus nitro-œreus*. In confirmation of this theory, Mayow covered a lighted taper with a glass globe and showed that the flame went out when the nitro-aerial spirit was exhausted and, further, that the volume of air remaining had diminished in quantity. Mayow

had already decided that the source of all heat was combustion or fermentation, the latter being a slow form of
burning, and that, in the living animal, heat was produced
in muscles. From this, he concluded that in respiration, the
"nitro-aerial spirit" was removed from the air in the lungs,
absorbed by the blood, and carried to all parts of the body
in the course of its circulation. He, therefore, repeated the
experiment detailed above, substituting a live mouse for the
lighted taper, and achieved an identical result.

Mayow did not isolate oxygen, but he proved its existence,
and his work ought to have been a beacon-light to those who
were to come after him.

Eighty years passed before the chemical nature of air was
further elucidated by Joseph Black, whose M.D. thesis of
1754 (published in 1756) described the discovery of carbon
dioxide, which he called "fixed air". In addition to the actual
re-discovery of van Helmont's "gas sylvestre", Black by
means of his quantitative experiments with chalk, laid the
basis for the atomic theory of John Dalton (1766–1844).

The actual isolation of oxygen was first achieved by Joseph
Priestley (1733–1804) in 1771. Priestley, a Unitarian Minister, had turned to teaching "natural science" as a means
of eking out his small stipend when he held a ministry at
Needham Market in Suffolk. The interest in science, thus
aroused, remained with Priestley throughout various appoint-
ments; for instance, when he held a ministry at Warrington,
he delivered a course of lectures on anatomy. He also made
numerous friendships in the scientific world, chief among
which was a lasting bond which he formed with Benjamin
Franklin. On removing to Mill Hill Chapel, Leeds, in 1767,
Priestley interested himself in the chemical nature of air and,
living next door to a brewery, carried out experiments with
the "fixed air" which was available in abundance on the
malting floor. Prevented because of his religious opinions
from accepting the post of naturalist to Captain Cook's

second voyage of discovery, Priestley remained at Mill Hill Chapel until, in 1773, he became Librarian to Lord Shelburne (later Marquess of Lansdowne), a post in which he was able to continue his scientific experiments without distraction.

In 1771 (as described in the *Philosophical Transactions* of the Royal Society (1772, **62**, 147), Priestley isolated a gas from nitre by heating it in a gun-barrel. He observed that a candle burned with an increased flame when immersed in this gas but, since he did not then possess a burning-glass, he was unable to produce the gas in sufficient quantities to examine its properties fully. It was not until August 1, 1774, that, having obtained a lens of 12 in. diameter and 20 in. focal length, Priestley obtained the same gas, which he called "dephlogisticated air" (oxygen) in considerable amount from *mercurius calcinatus*, and a full description of the gas and the methods of obtaining it from mercuric oxide ("red precipitate") and red lead appeared in the *Experiments and Observations on different kinds of air* (1774–75). In March, 1775, Priestley showed that mice could live in this gas, and the discovery of oxygen with its potential use in medicine was put on record.

Priestley's chemical discoveries were numerous, but friction between him and Lord Shelburne led to the resignation of his post, and he returned to the ministry in Birmingham. He was a pronounced liberal in his political opinions, and the support which he gave to a dinner to celebrate the anniversary of the French Revolution (July 14, 1791) led to an outbreak of mob violence in which his home was burned and the records of numerous experiments, never to be repeated or reported, were destroyed. In 1794, he emigrated to Virginia, where he continued his scientific work until just before his death in 1804.

Priority in the discovery of oxygen has often been claimed for the great Swedish chemist, Carl Wilhelm Scheele (1742–86). In fact, Scheele, by his own account, first isolated oxygen in 1772, and his first description of his discovery was not until 1777 (*Chemische Abhandlung von der Luft und dem Feuer*), so there seems to be no doubt that both Priestley's discovery and his publication of it were first in the field.

The importance of oxygen in the economy of nature was further elucidated by Jan Ingen-Housz (1730–99). Ingen-Housz was a physician of Dutch origin; educated abroad and at Edinburgh, he settled in London; becoming, in 1764, physician to the Emperor of Austria, he removed to Vienna. He contributed many papers to the Royal Society, and was elected a fellow on his return to England in 1778. In 1779 he published his *Experiments on vegetables*, in which he demonstrated the ability of green plants to absorb carbon dioxide when exposed to sunlight. This book is also important because, at the end of the preface, he wrote, "When this book was entirely printed, and nothing but the latter end of the preface unfinished, I was informed by my friend the Abbé Fontana (Felice Fontana, 1720–1805), that he discovered a few days ago a new method of procuring to a sick person the benefit of breathing any quantity of dephlogisticated air (oxygen) at a cheap rate". He goes on to describe the use of a solution of lime for the purpose of absorbing the "fixed air" (carbon dioxide), one of the earliest accounts of carbon dioxide absorption ever published. Scheele had also used "milk of lime" for absorbing "fixed air" from the atmosphere of "fire-air" (oxygen) in which he kept bees alive.

It would seem from the above that the use of oxygen was already being advocated in medicine, but unfortunately we have no information concerning the circumstances in which it was recommended. The medicinal use of carbon dioxide was also advised at this time. Matthew Dobson (? 1745–84), who is especially remembered for his discovery that the urine of diabetics contains sugar, in his *Medical Commentary* on *Fixed Air* (1779), particularly recommends the use of carbon dioxide in putrid fevers; it was usually administered in the form of an effervescent drink, but sometimes as an enema.

By 1780, Chaussier of Dijon was advocating the use of oxygen in the resuscitation of newborn babies, and he described a mask and bag of chamois leather for this purpose. In the following year, Henry Cavendish (1731–1810) demonstrated that the combustion of hydrogen in oxygen produced water.

In the years 1780 to 1793, the understanding of the nature of chemistry was fundamentally changed by the work of Antoine-Laurent Lavoisier (1743–94). This Frenchman, ably assisted by his young wife (she was 14 years his junior), set up one of the finest laboratories in the world at the French Arsenal. Among other great discoveries he showed the way in which acids and bases react to form salts, how oxygen and metals unite to form bases, and how oxygen and non-metals produce acids. It was this last discovery which caused him to rename dephlogisticated air "oxygène", the acid-producer. The work of Lavoisier completely overthrew the phlogiston theory of Stahl and initiated a new era in chemistry.

In the field of biology, Lavoisier, assisted by Pierre de la Place (1749–1827) measured the metabolic rate and respiratory quotient of a pig (1780) and, with Seguin, of a man (1793). His experiments with living organisms demonstrated the true nature of respiration and its analogy with combustion, and he achieved a quantitative analysis of these processes.

Lavoisier's last public service was to assist the commission which initiated the metric system of weights and measures. In 1793, he was arrested for his membership in the hated Ferme Générale, the tax-collecting authority of Royalist France, and he was executed early in the following year. His widow subsequently became the wife of another great scientist, Count Rumford.

By 1788, both Edmund Goodwyn and Charles Kite were advocating oxygen in the treatment of asphyxia, and, by the turn of the century, the rationale of this treatment was universally accepted, but the difficulty of obtaining and storing supplies of the gas prevented its use save in exceptional circumstances.

The foundation of the short-lived Pneumatic Institute at Clifton near Bristol increased the knowledge of gases, but the results in medical treatment were so unsatisfactory that the immediate effect was a withdrawal of interest from the subject. Thomas Beddoes (1760–1808), the founder of the Pneumatic Institute and the "discoverer" of Humphry Davy (1778–1829), was educated as a physician at Oxford, London and Edinburgh, in which latter University he obtained the degree of M.D. In 1787, he was appointed Lecturer in Chemistry at Oxford, a post which he was forced to resign after five years on account of his political opinions, which, like Priestley's, were "liberal"; like the latter he favoured the French Revolutionaries. While at Oxford, he published an account of the writings of John Mayow, and this work presumably drew his attention to the study of "airs" (gases). The Pneumatic Institute was founded with the idea of studying the medicinal uses of various gases in which Beddoes had interested himself both before and after leaving Oxford, and Beddoes had definite views on the function of oxygen in the animal economy. He followed Lavoisier, in opposition to many other scientists of his time, in believing that oxygen was removed from the air in the lungs and carried in the blood to different parts of the body, where it acted by increasing the "irritability" of living tissues; he also believed that sleep was caused by a reduction of oxygen in the body; and he considered pulmonary tuberculosis to be caused by an excess of oxygen; he therefore recommended treating that disease by inhalations of carbon dioxide. Scurvy, on the other hand, he thought was due to the removal of oxygen from the air by the action of intense sunlight. On the whole, he regarded pure oxygen as poisonous, although the presence of some oxygen in the atmosphere was essential to life; and Humphry Davy held similar views.

The fact that, unlike lighted tapers and living animals, green plants were not killed by enclosing them beneath a glass globe, puzzled John Mayow. As we have seen, Ingen-Housz had gone some way to explaining the paradox, but the full explanation came from Théodore de Saussure (1767–1845) of Geneva, who demonstrated the essentials of plant nutrition in 1804. He also showed that the seeds of plants will not germinate in the absence of oxygen, that carbon dioxide retards germination, and that light has no effect on germination until after green leaves have appeared.

In 1809, William Allen and W. H. Pepys read a paper entitled *On respiration* at the Royal Society, detailing careful quantitative experiments in which they showed that the only change which occurs to air during respiration is the substitution of carbon dioxide for a portion of the oxygen and that, when pure oxygen is breathed, nitrogen is excreted through the lungs. They also showed that the earliest scientists were wrong in believing that the lungs were completely collapsed after expiration and, in fact, still retained more than 100 cubic inches of air.

By the early nineteenth century, the value of oxygen in certain cardiac conditions was beginning to be recognized. In 1817, a Dr. R. Read delivered a paper in Dublin *On the use of oxygen gas in angina pectoris*; he described a typical case of angina in a man of 66 who was much relieved by the inhalation of several quarts of the gas. However, as was natural in the unsatisfactory state of medicine at that time, oxygen came to be used as a sort of panacea, and, failing in that purpose, was largely discarded. Thus, we have an account of one Daniel Hill, a practitioner in Bloomsbury in the early years of the nineteenth century: starting with the perfectly reasonable idea that "in all cases of debility, where the action of the heart and arteries was weak, it [oxygen] should prove extremely beneficial to the patient". He had some success in such cases, but Dr. Hill proceeded to use the gas in the treatment of all sorts of complaints, and claimed success with it in the treatment of epilepsy, paralysis, arthritis of the knee, tuberculosis of the hip, and other conditions. An account of one such case is too remarkable to be omitted here.

> "Hydrocephalus—Child of William Bennet, seventeen months old. At six months had small pox, succeeded by epilepsy; then inflammation of the eyes; after which the head began to enlarge until the sutures opened to a considerable extent and allowed the fluctuation of the water to be distinctly felt through the membranes. Pulse weak, beating 100 per minute, pressure on brain had caused total paralysis of extremities. Case was considered hopeless, oxygen treatment tried;—in one week the child began to show improvement;—in a month the head was reduced nearly to its natural size, the paralysis of the limbs was cured, and by continuing the treatment perfect recovery was soon accomplished".

We are not surprised to read that "Mr. Hill's treatment appears to have met with much hostility from his medical brotherhood"; honest physicians would not believe such reports, and hostility to such practitioners naturally entailed a decreased interest in the already proved virtues of oxygen.

However, the general public was becoming better informed of the truths of chemistry, and this interest was bound, sooner or later, to be reflected in medical practice. The biggest forward step was taken when, in 1844, Horace Wells made his ill-fated attempt to introduce anaesthesia with nitrous oxide. In 1845, George Wilson, M.D., F.R.S.E.,

Lecturer in Chemistry at Edinburgh, read a paper before the Royal Scottish Society of Arts *On the employment of oxygen as a means of resuscitation in asphyxia.* In this paper, he first argued the value of early and efficient artificial respiration and then went on to claim on physiological grounds the superiority of oxygen over common air for this purpose. He then proceeded to describe simple apparatus from which, by heating potassium chlorate mixed with ferric oxide, an adequate and cheap supply of oxygen could easily be obtained. Recognizing the difficulty of introducing the gas into the lungs of the patient, Wilson devised a species of oxygen "tent" which might be made of "wicker work covered with waterproof cloth. It should be large enough to contain the head and neck of the patient, and the front should be hinged so that it might be thrown open at once if necessary and glazed so as to permit the patient's face to be seen. The side of the box where the patient's head was introduced, might be terminated in a cylinder or loose tube of waterproof cloth, which could be tied round the neck by a ribbon or be attached to the skin by a piece of sticking plaster, so as to prevent escape of oxygen".

Allowance for the evacuation of the respired air was made, and artificial respiration, by compression of the chest, was not impeded by the apparatus. Wilson thought that all the above materials should be available at "our public hospitals, lying-in institutions, humane societies' rooms, police office stations and wherever else cases of asphyxia frequently come". He went on to say "The method appears particularly applicable to midwifery hospital practice. The quantity required for the inflation of the lungs of a still-born [sic] infant could easily be supplied by even a small apparatus. The method proposed would apply to every form of asphyxia occurring in hospital practice, to cases of poisoning with opium and to other states of disease or injury".

In spite of ingenious suggestions of this sort the use of

oxygen in medical practice, other than very occasionally, was limited by the size of gas-holders and the inability to transport gas other than for short distances and in small quantities in bladders. It is not known when oxygen was first compressed into metal cylinders although it is known that the Viennese Fire Brigade employed cylinders of compressed air as early as 1833. In London, cylinders of compressed oxygen were available at least as early as 1856, but it was not for another fifteen years that they were in much demand.

John Snow recorded one case of death under chloroform anaesthesia in 1849 in which oxygen was used in an unsuccessful attempt at resuscitation, but such cases must have been extremely rare at that date, for oxygen was prepared on the spot, and the requisite apparatus was usually lacking. The intensive use of cylinders began with the work of the firm of Barth in 1868, quickly followed by that of Coxeter.

Cylinders were apparently not in use in America at this time, for when E. Andrews, Professor of Surgery at Chicago introduced the idea of mixing nitrous oxide and oxygen in order to obtain improved "gas" anaesthesia in dentistry, he complained of the cumbersome bulk of balloons for storage and transport.

The revolutionary idea of combining oxygen with nitrous oxide did not at first meet with great success, and in 1872 we find Alfred Coleman writing "that mixtures of nitrous oxide and oxygen in various proportions had been employed, but that they had not been attended with success; they produced much struggling and excitement with but imperfect anaesthesia".

However, in 1878, Paul Bert (1833–86), Professor of Physiology at the Sorbonne, began to experiment with prolonged nitrous oxide anaesthesia, achieved by administering the gas mixed with air at a raised pressure. A year later, he was using 85% nitrous oxide with 15% oxygen at a pressure of 920 mm. Hg. with great success. Unfortunately the restrictions of the pressure chamber which had to be used as an operating theatre were such that by, 1883, the method was virtually abandoned, even by Bert, who, however, thought that "this method of anaesthesia as nearly as possible approached perfection".

The interest which had been aroused in prolonged anaesthesia by Bert's method led to several attempts to use a mixture of nitrous oxide and oxygen at normal pressure. The first to be successful was said, by Hewitt, to have been Klikowitch of St. Petersburg, probably in 1881. Hewitt himself experimented with the mixture, using for the purpose a calibrated gasometer which could be filled with the gases in any desired proportion. The first successful portable apparatus appeared in 1886; it was that of H. T. Hillischer, a Viennese dentist.

Hewitt found Hillischer's apparatus unsatisfactory because the regulating valve could not be adjusted "with that nicety which is necessary in actual practice" : he therefore set about designing an improved machine. This was first described in 1893 and was followed in 1897 by a still more satisfactory apparatus. As a result of all these endeavours, the idea of nitrous oxide–oxygen anaesthesia became wide-spread. Almost contemporaneously the idea of giving oxygen with other volatile anaesthetic agents was introduced. In 1887, Neudörfer of Vienna proposed the routine administration of oxygen with chloroform, and this suggestion was acted on by Kreutzmann of San Francisco, who employed Junker's vaporizer for this purpose. In 1895, a large series was reported by H. L. Northrop, and, at the same time, T. S. K. Morton of Philadelphia began using oxygen with ether, adopting an oxygen inhaler made by the S. S. White Dental Manufacturing Co., for this purpose. Meanwhile, in Europe, L. Prochownick of Hamburg began to use oxygen routinely at the end of anaesthesia with the idea of improving the patient's general condition in the immediate postoperative period. An important part of Prochownick's apparatus was the reducing valve. This apparatus was modified by Wohlgemuth in 1901; in 1902, Roth of Lübeck introduced a "bubble vaporizer", and added a reservoir bag to Wohlgemuth's oxygen–chloroform apparatus. The subsequent development of anaesthetic machines has been dealt with already in the section on Nitrous Oxide.

As early as 1588, de Acosta had reported that air above 14,000 ft. was not suitable for respiration. The introduction of the hot-air balloon by the Brothers Montgolfier in 1782 was to open a new era in the history of man's endeavour. The first human being to ascend in a balloon was de Rozier of Metz in 1783, but great heights were not easily obtained; in 1804, Gay-Lussac and Biot ascended to 13,000 ft, but it was not for another half-century that greater heights were reached. In 1862, Glaisher and Coxwell reached 29,000 ft. and suffered severely from oxygen want. Advised by Paul Bert, Croce-Spinelli, Sivel and Tissandier carried oxygen with them in their ascent of 1875, but it did not prevent the two former from dying of anoxia, since they became unconscious too suddenly to be able to avail themselves of the gas. Tissandier was more fortunate, and the oxygen undoubtedly contributed to his survival. In all later high ascents, oxygen was, of course, carried. With the advent of the aeroplane and the considerable heights achieved during the first world war, much ingenuity was used in designing suitable oxygen apparatus for aviators. Mountaineers benefited from this work, and oxygen apparatus was carried in the attempts to scale Mount Everest in 1922 and on subsequent occasions. It is not without interest that the "Everseal" masks (M. & I. E. Co. Ltd.), commonly used in this country in anaesthetic practice, were designed for use by Sir John Hunt's team which conquered Mount Everest in 1953.

Textbooks of anaesthesia in the nineteenth century have but few references to oxygen. A book published in 1879, for instance, merely mentions oxygen in order to deny that it is an anaesthetic. The first edition of Hewitt's text book (1893) does mention the use of oxygen in respiratory emergencies, but only very briefly and not much in its favour; the paragraph is unchanged in the second edition (1901). However, Dudley Buxton was, by 1900, advocating oxygen in the treatment of laryngeal spasm and of chloroform "syncope". Indeed, it was not until after the end of the first world war that the use of oxygen in resuscitation became at all normal. A certain "Captain Stokes" is credited by Barach as having introduced the use of oxygen by nasal catheter in the treatment of pulmonary oedema caused by gas poisoning, but this easy and efficient method of administration was soon forgotten and oxygen chambers were devised by Barcroft in England and Stadie of the Rockefeller Institute, largely as the result of the influential paper by J. S. Haldane in the *British Medical Journal* in 1917.

The first oxygen tent to fit over a bed was described by Leonard Hill in 1920, but this apparatus was not satisfactory since there was no means of removing excess moisture and heat. This difficulty was overcome by A. L. Barach, who constructed an oxygen tent in which oxygen enriched air was blown over ice, thus cooling and drying the atmosphere.

Efficient masks for the administration of oxygen were introduced in 1938 when the "B. L. B." (Boothby, Lovelace and Bulbulian) apparatus was described, and there have been modifications and improvements in such devices at frequent intervals ever since.

As the value of oxygen has become more apparent, the price has been reduced, and the means of supply have been improved. Many hospitals now have a piped oxygen supply not only to the operating theatres, but also to the wards. It is a far cry to the days when Charles Kite (1788) wrote of the

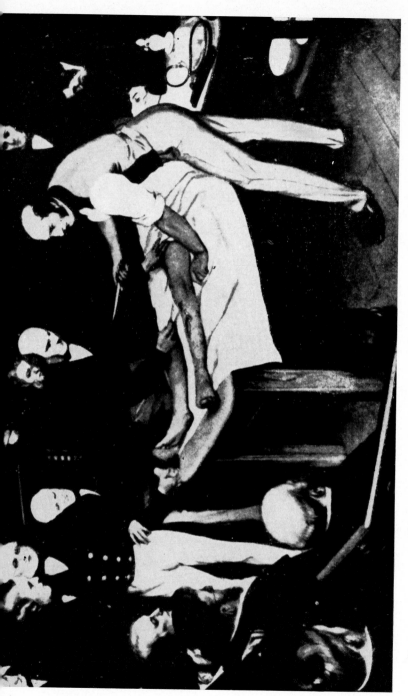

Figure 24. 21st December, 1846. Robert Liston (1794–1847) performs the first surgical operation under anaesthesia in England.

Figure 25. John Snow (1813–1858), the first physician-anaesthetist. From a painting in the possession of

Figure 26. David Waldie (1813–1889), who recommended chloroform as an anaesthetic to James Young

costliness of procuring sufficient oxygen ("about two hogs-heads") for a single case of respiratory failure.

HELIUM

The discovery of helium, identified in the sun 27 years before it was isolated on earth, is one of the most remarkable passages in the history of science. It was in 1868 that Sir Norman Lockyer investigated the rays of the sun with a spectroscope; he noticed a fine yellow line close to the sodium pair, and, since no other substance known to science gave this line, he concluded that he had found a new element, which he named Helium, from the Greek word for the sun. In 1895, Sir William Ramsay, examining a rare Norwegian mineral called "cleveite", obtained from it a gas which gave an identical spectrogram.

Helium, one of the "inert" gases, is non-inflammable. At the outbreak of the first world war, observation balloons were filled with hydrogen and were consequently extremely dangerous and easily destroyed by enemy action. Helium occurs naturally in large quantities only in the natural gas fields of North America whence it was imported into England in large quantities to replace hydrogen for balloons.

Mixtures of helium and oxygen were first used for inhalation by the American chemist and physicist, Elihu Thompson, who found that it was ideal for use by deep divers. A mixture of helium 80% and oxygen 20% has a density roughly one third that of air or pure oxygen, hence in conditions of turbulent flow, when the density of the gas is important, the helium mixture can be made to flow with much less effort than either air or pure oxygen. On these grounds Barach, in 1934, recommended the use of this mixture for the treatment of asthma and allied conditions. Since masks at that date were not satisfactory, and the high diffusibility of helium renders a tight-fitting mask essential, Barach and Eckman designed a helmet, fitting closely round the neck, for use with helium mixtures. The enthusiasm with which this gas was first hailed has waned considerably; it is now recognized that, even in asthma, laminar flow, in which the viscosity of the gas is more important than its density, is present in a large component of the respiratory passages. Since the viscosity of helium is very high, its advantages in inhalational therapy are negligible.

Chapter Eleven

BLOOD TRANSFUSION &
INTRAVENOUS ANAESTHESIA

BLOOD TRANSFUSION

Although the first attempts at blood transfusion and intravenous therapy began in the seventeenth century, there is
one isolated example of the conception of the intravenous
administration of remedial drugs dating from the very beginning of the Christian era. This account comes from the
Metamorphoses (Bk. 7) of Ovid (43 B.C.–A.D. 17). Jason,
seeing his father, Aeson, grow old and feeble, begs his wife,
Medea, to exercise her magic powers and restore the old
man's youth. Medea, after suitable prayers, repairs to the
home of the gods, where she gathers magical herbs. Aeson
is brought to the altars which Medea has erected and where
a decoction of the herbs "bubbled and boiled, white-foam-
ing in a brazen vessel" and "wherever the boiling broth
spat forth its hissing drops, the earth grew bright with soft
grass and sweet-smelling flowers". Medea then "drew her
knife across Aeson's throat and drained out the thin blood,
and, in its place, infused that life-giving juice. As his lips
and wounded throat imbibed it, his hair and beard shed their
silver and shone with the glossy, raven hue of youth; his
muscles swelled, the wrinkles filled, the rose, long faded,
bloomed in his cheek anew, and every limb was lithe.
Wondering Aeson woke to find himself as he had been some
forty years before".

It is not, however, to be thought that such infusions were ever attempted by the ancients: Ovid's story is merely a flight of fancy, unconnected with medical practice.

However, the doctors of the Scientific Period (585 B.C.–A.D. 200) were well aware of the importance of the blood in maintaining life. The doctrine of the four humours, of which blood was one, had been modified by Erasistratus of Chios (c. 300 B.C.), who believed that disease was usually caused by a plethora or excess of blood in a particular region. The followers of Erasistratus introduced blood-letting as a form of treatment, and this therapy was used and abused until almost the end of the nineteenth century.

It was natural that the idea of the circulation of the blood, first promulgated by William Harvey in lectures at the Royal College of Physicians of London in 1616, should stimulate experiments with blood, but it seems likely that the idea of blood transfusion had already occurred to some. Thus Pegelius of Rostock may have mentioned it as early as 1604, and Andreas Libavius certainly referred to it in 1615. Again, in 1628, the year of the publication of Harvey's *De Motu Cordis*, Colle of Padua suggested transfusion as a method of prolonging life.

Developments in England, where Harvey's doctrine naturally gained greatest currency, were delayed by the political turmoil which preceded and accompanied the Civil War (1642–49). In the latter year, Francis Potter, a Somersetshire parson, attempted unsuccessfully to transfuse blood into a hen; the idea of curing disease by this method had apparently been in his mind for some ten years.

In 1656, (Sir) Christopher Wren experimented with the intravenous administration of drugs to animals. The first authenticated experiments were carried out by the Royal Society, which had been incorporated in 1662. In May, 1665, at a meeting of that body, Thomas Cox related how he had transfused blood from one pigeon to another; in June, Dr.

Wilkins reported a similar experiment on dogs; and, in April 1666, Robert Boyle described another attempt. In none of these cases was more than a very small quantity of blood introduced.

Richard Lower, in his *Tractatus de Corde* (1669) describes in detail how in February 1665 (N.S.) he carried out a series of successful massive transfusions on dogs by the direct artery to vein technique, and this account is confirmed in the *Philosophical Transactions* of the Royal Society. To Lower, therefore, must go the credit of the first successful transfusion.

A year later, Denis of Montpellier carried out similar experiments, not always using animals of the same species and, in June 1667, transfused 3 oz. of lamb's blood into the veins of a youth suffering from a chronic fever, apparently a successful form of therapy. Denis continued to use this method of treatment until, in 1668, one of his patients died. A court case ensued, and, by an Act of the Parlement of Paris of 1670, blood transfusion was made illegal in France.

Experiments, however, continued in England, and, in November 1667, Samuel Pepys described how a "poor and debauched man" was transfused with 12 oz. of sheep's blood without ill-effects.

The first book on blood transfusion appeared in 1665; it was written in German by J. S. Elsholtz. An enlarged edition of the book reappeared in Latin in 1667, under the title *Clysmatica Nova*; it contained a diagrammatic representation, the first illustration, of blood transfusion. Other books, dealing in whole or in part with transfusion, some of them illustrated, were soon published: the anonymous *Relazione del' Esperienze* (1668), Mercklin's *De Ortu et Occasu Transfusionis Sanguinis* (1679), Folli's *Stadera Medica* (1680), Scultetus', *Armamentarium Chirurgicum* (1693), and Purmann's *Lorbeer Krantz oder Wund Artznei* (1705).

During the eighteenth century, comparatively little seems to have been done in the field of blood transfusion. In his *Zoonomia* (1794), Erasmus Darwin states that he had advised daily transfusions of human or animal blood to "an old gentleman whose throat was entirely impervious", but the patient refused. The matter was, however, taken up with enthusiasm by James Blundell (1790–1877), who performed a number of transfusions with human blood and invented some ingenious apparatus for the purpose. He reported a case of postpartum haemorrhage, successfully treated in 1829; the patient received 8 oz. of blood. Other occasionally successful operators were Blundell's collaborators, Charles Waller and E. Doubleday. Meanwhile, during the epidemic of Asiatic Cholera in 1831, O'Shaughnessy discovered that the blood of the victims was depleted of both salt and water. This observation was put to practical use by T. A. Latta of Leith in the following year, when he introduced, with great success, the practice of intravenous saline infusion for this disease.

The year 1873 was marked by the discovery of the species specificity of blood by Landois, thus terminating experiments in the transfusion of animal blood to man. In the same year, Aveling described a simple and efficient apparatus for the direct transfusion of blood from donor to patient, thus eliminating the problem of clotting. Three years later, Noel described a rotary pump, similar to those in use today, which simplified even more the direct transfusion of blood.

In spite of these improvements, J. B. Murphy, in 1907, described a method of direct anastomosis of the vessels of donor and patient, but this highly technical procedure never became popular.

With the first year of the twentieth century, the practice of blood transfusion was placed on a sound basis by the discovery of agglutinins and iso-agglutinins by Landsteiner in

Vienna and Shattock in London. The former described three groups; a fourth was added in the following year by von Decastello and Sturli. Further work on the ABO blood groups was done by Jansky of Prague (1907) and Moss (1909), but the numerical notations which they introduced have been supplanted by the international nomenclature. In 1910, von Dugern and Hirschfeld discovered that the inheritance of blood groups was in accordance with the Mendelian theory. By 1911, Ottenberg had drawn attention to the possibility of persons of Group O being used as "universal donors", and two years later, he and his co-workers described in vitro tests for the cross-matching of blood.

The question of the blood groups was, however, complicated by the discovery of the independent M and N antigens by Landsteiner and Levine (1927). In the following year, the same workers described the agglutinogen P and, since 1945, numerous other agglutinogens have been described (e.g. "Lutheran", 1945; "Lewis", 1946; "Kell", 1946; "Gr", 1946; and "Jobbins", 1947). The first of these, P, is widely distributed, but the remainder are only very rarely encountered. The discovery of "cold" agglutinins, both specific and non-specific, dates from the same period, as does the introduction of Coombs sensitization test (1945).

The use of intravenous saline in the treatment of burns was begun by Weidenfeld in 1902; by 1912, attention was drawn to fluid loss by other means, such as vomiting, and the study of blood fluids and electrolytes was well advanced.

In 1909, Brewer and Leggett had recognized that the co-agulation of blood could be delayed by the use of paraffin-coated glass tubes; this led to the development of the Kimpton-Brown tube (1917), employed successfully by the Harvard Medical Unit in France. Experiments in preventing clotting had begun much earlier; Wright (1891) had tried oxalate; and Leopinasse (1908–9) used hirudin, peptone and sodium citrate, but regarded them all as too toxic. The successful use of citrated blood was first described by Hustin in Belgium (1915), and this work was further advanced by Agote of Buenos Aires. The technique was much improved by Robertson towards the end of World War I. Curiously enough, there was a simultaneous revival of the method of direct transfusion of unmodified blood by Lindemann, who employed a "multiple syringe" technique. The use of heparin as an anticoagulant was advocated by Skold in 1936.

Although there had been some organization of blood donors during World War I, the first real steps in the formation of a proper service began with the foundation of the London Blood Transfusion Service in 1921. By 1939, more than 5,000 transfusions a year were being provided. The work was further advanced by the British Red Cross Society. At the outbreak of World War II, Regional Transfusion Centres were organized by the Medical Research Council, and these bodies have now become permanent institutions in the National Transfusion Service. The present apparatus for blood transfusion derives from that designed by Marriott and Kekwick in 1935. During all this period, the use of blood and blood substitutes has greatly expanded. Thus, while Weil had recognized that blood was important in the treatment of haemophilia as early as 1906, it was left to Feissly (1928) to show that plasma was equally valuable in this condition. Ward in 1918 had shown also that animals dying of haemorrhage were suffering more from loss of blood volume than from loss of haemoglobin. The value of plasma in the treatment of burns was pointed out by Elkinton in 1939. An interesting development was the dilution of blood with a solution of various salts to ten times its own volume, a device employed by Petrov in 1943; while the great demands for blood also led to the exploitation of that of cadavers by Yudin (1936) and Shamov (1937).

On the other hand, the use of "packed-cells" has been

shown to be of great value in the treatment of anaemia without reduction in blood volume. The first to describe the advantages of this method were MacQuaide and Mollison (1940).

Although there have been occasional reports of diseases such as typhoid fever and smallpox being conveyed to the recipient by blood transfusion, by far the commonest disease so spread is virus hepatitis (homologous serum jaundice). This disease and its method of propagation have been recognized since 1885, when there was a severe outbreak following vaccination with human serum in Bremen. The first case after blood transfusion was reported by Junet and Junet in 1938, and the danger of this complication has been underlined by repeated outbreaks. One result has been the introduction of "small group" pooled plasma, which has now entirely replaced the older "large group" pooling.

A dramatic and important step forward in the use of blood transfusion was taken when, in 1940, Landsteiner and Wiener observed that the serum of a rabbit, previously inoculated with the red cells of a rhesus monkey, developed an immune agglutinin, which reacted with the red cells of most, but not all, human subjects. The importance of this "Rh" factor was quickly appreciated, and the connexion between it and neonatal haemolytic disease was reported by Levine in 1941. Fisher (1944) introduced his ingenious theory that the various Rh sub-types comprise different combinations of three closely linked elementary genes, inherited by Mendelian laws, one from each of three allelomorphic pairs. Wiener, however, has never accepted the classification of Fisher; but it is fair to say that it forms a convenient working hypothesis.

Blood transfusion has usually been given by the intravenous route. In 1941, Tocantins and O'Neill introduced the technique of intramedullary transfusion; in 1954, intra-arterial transfusion became temporarily popular; and, recently, the intraperitoneal administration of blood has been advocated in certain circumstances. A particular aspect of intra-arterial transfusion was the practice of arteriotomy introduced by Gardner in 1946 for the control of blood loss, especially in cerebral surgery. Blood was removed by means of an intra-arterial cannula, and, after addition of heparin, stored until the need for haemostasis had passed; the blood was then re-introduced through the same cannula. The experimental work of Kohlstaedt (1943) on animals had shown that resuscitation was quicker when this route was employed than when the blood was returned intravenously.

A number of so-called "plasma expanders" have been introduced from time to time. Solution of gum acacia, used during World War I, was the first; this was followed by bovine serum treated so as to reduce the risk of an anaphylactic response, but none was completely satisfactory. In 1949, Thorsen introduced dextran, a polysaccharide produced by the fermentation of sucrose by the micro-organism, *Leuconostoc mesenteroides*. This has proved a useful blood-substitute, especially since the preparation of large molecule fractions. One difficulty caused by dextran was that, because it might lead to rouleaux formation in vitro, it was liable to interfere with the subsequent cross-matching of the patient's serum with blood. Fortunately, this difficulty has been recently overcome.

The history of extracorporeal circulation with the aid of pumps and oxygenators is so recent that what follows must not be considered as the final word on the subject. It has its roots in the crossed-circulation experiments of Starling, so well known to students of physiology, and the impetus for their development lay in the desire of surgeons to perform "open heart" operations.

The first practical oxygenator to be described seems to have been the rotating disk oxygenator of Melrose, developed at the Postgraduate Medical School, Hammersmith, in 1949. Bubble-oxygenators were described in the following year by Clark and his co-workers, and were used by Lillehei, while similar oxygenators using a higher flow were also developed at the Mayo clinic. The vertical screen oxygenator of Miller, Gibbon and Gibbon was described in 1951. It was in this year that the first pump-oxygenator seems to have been used in man by Dennis et al. (*Annals of Surgery*, 1951, **134**, 709), but cases were comparatively rarely described before 1954.

The major problems involved in the construction of this sort of apparatus were concerned mainly with the difficulty of building either pumps or oxygenators capable of maintaining an adequate flow of arterial blood. The newest development in this direction has recently been described by Drew and his co-workers. This technique involves the use of a pump-heart-by-pass, enabling the blood to be oxygenated in the patient's own lungs, combined with profound hypothermia which lessens the body's oxygen requirement.

An important stage in the development of extra-corporeal circulation was reached when, in 1952, Delorme described his method of arterio-venous shunt with cooling of the blood, in order to produce hypothermia.

Intravenous infusion and transfusion, extra-corporeal circulation and even the intravenous administration of drugs are all the direct outcome of the work of William Harvey, who may be considered as the Father of Modern Medicine and who has had an especial influence on the science of resuscitation. Yet, after the publication of his great work on the circulation of the blood, his patients, says Aubrey, "did think him crack-brained". Although we may frequently deplore the sensationalism of the press in medical matters, we may be thankful that we work in a very different climate of public opinion, and it is satisfactory to know that encouragement and acclaim have been awarded to those who have furthered the important work in extracorporeal circulation.

INTRAVENOUS ANAESTHESIA

The intravenous administration of drugs is closely related to the subject of blood transfusion which, being derived from the work of William Harvey, dates from the same period: its history is, however, much less coherent than that of transfusion, for the intravenous route seems to have been entirely neglected for more than two hundred years after the first experiments. No doubt this hiatus is largely due to the lack of a suitable syringe: the invention of the hypodermic syringe by Pravaz, and of the detachable needle by Alexander Wood, both in 1853, provided the tools required by the clinician. Even so, the intravenous use of anaesthetic agents was delayed for a further twenty years.

The earliest experiments of which we have any record were made by (Sir) Christopher Wren in 1656, and were referred to by Oldenburg and Clarck in the *Philosophical Transactions* of the Royal Society, in 1665. The influence of William Harvey on Wren is to be traced in the fact that, at the time of these researches, Wren was assistant to the celebrated physician, Sir Charles Scarborough, who was a close friend of Harvey. In default of a syringe, Wren made use of a quill attached to a piece of pig's bladder, and, with this crude apparatus he demonstrated the effects of a solution of opium, of *crocus metallorum* and, according to one authority, of wine and beer when given intravenously to dogs. In 1665, Sigismond Elsholtz confirmed the first of these experiments, bringing about the narcosis of a dog by the intravenous administration of opium.

It was not until twenty-five years after the discovery of anaesthetics that the subject received any further attention. In 1872, Pierre-Cyprien Oré, Professor of Physiology at Bordeaux, described anaesthesia in animals by the intravenous administration of a solution of chloral; two years later, he reported to the French Academy of Sciences the first use of this anaesthetic in man. Chloral, however, is not a satisfactory anaesthetic agent, and the method did not prove popular, in spite of Oré's continued advocacy. The intravenous route was, however, revived in 1898 by E. Dreser of Munich, who employed methyl propyl carbinol urethane (Hedonal); this drug achieved a measure of success, being used, frequently in conjunction with chloroform, by N. F. Krakow of St. Petersburg until at least 1908.

In 1909, Ludwig Burkhardt used a solution of chloroform as an intravenous anaesthetic and, four years later, Noel and Souttar were using paraldehyde by the same route. Soon afterward, trichloro-iso-propyl alcohol (Isopral) was introduced, and Graefe reported on a series of 359 cases in which anaesthesia had been induced with Isopral and continued with ether.

Meanwhile, the routine use of premedication with morphine and atropine or hyoscine was coming into fashion: the intravenous administration of these drugs was first reported by Elisabeth Bredenfeld of Switzerland in 1916. It was also in this year that Peck and Meltzer advocated the intravenous use of magnesium sulphate as an adjunct to anaesthesia, on the ground that less anaesthetic was then required to achieve suitable operating conditions. It was in 1921 that Nakagawa first recommended ethyl alcohol as an intravenous anaesthetic, but the use of this agent did not become popular until after the work of M. G. Marin of Mexico, in 1929.

Until the third decade of the twentieth century, the advocates of the intravenous route had tried various types of drug and had achieved only moderate success. It was in 1924 that a new chapter opened with the introduction of the first intravenous barbiturate, the forerunner of a large group of drugs of this type which has proved extremely valuable to the anaesthetist. The first barbiturate, barbitone (Veronal) had been synthesized in 1903 by Fischer and von Mering; this drug was later combined with di-allyl barbituric acid (Dial) to form a new compound, Somnifene. Animal experiments were begun with Somnifene by Bardet in 1920, its use in man being first reported by Fredet and Perlis in 1924. It was in this same year that L. Bogendörfer of Würzburg used di-allyl barbituric acid alone by the same route. The barbiturates had arrived, and in the following years they have appeared in increasing numbers, and have occupied the centre of the stage. Thus, in 1927, Bumm introduced sodium butyl brom-allyl barbiturate (Pernocton), and, in 1929, Weiss tried phenyl ethyl barbituric acid (Luminal); the use of sodium amytal was also described in 1929 by Zerfas and MacCallum. In the following year, Fitch, Waters, and Tatum reported on the use of pentobarbitone sodium (Nembutal), and, in 1933, Döring introduced sodium iso-propyl bromallyl barbiturate (Eunarcon), which latter was favourably received as an intravenous anaesthetic agent.

All these drugs were, however, quickly over-shadowed by the first "ultra-short acting" barbiturate, hexobarbitone sodium (Evipan Sodium), which was first employed by Weese and Scharpff in 1932 : this agent at once leapt into prominence and favour, so that the introduction of butyl ethyl barbituric acid (Soneryl) as an anaesthetic by Desplas and Chevillon in 1934 passed almost unnoticed. It was in the latter year that J. S. Lundy of the Mayo Clinic introduced sodium thiopentone (Pentothal Sodium), which was soon to surpass even hexobarbitone in popularity, and which has so far remained the intravenous agent most commonly used, in spite of the débâcle of Pearl Harbour and the discovery in recent years of several other barbiturates suitable for intravenous use.

Although the barbiturates have deservedly gained the greatest popularity, there are other drugs which have also been used with considerable success in recent years. Thus, tribromethanol (Avertin), introduced by Butzengeiger in 1926, was employed intravenously by Kirschner in 1929: during the second world war, it found its place as a satisfactory agent for the induction of anaesthesia in patients with "floating tongue", the result of bilateral fracture of the mandible; such patients were notoriously difficult to anaesthetize safely by any other means, but the introduction of the relaxants has rendered this technique obsolete. In recent years, attention has been given to the steroids, which have been shown to have considerable possibilities as anaesthetic agents, but the slowness of onset of unconsciousness and the risk of venous thrombosis have militated against their acceptance by clinicians.

The intravenous use of procaine is in a rather different category. Synthesized by Alfred Einhorn in 1899, it was first used intravenously by August Bier in 1908. Bier described a method of regional analgesia in which part of a limb was exsanguinated and isolated between tourniquets, the veins then being filled with a dilute solution of procaine. In the same year, J. Goyanès of Madrid used a rather similar technique, employing intra-arterial instead of intravenous injection; this latter method was further modified in 1910 by J. L. Ransohoff, who appreciated the relative lack of toxicity of intra-arterial, as compared with intravenous, procaine, and therefore discarded the tourniquets. The systemic use of intravenous procaine, however, began with the observation of its beneficial action in arteritis obliterans by Leriche and Fontaine in 1935. In 1942, Lundy recommended its use for the relief of the pruritus of jaundice, and Gordon employed it as a general analgesic in the treatment of burns in the following year. Intravenous procaine was first used as a general anaesthetic by Bigelow and Harrison in 1944, and its use in the postoperative control of pain was begun by Burstein in 1947.

The pharmacological importance of the intravenous route for the administration of drugs is that it enables nonvolatile agents to be given in such a way that their effects are rapidly observable, and the administration is thus made safer; from the point of view of the patient, however their advantage lies in the ease and comfort with which anaesthesia can now be induced. The anaesthetist of today owes a great debt of gratitude to the pioneers of the intravenous route, and those who remember anaesthesia as it was in the days when intravenous injections were by no means a commonplace must often look back with amazement and pleasure on the change which has overtaken our specialty in the last quarter of a century.

Figure 27. Sir James Young Simpson (1811–1870), who was the first to use anaesthesia in midwifery.

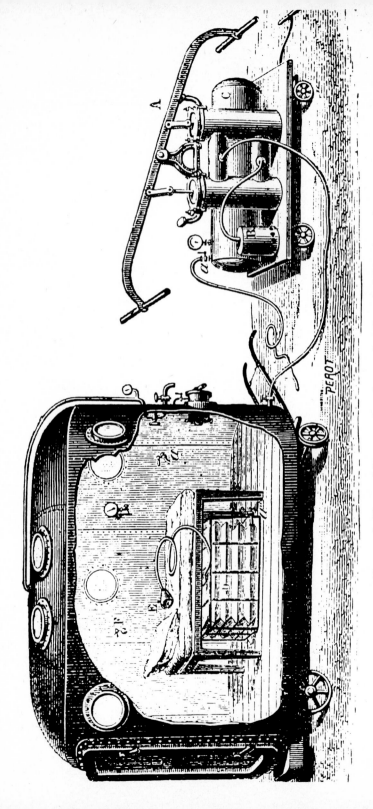

Figure 28. The mobile operating theatre for the administration of nitrous oxide under pressure, designed by Paul Bert (1878).

Appendix A

THE DISCOVERY OF ETHER

The discovery of ether is attributed by some authors to an Arabian whom they call Djafar Yeber. An investigation reveals no Arab known to history bearing this name; the allusion is to the famous alchemist Geber (Jābir) and the curious spelling of the former name is no doubt attributable to transliteration through several languages, of which French was one. The similarity, or transposition, of "B" and "V" in Spanish may possibly account for the introduction of the name "Ja'far" as a misreading of "Jābir".

Abu Abdullah (or Mūsa) Jābir ibn Hayyām (or Hayyān), known also as al-Kūfi, at-Tūsi, al-Harrāni and al-Azdi, was born at Tūs in A.D. 721 or 722. His father was a druggist of the tribe of Azd, and plied his trade at Kūfa (the home of the so-called Kufic script). Jābir later became a close friend of Ja'far al-Barmāki, Wazīr of Harūn ar-Rashīd, immortalized in the *Thousand and One Nights*, and was banished from Baghdad when that minister was executed in 803. He retired to Kūfa and finished his days in obscurity.

He studied occultism under a Shi'ite sheikh, Ja'far as-Sādiq, 700–765, which may account for the addition of Ja'far to his name. An account of his writings and life is given in the Kitab al-Fihrist of the tenth century. He is credited with formulating the chemical hypothesis, universally believed in the Middle Ages that all metals were compounded of mercury and sulphur, the proportions varying with the different metals; gold could thus be made from any metal by altering these proportions.

Jābir is said to have written more than one hundred books, nearly all still extant. However, the authorship of many is dubious in the extreme, some being of definitely later period and others being certainly of European origin. All but a few of his works remain unedited, and the full extent of his knowledge and attainments is not known. The belief that he discovered ether is due to confusion between the terms "oil of vitriol", by which sulphuric acid was known, and "sweet oil of vitriol", the name applied to ether.

Bertholet, in the introduction to the translation of several of the works attributed to Jābir, states, "In the Arabic books bearing the name Jābir, there is no mention of the discoveries which figure in the Latin books, such as nitric acid, aqua regia, oil of vitriol" (etc.). In a note to this passage, he states: "Oil of Vitriol. In the texts which follow there exists no precise mention relative to this oil, since identified with sulphuric acid. Even the preparation of this" (red liquid) "is added at the end of a work of Jābir with which it has no connexion; it is a later interpolation. In any case, with such a confused description, one would not be able to corroborate the discovery of sulphuric acid." It therefore seems certain that Jābir discovered neither ether nor oil of vitriol (sulphuric acid).

The evidence that Raymond Lully, another celebrated alchemist, discovered ether is also feeble. He is credited with discovering a white fluid which he named "oleum vitrioli dulce". Keys throws doubt on the suggestion. This Raymond Lully, Doctor illuminatus, was the son of a Majorcan nobleman, also named Raymond, Seneschal of the Isles, who had fallen in love with a Genoese lady of good birth, Ambrosia di Castello. As, however, both he and she were already married, his overtures were rejected, but she told him that she would receive him when both his wife and her husband were dead. More than 30 years later, it is said, Ambrosia's husband died; Lully's wife had died some time before. One day, Lully called on her; he was old, worn and wrinkled, and he held in his hand a glass phial. He had spent the intervening years in discovering the Elixir of Life, he said, and this phial would give them eternal life in which to enjoy their mutual love. Ambrosia took a mirror and showed him his aged appearance; then, disclosing a fungating cancer of the breast, she said: "Your elixir may be able to prolong life, but it cannot restore youth or beauty. Would you care to perpetuate horrors like this?" Lully let fall the phial, which broke on the stone floor, and no one has succeeded in making the Elixir Vitæ since.

His son, Raymond, was born in 1234. He led a dissolute life until be became "converted" in 1266. His discovery of sweet oil of vitriol is placed in the year 1275. It has been suggested that he was employed to purify the gold used for minting the Rose Nobles of Edward III, some of which are still extant, and are called "Raymundins". In 1276 he established a College of Franciscans at Padua for the study of Oriental languages, in order to refute the works of Muslim doctors and to preach Christianity to the Moors. He received encouragement from the Pope (Nicholas IV) and from several European monarchs. He attempted also to found a new religious order to replace the Knights Templar after their dissolution. He died in 1314 or 1315, having expounded much mysticism and being, no doubt, as his wife maintained, more than a little mad. Ellis states that he was martyred at Bugia, but this may perhaps be a confusion with the father, who became a monk after the death of Ambrosia and was martyred by the Muslimīn.

It is usually stated that the preparation of ether was placed upon a scientific basis by Valerius Cordus (1515–44) in 1540. Lee states that it was "originally prepared" by him, and Garrison calls him the "discoverer". It seems likely that a description of the way in which sweet oil of vitriol is prepared first appeared in his posthumous writings. He had been apprenticed to Paracelsus, who tells us that he himself prepared sweet oil of vitriol from alcohol and sulphuric acid in 1540, the year before his death, but his notes were not unearthed until 1730. This distillate he gave to his poultry and observed that it threw them into a deep sleep from which they later awakened unharmed. He recommended that sweet oil of vitriol should be used to allay painful diseases, and it is likely that further investigations of its use in medicine and surgery was only prevented by his untimely death.

Aureolus Phillipus Theophrastus Bombastus von Hohenheim, self-named Paracelsus, was a migratory physician. His manner was such that he is said to be the eponymous originator of the word "bombastic", although the Oxford English Dictionary does not concur in this derivation. He was, however, a keen observer and had been "taught the healing art by the greatest of all teachers, experience".

He was born near Zurich in 1493 and travelled very extensively from Poland to Egypt and from England to Samarkand. He early turned his attention to alchemy and attempted to turn lead into gold. He soon realized that alchemy was an empty subject and his writings were its death blow. He turned his work to good account, however, by becoming one of the first real chemists. In 1526, at the age of only 33, he was appointed to the double Chair of Medicine and Chemistry at Basle. Here, he caused a sensation by burning works of Galen, Avicenna, Averroes and Aristotle at the beginning of his course of lectures. A further sensation was caused by his lecturing in German; he was the first to discard Latin and employ the vernacular in teaching. However, his energy and self-confidence soon degenerated into arrogance and boasting, and, although he made many almost miraculous cures, he became unpopular. His interest in science was accompanied by delight in sensual pleasures, and he gradually descended into drunkenness and debauch. He left Basle in a temper after only two years, and wandered from place to place, dying at Salzburg at the age of 48.

He was a clear thinker; these words show him to be a man who saw past the barriers of contemporary philosophy. "What is now deemed mysterious," he wrote, "will, in time to come, be found to spring from natural causes". Besides being a great practitioner of medicine, he was a chemist not to be despised; he perceived the part played by the atmosphere in combustion and recognized the analogy between combustion and respiration. He saw that, in the living organism, chemical processes are going on. His main fault lay in the fact that he sought not to teach, but to thunderstrike and dazzle. Osler called him "the Luther of Medicine", for, when authority was paramount, he stood out for independent study.

If Valerius Cordus must be displaced from the position of discoverer of ether, yet he still claims a place in history. Dying three years after Paracelsus at the early age of 29, he nevertheless found time to edit and expand, by the description of 600 fresh plants, the Materia Medica of Dioscorides, which had been the standard text-book for a millennium and a half.

The contributions to our knowledge of ether made by these early investigators was brought to light and summed up by the German-born apothecary, Sigismund August Frobenius, who was a Fellow of the Royal Society and who died in London in 1743. He originated the name "ether" by calling the sweet oil of vitriol, "spiritus æthereus".

The later history of ether is common knowledge and, apart from the importance of C. T. Jackson in its introduction as an anaesthetic, is but little in dispute. The early history, however, is confused and doubtful. In the absence of adequate evidence for the discovery of sweet oil of vitriol by Lully, Paracelsus must be considered, not only the first to prepare this valuable agent, but also the first to appreciate its anaesthetic properties.

Appendix B

THE FATE OF
EUFAME MacCALZEAN

It has been stated that a certain Eufame MacCalzean or McAlyane was executed in Scotland in the reign of James VI for attempting to relieve the pains of childbirth. Such a bald statement is misleading, and the more important events which led to her trial and execution deserve some attention. These events are set out in a contemporary pamphlet, printed in 1591 and entitled "Newes from Scotland".

In October 1589, James VI, throwing off his more customary cowardice, braved the terrors of the deep in order to voyage to Norway and bring back his bride, the 15-year-old Anne of Denmark. The return journey was made in May of the following year, but the King's ship was beset by storms, and there was some danger of shipwreck.

The disclosures of a girl suspected of witchcraft led to the arrest of numerous persons for having been involved in Satanic rites at the Kirk of North Berwick, whither they had sailed in sieves. The Devil attended the church in person and, after a lewd penance had been enjoined, urged the witches to attempt the destruction of the King. Various attempts by poison and witchcraft were made without success, and the witches eventually took a cat, christened it, tied parts of a dead man to it, and then deposited it in the sea off Leith, having sailed thither in their sieves for this purpose. This resulted in the springing up of a great storm which sank at least one boat and imperilled the King's ship.

Many of the accused witches, having confessed their crimes under torture, were executed by strangling, their bodies being afterwards burned. One who did not confess was Euphemia MacCalyean ("z" is often written for "y" in old Scots manuscripts). This lady was the daughter of Thomas MacCalyean, Lord Cliftonhall, a Senator of the College of Justice and a man distinguished for his erudition and attainments. He had died ten years before these events, having incurred the dislike of the Queen Regent, Mary of Guise, for his spirited defence of the rights of Edinburgh.

William Roughead (*The Riddle of the Ruthvens*) states of the fair Euphemia that the offences with which this lady was charged are no less astonishing than varied. They embrace the attempted poisoning of her husband in the first year of her marriage to the end that she "mycht gett ane utheir guidman", as a result of which he "brak out in reid spottis" and was compelled to seek safety in France, his disappointed spouse bidding "the ffiend ga with him"; bribing with her own jewels her daughter's lover to transfer his affections to herself, and, on his declining either to do so or to return the gifts, attempting to recover these by witchcraft; destroying by the same means several persons, including her father-in-law; and, finally, participating in "the Conventicle at North-Berwick Kirk".

From Pitcairn (*Ancient Criminal Trials in Scotland*, 1833), we learn that Ewfame Makcalyane alias Moscrop (her married name) was tried on June 9 to 12, in the twenty-fourth year of James VI. The dittay, or indictment, included twenty-eight counts, all concerning witchcraft and some being for murder as well. The eighteenth count reads thus: "Indicted of consulting and seeking help of the said Annie Sampson, a notorious witch, for relief of your pain in the time of your birth of your two sons, and the receiving from her to that effect a "bordstone" (presumably a stone with a natural hole in it and thus thought to have magical powers; a bored-stone) to be laid under the bolster, put under your head; enchanted mould (i.e., soil from a cemetery) and powder put in a piece of paper to be used and "rowit" (i.e., rolled) in your hair at the time of your "droweis" (i.e., birth pangs); your "guidman's" (i.e., husband's) "sark" (i.e., shirt) to be presently taken off him and laid "woumplit" (i.e., rumpled) under your bed-side; the which being practised by you as you had received the same from the said Annie. By the information and the use thereof, your sickness was cast off you unnaturally in the birth of your first son upon a dog which ran away forthwith and was never seen again. And in the birth of your last son, the same practice aforesaid was used and your natural and kindly pain unnaturally cast off you upon the wanton cat in the house, which likewise was never seen thereafter".

The verdict of the assize (i.e., jury) was returned on June 12 by the chancellor (i.e., foreman), James Johnstone of Elphinstone, who was not "chased from the assize", as is wrongly stated by Roughead. In the "Articles of Conviction" (or verdict), she was found guilty on ten of the twenty-eight counts, the fifth reading: "Item, for consulting with Annie Sampson, a witch, for getting of moulds from her to be used by the said Effie in relief of her pain in her birth of her two sons".

The doom (or judgment) was passed on her on June 15, all her goods being forfeited to the crown and she herself sentenced to be "brunt in assis, quick" (i.e., to be burnt to ashes alive), without the humanity of previous strangling, which sentence was duly carried into effect on Castle Hill.

The above account reveals the prevalence of witchcraft 350 years ago. Belief in the powers of sorcerers was almost universal. King James VI himself wrote a highly authoritative book on the subject in which he expressly points out that to obtain good ends by witchcraft is a heinous sin. Even the most outwardly respectable were wont to resort to witches to obtain their ends, and this was particularly brought to the notice of the world by the proceedings of the Chambre Ardente in Paris in the 1680s.

It was then shown that nearly all the great ones of the court of "Le Roi Soleil" were either actively engaged in poisoning and witchcraft or were the passive victims of these nefarious machinations.

These proceedings likewise disclosed the traditional connexion between midwifery and witchcraft, of which more than a hint comes to us from the trial of the wretched Euphemia and her confrères.

Without in any way wishing to whitewash the justice dispensed by James VI, whose dealings with Arabella Stewart, Raleigh and Robert Carr speak for themselves, it is worth notice that Euphemia suffered the penalty of using witchcraft, and the real charge against her was of attempting the death of the King by her participation in the "Conventicle at the Kirk of North-Berwick". No mention would have been made of her attempts at self-administered obstetrical analgesia, had they been undertaken by legal means; her use of witchcraft on these occasions, however, was a useful point for the prosecution, as showing that she did consort with known witches.

It therefore seems that the statement that she was done to death for attempting to allay the pains of childbirth is a terminological inexactitude, and we may rest content that, whatever the people of an enlightened age may think of witchcraft and such barbarous punishment, Euphemia Mac-Calyean was a thoroughly vicious woman, whose death is not greatly to be mourned.

Appendix C

ENDOTRACHEAL AND OTHER MODERN METHODS IN THE EIGHTEENTH CENTURY

The endotracheal technique was illustrated and described by Vesalius, but his method entailed preliminary tracheotomy, as did the endotracheal technique of Trendelenburg (1871). The first accepted account of intubation through the glottis for anaesthesia is by Macewen in 1880.

It is interesting, therefore, that endotracheal intubation, by the oral and nasal routes, was described by Kite in 1788, a hundred years before Macewen; and Kite himself does not claim to be the originator of the technique, which he used in resuscitation of the apparently dead.

In the year 1787, the Humane Society (now the Royal Humane Society) decided to offer prizes for the best essays on the Recovery of the Apparently Dead. The essay submitted by a surgeon practising at Gravesend, Charles Kite, Member of the Corporation of Surgeons in London, was awarded the silver medal, and this essay was published in 1788 in book form. As an appendix, there is a description of a pocket case of instruments to be used in the resuscitation of the drowned, of whom Kite apparently saw a great many in his work by the Thames Estuary.

A folding plate illustrates the contents of this case. One of the items, "shaped like a male catheter", is labelled, "An instrument to pass beyond the glottis". In a second plate, this instrument is shown attached to the "elastic tube", which could be used, either with this catheter, or with an ivory nozzle to fit the nostril, for the inflation of the lungs.

In the text, the use of the catheter is mentioned thus:

"If any difficulty should arise in distending the lungs, it must proceed either from water in the windpipe or a contraction or adhesion of the epiglottis. We have already pointed out the method of discovering when the first circumstance occurs; and when the latter is the case, we shall generally remedy the inconvenience by bringing the tongue forwards, which, being connected to the epiglottis by inelastic ligaments, must of course be elevated. Should any further impediment however occur, the crooked tube, bent like a male catheter, recommended by Dr. Monro, and mentioned by Mr. Portal, Mr. le Cat, and others, should be introduced into the glottis, through the mouth or one nostril; the end should be connected to a blow-pipe, or, what will be more convenient, the pipe for the nose belonging to the elastic tube may be removed, and this instrument screwed in its place, according to the plan mentioned in the description of a pocket case of instruments for the recovery of the apparently dead, by Mr. Savigny" (the instrument maker).

The following description occurs in the Appendix:

"Should further impediments however occur, the pipe for the nose is to be removed, and the crooked tube bent like a male catheter, recommended by Dr. Munro, and mentioned by Mr. Portal, Mr. le Cat, and others, is to be screwed on the tube in its place: this is to be introduced through the mouth, or one nostril, into the glottis, when, on blowing through the mouth-piece, or applying the bellows, the lungs will be dilated".

The reference to "Dr. Munro" cannot be identified, but it may be to Alexander Munro, primus, of Edinburgh, who apparently advocated the inflation of the lungs by artificial means as a method of resuscitation. Antoine Portal (1742–1832) apparently advocated intubation by tracheotomy, but only as a last, desperate resource. It appears that Claude-Nicolas le Cat (1700–68) expressed a desire to see a tube designed which could be passed through the glottis to assist in artificial respiration.

From what has been written, it is obvious that Kite was a man of considerable ability, and a perusal of his book shows that he had a remarkable grasp on the subject of resuscitation. He recognized that laryngeal spasm, as distinct from closure of the glottis by the lowering of the epiglottis, could occur. After stressing that water is not generally found in the lungs of animals recently drowned, he writes, "Allowing then, what is, I think, clearly proved, that death is caused by contraction of the parts about the larynx stopping respiration—it still remains to enquire, concerning the manner in which this stoppage of respiration acts, so as to occasion that effect". Earlier, he shows that he was aware that pulmonary oedema could occur in these circumstances, and that this might mislead investigators into thinking that water had been aspirated into the lungs:

"In answer to those who maintain the third opinion, it will be proper to observe, that although water has, beyond doubt, often been found in the lungs of drowned animals; yet that it is frequently absent, is evident from the experiments of men of undoubted authority. Frothy mucus, now and then mixed with blood, is very generally to be met with in the lungs, and sometimes in considerable quantity, owing to the blood and mucus being forced through the vessels by the great distension of the pulmonary artery; and this, I have no doubt, has frequently been taken for water: but if the animals are drowned in water tinged with a colouring substance, the fact will then be readily ascertained. Of ten kittens drowned in this manner, not one drop of the liquor was found in, or to be pressed out of the lungs".

As a further extension of this belief, he describes similar experiments to show that water never enters the lungs until death has occurred, and he points out that the spasm will relax at that moment, allowing water to "fall in". This may not be entirely in line with modern belief, but it is not far removed from it.

It is not surprising to find that Kite had some, to us, curious notions concerning respiration. The following passage at least shows that Kite used the lancet less than his colleagues, and that he attempted to give reasons for his actions:

"It is, however, to be observed, that large and repeated bleedings do not seem so indispensably necessary in the present instance, as in apoplexies arising from some other causes, as artificial respiration will in general answer the purpose of removing the over-distension of the venal system, consequently the compression of the brain, nearly as effectually and expeditiously; and is not liable to be attended with any disadvantages. In a full inspiration, the vesicles of the lungs are expanded, and at the same time the capacity of the pulmonary blood-vessels is considerably increased, so as to receive a larger quantity of blood from the right ventricle. In expiration, the vesicles are collapsed, and the contents of the blood-vessels are, in consequence, driven into the left auricle and ventricle. This process, frequently repeated, will in a short time remove the congestion in the great vessels; and the compression of the brain, which depended upon that congestion, will, I conceive, be as readily overcome as by opening a vein. On this account, and particularly as it is removing the cause of death, we cannot hesitate one moment in pronouncing, the restoring of the action of the lungs to be of the very first importance in all our attempts to recover the apparently dead. Dr. Fothergill, with great propriety, compares the lungs of drowned people to a clock whose pendulum has stopped; yet, says he, renew but the action of the lungs in the one, and touch but the pendulum in the other, and all again is life and motion. The same gentleman observes, in another place, that to inflate the lungs, especially of drowned persons, completely, requires no inconsiderable share of skill and dexterity".

Yet none can deny the wisdom and truth of the principles which he laid down. Although he described various methods of "removing the compression of the brain, and the congestion about the heart and lungs", and of "exciting the irritability of the muscular fibres", yet he states categorically:

> "Let it be observed, as an invariable rule, that in all attempts to recover the drowned, our attention should be principally and primarily directed to—the administration and proper regulation of the inflation of the lungs—and the application of heat".

Concerning the inflation of the lungs by the insertion of a tube into the nostril or by mouth-to-mouth breathing, he suggests a manoeuvre which might well be adopted by modern anaesthetists who wish to perform so-called "controlled" respiration in the absence of an endotracheal tube; namely, "by making a suitable pressure on the prominent part of the wind-pipe, he prevents the air passing into the stomach".

Should all other methods of inflation fail, tracheotomy is advocated as a last resort, a tube to be inserted and the lungs inflated by a bellows; "I acknowledge, however, I should not expect it would succeed when the other means have failed".

There are other points on which Kite held extraordinarily advanced views. For instance, he foreshadows the more recent knowledge of the stimulation of respiration by exciting reflexes from the tracheo-bronchial tree: "Air loaded with the vapour of tobacco—of the volatile alkali—of the spirit of sea salt—and spirit of sulphur, have been recommended with the view of exciting the action of the lungs with greater expedition." However, he casts doubts on the advisability of using these stimulants, and continues:

"With fairer prospects of success, is the dephlogisticated air of Dr. Priestley recommended for the same purpose. Dr. Fothergill, in particular, has distinguished himself by his truly ingenious remarks on its application to the subject now under our consideration. It must be observed, however, that in this instance the Doctor's practice seems entirely influenced by a theory, which supposes the cause of death, in drowned people to be noxious air stagnant in the cells of the windpipe; and as this species of air neutralizes mephitic air, and renders it respirable, 'it seems', says the Doctor, 'to be the direct anti-dote supplied by nature for correcting the contaminated air stagnant in the bronchial cells, and also for inflating the lungs, in preference to common air' ".

He is not convinced of the efficacy of dephlogisticated air, but is willing to give it a trial. He points out the difficulties, however, because, for only 10 minutes of artificial respiration at 10 inflations per minute, no less than 30,000 cu. inches of gas (two hogsheads) would be required. This would be very expensive, but, he writes, and those in charge of health services might well consider, "The costliness of the article, however, is the most trifling objection which can be brought against it, and could not require one moment's consideration, was it found to answer, and could it be readily procured and conveniently administered".

It should be remembered that, at the time Kite wrote, the discovery of oxygen (dephlogisticated air) had only been published thirteen years before, and its part in respiration was yet unknown; a somewhat conservative outlook was therefore natural.

Like those in our own day, Kite realized the difficulty of determining whether death had or had not occurred. He relied upon no one sign, but thought that lack of response of muscles to electrical stimulation was proof that the state of death was irreversible. He also used the electric current to hasten recovery and noticed that the diaphragm could be brought into action by it. He writes:

"The part which in my experiments on drowned animals, I found to be the most readily excited to action, was the diaphragm; and although the shocks were directed so as to pass through the auricles of the heart, consequently much above that muscle, yet it was always brought into great contractions".

He could hardly be aware that the shocks he was administering were probably exciting diaphragmatic action by stimulating the phrenic nerves in their course past the heart. It was not until 1863 that Kidd and Lobb showed that electrical stimulation of the phrenic nerves was a practical method of performing artificial respiration.

Kite in his book, deals mainly with the recovery of the apparently dead from drowning, but he also discusses the similar state of those who have been hanged, struck by lightning, or are suffering from syncope. In each case, he stresses the importance of artificial respiration by inflation. There is no doubt that he was a great practitioner of medicine, and his greatness is enhanced by his modesty. Every theory and every method are weighed in the balance. The extracts given above show that, although his references are unfortunately incomplete, he never fails to acknowledge the source of all his ideas.

Kite's book was published 175 years ago; medical science has risen to great heights since then, but there can be little doubt that an intelligent person, who had read no other work on the subject save Kite's, would be able to render better aid to a drowned man than most medical practitioners of today.

Index

OF DRUGS AND TECHNIQUES

A.C.E., 145
Acetone, 145
Alcohol, 94, 145, 202, 203
Artificial Respiration, 69, 79, 80, 81, 83, 84, 85, 89, 92, 109, 150, 151, 155, 186, 217–220
Atropine, 105, 140, 159, 160, 203

Baaras, 38, 44
Barbiturates, 107, 109, 161, 203, 204
Basal Narcosis, 161
Bleeding to Syncope, 77, 93
Blood Transfusion, 65, 67, 68, 69, 70, 71, 85, 90, 92, 104, 107, 109, 193–202
Bromethol, 161, 205

Carbon Dioxide, 67, 77, 78, 79, 82, 89, 91, 92, 171, 178, 179, 181, 182, 184
Carbon Dioxide Absorption, 81, 82, 95, 108, 129, 147, 181
Chloral, 92, 104, 203
Chloric Ether (Dutch Oil), 135, 136, 144, 145
Chloroform, 92, 94, 99, 101, 102, 103, 106, 107, 118, 120, 127, 129, 135-144, 145, 147, 148, 149, 159, 160, 187, 189, 203

Chlorpromazine, 109, 169
Compression of Nerves, 28, 62, 66, 84, 93, 171
Curare (& other Muscle Relaxants), 58, 63, 64, 83, 88, 89, 92, 93, 102, 109, 123, 154–158, 205
Cyclopropane, 108.

Divinyl Ether, 109, 122, 148

Endotracheal Intubation, 84, 85, 86, 87, 88, 95, 99, 104, 105, 106, 107, 108, 149–153, 216–220
Ether, 17, 45, 48, 56, 58, 59, 62, 70, 71, 72, 78, 87, 89, 90, 91, 94, 95, 96, 99, 100, 101, 103, 110–122, 123, 127, 129, 136, 137, 140, 142, 143, 144, 145, 146, 158, 160, 166, 207–211
Ethidine Dichloride, 140, 145
Ethyl Bromide, 146, 147
Ethyl Chloride, 106, 145–147, 166
Ethylene, 122, 133

Halothane, 100, 109, 147, 148
Hedonal, 203
Helium, 191, 192
Hemp, 15

P

Hypnotism, 69, 75, 76, 77, 82, 83, 88, 91, 92, 94, 95, 116
Hypodermic Injection, 93, 94, 101, 102
Hypothermia, 99, 109, 165, 167–171

Intravenous Anaesthesia, 56, 67, 68, 69, 70, 104, 176, 202-205
Isopral, 203

Kelene, 146

Lettuce, 91
Local (& Spinal) Anaesthesia, 63, 99, 102, 103, 105, 106, 107, 109, 157, 166, 167, 171–177

Magnesium Sulphate, 203
Mandragora (Mandrake), 17, 27, 30, 34, 35, 36, 37, 38, 41–43, 44, 46, 48, 49, 50, 62, 63, 66, 68, 72
Mayo, 43
Methyl Chloride, 147
Moly, 31
Morphine, 88, 91, 93, 94, 104, 107, 140, 159, 160, 203
Nitric Ether, 145

Nitrous Oxide, 77, 78, 80, 87, 88, 90, 93, 95, 99, 104, 105, 109, 112, 113, 115, 120, 121, 122, 124–134, 139, 140, 143, 185, 187, 188

Opium, 34, 35, 37, 38, 39, 46, 48, 49, 58, 63, 68, 73, 95, 114, 202
Oxygen, 70, 78, 80, 82, 83, 89, 95, 105, 122, 129, 130, 131, 132, 139, 168, 178–191, 221

Papaveretum, 161
Pentamethonium, 157

Rectal Anaesthesia, 119, 121, 122, 161
Refrigeration Anaesthesia, 14, 46, 56, 64, 65, 67, 68, 77, 81, 88, 109, 120, 146, 162–170, 171
Rhigolene, 120, 166

Scopolamine (Hyoscine), 68, 107, 160, 203
Somnoform, 147
Spongia Somnifera, 45, 47, 48, 49, 63

Trichloroethylene, 109, 147

Vienna Mixture, 145

Index

OF PERSONAL NAMES

Abbott, Gilbert, 96, 116
Acosta, de, 64, 189
Adam, 35
Adams, Francis, 163
Ælianus, Claudius, 43, 44
Æson, 193
Aëtius of Amida, 44
Agote, L., 198
Albinus, B. S., 155
Albucasis, 46
Alcuin, 163
Alexander the Great, 33, 36
Alfred, 168
Allen, F. M., 109, 167
Allen, Mrs., 94
Allen, William, 87, 88, 89, 184
Allis, O. H., 121
Amenhotep IV, King, 30
Andrews, C. F., 167
Andrews, Edmund, 129, 187
Annandale, J., 151
Anrep, V. K. (von), 173
Apuleius (Lucius Apuleius Barbarus), 44
Arago, F. J. D., 114
Archibald, E., 153
Arderne, John, 43, 48, 49
Argumosa y Obregon, de, 118
Aristotle, 34, 35, 36, 39, 40, 47, 51, 52, 53, 54, 58, 64, 65, 210
Arnott, James, 166

Arrowood, Julia, G., 175
Arthur, Prince, 142
Ashurbanipal, King, 31, 32
Ashur-nasir-pal II, King, 31, 32
Asklepiades of Bithynia, 33, 149
Asklepios, 32
Athanasius, St., 43
Aubrey, John, 67, 201
Aubert, P., 160
Auenbrugger, Leopold, 74, 80
Auer, J., 107, 152
Augustus II, King, 72
Aveling, J. H., 196
Avenzoar, 149
Averroës, 47, 210
Avicenna, 41, 46, 210

Babcock, Wayne, 175
Bacon, Sir Francis, Viscount St. Albans, 65, 66, 165
Bacon, Roger, 48, 51, 163
Bailey, C. P., 109
Bailly, Maire of Paris, 76
Bancroft, Edward, 155
Bancroft, 168
Bannister, Freda K., 21
Barach, A. L., 190, 191
Barcroft, J., 190
Bardet, D., 204
Barlow, R. B., 157

225

Bartas, G. de S. du, 63
Barth, George, 104, 129, 187
Barthélemy, 107, 152
Bartholin, Thomas, 68, 88, 164, 165
Barton, William P. C., 88
Beatrice, Princess, 102, 142
Beatty, Sir Chester, 30
Beaumont, William, 75
Beddoes, Thomas, 78, 86, 87, 125, 183
Bede, The Venerable, 45, 163
Beethoven, L. van, 74, 80
Behrend, 118
Bell, Sir Charles, 74
Bell, Jacob, 144
Benedict, St., 46
Bennett, A. E., 157
Bennett, A. H., 172
Bernard, Claude, 102, 156, 159
Bert, Paul, 130, 131, 187, 188, 189
Bibra, E. von, 146
Bickford, R. G., 130
Bier, August, 107, 175, 176, 205
Bigelow, Henry Jacob, 17, 96, 100, 117, 127, 143
Bigelow, Jacob, 18
Bigelow, N., 168
Bigelow, W. G., 205
Biot, 189
Bird, Marcus, 166
Bjork, V. O., 153
Black, Joseph, 77, 78, 79, 178, 179
Blalock, A., 168
Blundell, James, 90, 196
Boccaccio, Giovanni, 51
Boehm, R., 156, 157
Bodmin, R. I., 158
Boerema, J., 169

Boerhaave, Hermann, 55, 66, 71
Bogendörfer, N., 204
Bonpland, A., 88
Boothby, W. M., 132, 190
Boott, Francis, 100, 101, 117
Borderan, 173
Borelli, G. A., 54, 67, 68, 70
Borlase, J. B., 125
Boswell, James, 80, 165
Bouchut, Eugène, 151
Boussingault, J. B., 92
Bovet, Daniel, 157, 158
Boyle, H. E. G., 108, 122, 132, 147
Boyle, the Hon. Robert, 54, 68, 69, 70, 111, 195
Brahé, Tycho, 54, 64
Braid, James, 83, 94
Braun, Heinrich F. W., 107, 174
Bredenfeld, Elisabeth, 203
Brewer, G. E., 197
Brocklesby, Richard, 155
Brodie, Sir Benjamin, 84, 89, 155, 156
Brown, G., 161
Brown, John, 76, 82
Bruno, Giordano, 53, 64, 65
Brunton, Sir Thomas Lauder, 140, 141
Bulbulian, A. H., 190
Bullein, William, 52, 62
Bumm, R., 204
Burke, Edmund, 124
Burkhardt, Ludwig, 203
Burnett, 115
Burns, Robert, 74, 79, 85
Burstein, C. L., 205
Butzengeiger, O., 205
Buxton, Dudley, 161, 190
Byron, Lord, 74, 84

Calcar, J. van, 61
Cap, 92
Carlens, E., 153
Carlson, H., 146, 167
Carter, R. W., 121
Cartwright, F. F., 20, 87
Cat, Claude-Nicolas le, 84, 85, 150, 217, 218
Cathelin, F., 107, 176
Catherine of Aragon, Queen, 52
Caxton, William, 57
Cavendish, Henry, 74, 80, 83, 182
Celsus, 33, 37, 38, 51
Cerna, David, 146
Chamberlain, 116
Chadwick, Edwin, 77, 93
Channing, Walter, 118
Charles IX, King, 62
Charles X, King, 78, 91
Charrière, 118, 138
Chaucer, Geoffrey, 49
Chauliac, Guy de, 48
Chaussier, François, 83, 88, 95, 150, 182
Chen, M. Y., 109, 122
Chevillon, G., 204
Chopin, Frédéric F., 88, 97
Christison, Sir Robert, 112
Cieza de Leon, Pedro, 172
Clark, 132
Clark, 201
Clarke, William E., 78, 94, 112, 113
Cloquet, Jules, 77, 92
Clover, Joseph, 103, 120, 122, 128, 129, 131, 139
Clutterbuck, 93
Cole, Leslie, 157
Coleman, Alfred, 128, 129, 131, 132, 187

Colle, Johann, 194
Collyer, Robert A., 94
Colton, Gardner Quincy, 95, 125, 126, 127, 128
Colombo, Realdo, 61
Columbus, Christopher, 57, 60
Condamine, de la, 155
Condemberg, Peter, 110
Constable, John, 74
Cookson, B. A., 109
Cooper, Sir Astley, 87, 93, 126
Copernicus, Nicolas, 53, 60, 65
Cordus, Valerius, 59, 62, 110, 111, 209, 210, 211
Corning, James Leonard, 105, 173, 175
Cosmas, St., 43
Costaeus, Johannes, 64, 164
Cotton, F. J., 132
Coupart, 173
Courtois, Hans, 85, 150
Courville, C. B., 133
Cox, Thomas, 194
Coxeter, 129, 187
Coxon, S. A., 131
Coxwell, H. T., 189
Crafoord, C., 109
Crile, George Washington, 174
Croce-Spinelli, 189
Cromwell, Oliver, Lord Protector, 54
Cullen, William, 18, 74, 81, 165
Currie, James, 85, 165
Curry, James, 85, 150
Cushing, Harvey, 174
Cushny, A. H., 141

Dalton, John, 91, 112, 179
Damian, St., 43
Dante (Alighieri), 48, 51
Darwin, Erasmus, 85, 196

Dastre, A., 159, 160
Davies, Morriston, 151
Davison, M. H. Armstrong, 157
Davy, Sir Humphry, 20, 74, 78, 86, 87, 112, 125, 183, 184
Dean, H. P., 175
Decastello, von, 197
Delorme, E. J., 168, 197, 201
Demarquay, J. N., 159
Demosthenes, 36
Denis (Denys), Jean, 70, 195
Dennis, C., 201
Depaul, A. J. H., 95
Desault, P. J., 150
Descartes, René, 54
Desgranges, 84
Desplas, Bernard, 204
Dieffenbach, J. F., 118
Diocletian, Emperor, 43
Dioscorides, Ped., 16, 37, 38, 43, 171, 211
Dirk, A, von, 160
Dobson, Matthew, 82, 181
Dodoens, R., 63
Döring, Oskar, 204
Dorrance, G. M., 151
Doubleday, E., 92, 196
Dresser, E., 203
Drew, C. E., 201
Dubois, P., 118
Ducos, 96, 114
Dufour, 107, 152
Dugern, von, 197
Dumas, J. B. A., 93, 136
Duncan Flockhart & Co., 137
Duncan, James Matthews, 137
Duncum, Barbara M., 20
Dundee, John W., 144
Dunham, 127
Duprey, 119
Dupuytren, G., 126
Dürer, Albrecht, 56, 57

Dutcher, J. D., 156

Ebers, G., 25, 29
Eckman, M., 191
Edwards, W. B., 109, 176
Eichna, I. W., 168
Einhorn, Alfred, 107, 174, 205
Eisenmenger, V., 151
Elkinton, J. R., 198
Elliotson, John, 17, 77, 94
Ellis, E. S., 20, 72, 209
Elsberg, C. A., 107, 152
Elsholtz, J. S., 69, 107, 195, 202
Embley, E. H., 160
Enderby, G. E. Hale, 157
Erasistratus of Chios, 33, 34, 36, 194
Erichsen, Sir John, 95
Esdaile, James, 77, 95
Eslon, C. d', 82, 83
Eurypylos, 171
Evans, T. W., 128
Eve, 35, 63, 142

Fabri, L. C., 73
Fabrizi of Aquapendente, 61, 66
Falloppio, G., 61
Faraday, Sir Michael, 74, 87, 90
Faulconer, Albert jr., 130
Fauvel, Charles, 172
Fay, T., 167
Feissly, R., 198
Fernel, J. F., 53, 60
Filliâtre, Le, 175
Fine, 87
Fischer, Emil, 107, 204
Fisher, R. A., 199
Fitch, R. H., 204
Flourens, M. J. P., 136, 145, 156
Floyer, Sir John, 71

Folli, Francesco, 195
Fontaine, R., 176, 205
Fontana, Abbé Felice, 81, 82, 83, 129, 155, 181
Foregger, Richard, 132
Formby, Richard, 144
Fothergill, John, 219
Fourneau, Ernest, 173
Foy, George, 172, 173
Fracastoro, G., 53, 59
Frampton, John, 63, 154, 172
François, 91
Franken, 50
Franklin, Benjamin, 76, 80, 83, 179
Frazer, William, 117
Fredet, Pierre, 204
Frenckner, P., 152
Froben, A. S., 72, 111, 211
Frost, Eben, 96, 115
Fuchs, Leonhard, 60
Fuller, 168
Fülöp-Miller, R., 20

Gabb, John, 145
Gaedicke, 102, 172
Gale, J. W., 152
Galen of Pergamum, 32, 33, 34, 39, 40, 41, 46, 51, 52, 53, 55, 58, 60, 61, 69, 210
Galilei, Galileo, 54, 64, 65
Galvani, Luigi, 74, 85
Gandhi, Mahatma, 167
Garcia, Manuel, 102, 150
Gardanne, de, 84
Gardner, H. Bellamy, 121
Gardner, W. J., 200
Garrison, Fielding H., 19, 209
Gatch, W. D., 121, 132
Gay-Lussac, J. L., 189
George IV, King, 87
Gesner, Conrad, 110

Gibbon & Gibbon, 201
Giesel, 173
Gilbert, William, 53, 64, 65
Gill, R. C., 154
Gillespie, Noel, 21
Gillies, John, 144, 158, 175, 176
Gillies, Sir Harold, 149
Glaisher, James, 189
Glover, R. M., 94, 96, 136
Goethe, J. W. von, 74, 78
Goodrich, F. C., 113
Goodwyn, Edmund, 84, 183
Gordon, R. A., 205
Gould, A. A., 17
Goyanes, J., 176, 205
Graefe, Wilhelm, 203
"Graham, Harvey", 20
Gratton, J. H. G., 163
Graubard, D. J., 176
Gream, G. T., 142
Greatrakes, Valentine, 69
Greene, W. W., 104
Greener, Hannah, 101
Griffith, Harold R., 109, 154, 157
Griffiths, H. W. C., 157, 175, 176
Griffiths, R., 67
Guedel, Arthur E., 119, 122, 131, 152
Guillotin, J. I., 75, 83
Gutenberg, Johannes, 50, 56
Guthrie, Douglas, 19, 90
Guthrie, Samuel, 92, 135, 144
Guyon, E., 159
Gwathmey, John Tayloe, 122, 132

Hadfield, C. F., 147
Haldane, J. B. S., 190
Hall, Marshall, 93

Halla, 118
Haller, A. von, 55, 72
Halsted, William Stewart, 105, 106, 174
Haly Abbas, 46
Harcourt, Vernon, 107, 141
Harless, E., 146
Harley, George, 145
Harley, John, 159
Harūn ar-Rasheed, Caliph, 45, 110, 207
Harrison, I., 205
Hart, Ernest, 129
Harvey, William, 39, 54, 65, 68, 163, 194, 201, 202
Haward, J. W., 120
Hawkins, Sir John, 154
Hayden, G. G., 116
Haydn, F. J., 74, 85
Head, H., 152
Hearst, 30
Heidbrink, J. A., 132
Helmont, J. B. van, 67, 178, 179
Henri II, King, 60, 62
Henri III, King, 62
Henry VIII, King, 52, 57, 58, 59
Hermes, 31
Herodotus, 15, 34
Herophilus of Chalcedon, 33, 36
Herring, P. T., 167
Herzberg, M., 147
Hewer, C. Langton, 109, 147
Hewitt, Sir Frederic, 105, 121, 131, 132, 139, 188, 190
Heyfelder, F., 118, 146
Hickman, Henry Hill, 20, 78, 91, 125
Hildegarde, "St.", 47
Hill, Daniel, 185

Hill, Sir Leonard, 190
Hill, W., 150, 151
Hilliard, Harvey, 131
Hillischer, H. T., 131, 188
Hingson, R. A., 109, 176
Hippocrates of Cos, 33, 35, 149, 162, 163
Hirschfeld, L., 197
Hoche, A., 157
Hobbie, Miss, 94, 113
Hoffman, 27, 66
Holmes, Oliver Wendell, 15, 17, 18, 75, 94
Homer, 31, 41, 171
Hooke, Robert, 69, 149
Hooper, 101, 117, 118
Horsley, Sir Victor, 160
Hua-T'o, 43
Hugo of Lucca, 47
Huguenard, P., 109, 169
Humboldt, F. H. A. von, 88, 155
Hunt, Sir John, 189
Hunt, R., 158
Hunter, John, 74, 79, 81, 84, 165, 170
Hunter, William, 71, 74, 81
Hustin, A., 198
Hyderabad, the Nizam of, 140
Hyksos, the, 28

Imhotep, 28
Ing, H. R., 157
Ingen-Housz, Jan, 81, 82, 181, 184
Isidorus, Bishop, 44
Isaacs, Jasper, 50
Isla, R. de, 60
Ives, Eli, 136

Jābir ibn Hayyān, 45, 110, 207–208

Jackson, Charles T., 100, 104, 114, 115, 116, 211
Jackson, Chevalier, 150
Jackson, Dennis E., 108, 147
Janeway, H. H., 150, 151
Jansky, J., 197
Jason, 67, 193
Jeffries, B. J., 120
Jenner, Edward, 75, 86
Joan of Arc, 43, 50
Johnson, Alexander, 80, 81
Johnson, G. Enid, 109, 154, 157
Johnson, John, 95, 114
Johnson, Samuel, 71, 74, 80, 165
Jones, Howard, 175
Jonesco, J., 175
Josephus, Flavius, 37, 38, 44
Joshua, 35
Julliard, Gustave, 121
Junet & Junet, 199
Junker, F. E., 188

Kanaar, A. G., 168
Kant, Immanuel, 74, 83
Keep, Nathan C., 118
Keith, Thomas, 137
Kekwick, A., 198
Kelly, Sir Robert E., 108, 152
Kepler, Johann, 54, 64
Keynes, Sir Geoffrey, 86
Keys, Thomas E., 20, 87
Khammurabi, 26, 29
Kidd, 222
Killian, G., 106, 150
Kimpton-Brown, 197
King, H., 109, 156, 157
Kirke, 31
Kirschner, M., 205
Kirstein, Alfred, 106, 150
Kite, Charles, 84, 85, 88, 150, 183, 190, 216–222

Klikowitch, S., 105, 131, 188
Knapp, H. J., 173
Knox, John, 52, 62, 63, 97
Kohlstaedt, 200
Koller, Carl, 105, 173
Korff, Berthold, 107
Krakow, N. F., 203
Krantz, J. C. jr., 123
Kreutzmann, 188
Kuhn, F., 151

Labbé, L., 159
Labordt, 173, 176
Laborit, H., 109, 169
Laennec, R. T. H., 74, 90
Lafargue, 93
Lake, N. C., 175
Lamballe, de, 117
Landois, Leonhard, 104, 196
Landsteiner, Karl, 107, 109, 196, 197, 199
Lang, Andrew, 42
Lange, 168
Laplace, P. S. de, 78, 84, 182
Larrey, Baron Dominique-Jean, 77, 88, 91, 165
Lassen, H. C. A., 133
Latta, Thomas Aitchison, 92, 196
Lavoisier, Antoine-Laurent, 74, 75, 78, 81, 82, 83, 86, 178, 182, 183
Lausitz, 67
Lawrie, Edward, 140
Leake, Chauncey D., 109, 122
Leavitt, William P., 115
Leeuwenhoek, A. van, 54, 70
Lee, J. Alfred, 21
Leggett, N. B., 197
Lehmann, K. B., 147
Leipoldt, C. L., 161

Lemmon, W. T., 175
Lemnius, 63
Leopinasse, 197
Leopold, Prince, 102, 142
Leriche, Réné, 176, 205
Leroy d'Estoilles, J. J. J., 92, 150
Levine, P., 197, 199
Levy, A. Goodman, 107, 141
Levy, R. B., 176
Libavius, Andreas, 65, 67, 194
Liebig, Justus von, 92, 135, 136
Liégard, 93, 171
Lillehei, C. W., 201
Lind, James, 73, 74
Lindeman, E., 198
Linné (Linnaeus), K. von, 18, 73, 78
Lister, Joseph, Baron of Lyme Regis, 98, 103, 104, 106, 108, 139
Liston, Robert, 74, 101, 117
Lloyd, Meredith, 67
Lobb, Harry, 222
Lockyer, Sir Norman, 191
Löfgren, N., 174
Long, Crawford Williamson, 20, 78, 94, 103, 113
Lonsdale, Miss, 101, 117
Lotheissen, Georg, 146, 167
Louis XVI, King, 75, 83
Lovelace, W. R., 190
Lower, Richard, 67, 68, 69, 70, 195
Luckhardt, Arno B., 133
Lully (or Lull), Raymond, 48, 110, 208–209
Lundqvist, B., 174
Lundy, J. S., 109, 176, 204, 205

MacCallum, J. T. C., 204

MacCalyean, Eufame, 64, 212–215
McDowell, Ephraim, 75, 89
Macewen, Sir William, 105, 108, 151, 216
Macintosh, Sir Robert R., 21, 132, 151, 175
McIntyre, R. A., 154, 157
McKesson, Elmer I., 132
MacMechan, F. H., 161
Macnaughten-Jones, H., 160
MacQuaide, D. H. G., 199
Magaw, Alice, 121
Magill, Sir Ivan Whiteside, 99, 108, 133, 149, 150, 152
Maimonides, 47
Major, J. D., 68, 70
Major, Ralph H., 20, 29
Malgaigne, J. F., 101, 117
Malpighi, Marcello, 54, 68
Marcus Aurelius, Emperor, 39
Marcy, E. E., 95, 113, 114
Marggraff, Jorg, 155
Marin, M. G., 203
Marriott, H. L., 198
Mart, W. D., 151
Martyr, Peter, 58, 154
Mary, Queen of Scots, 52, 62
Mason, 168
Matas, Rudolph, 151, 174
Mattison, J. B., 173
Maxson, Louis H., 175
Maydl, Karel, 151
Mayow, John, 54, 70, 178, 179, 183, 184
Medea, 67, 193
Meisser, A. G., 72
Melrose, D. G., 200
Meltzer, S. J., 107, 152, 203
Mendelssohn (-Bartholdy), Felix, 83, 88, 97
Mercklin, G. A., 70, 195

Mering, J. von, 107, 204
Mesmer, Franz Anton, 69, 75, 76, 82, 83
Miller, H., 201
Minnitt, R. J., 109, 131
Mitchill, S. Latham, 87, 125
Mollière, Daniel, 121
Mollison, P. L., 199
Monardes, Nicolas, 63, 154, 155
Mondino, 48
Montgolfier Brothers, 189
Moore, James, 84, 171
Morton, H. J. V., 158
Morton, T. S. K., 188
Morton, William Thomas Green, 15, 17, 18, 78, 94, 96, 100, 104, 113, 114, 115, 116, 117, 118, 123, 127, 142
Moss, W. L., 197
Mozart, Wolfgang, 74, 79, 83
Munro, Alexander, primus, 71, 84, 150, 217
Murphy, J. B., 196
Murray, J., 128, 130
Mushin, William W., 21

Nakagawa, K., 203
Napoleon I, Emperor, 73, 74, 87, 88, 165, 168
Neptune, W. B., 109
Nero, Emperor, 37, 38
Neu, M., 133
Neudörfer, 188
Newton, Sir Isaac, 54, 70, 71, 111
Newton, T., 63
Nicholas of Salerno, 47, 48
Nichols, T., 172
Niemann, Albert, 103, 172
Noel, H., 196, 203
Nooth, 84
Northrop, Thomas, 188

Nunneley, Thomas, 127, 145, 146
Nussbaum, J. N. von, 159
Nysten, P. H., 89, 112

O'Dwyer, J. P., 151
Odysseus, 31
O'Neill, J. F., 199
Oporinus, 61
Oppenheim, H., 147
Oré, P. C., 104, 202, 203
O'Shaughnessy, W. B., 92, 196
Osler, Sir William, 53, 59, 68, 106, 164, 211
Ostlere, G., 147
Ottenberg, R., 197
Ovid, 67, 193, 194

Pagès, Fidel, 176
Palmgren, E. C., 118
Paracelsus, 53, 58, 59, 65, 110, 111, 178, 210, 211
Paré Ambroise, 62, 84, 171
Parker, Peter, 118
Parkinson, John, 66
Paton, W. D. M., 157
Patroclus, 171
Paul of Ægina, 45
Pawling, J. R., 135
Pearson, Richard, 78, 86, 111, 112
Peck, C. H., 203
Pegelius, 194
Pender, J. W., 130
Pepys, Samuel, 54, 195
Pepys, W. H., 88, 89, 184
Pericles, 33, 35
Perlis, Régine, 204
Peterson, M. C., 176
Petrov, I. R., 198
Phillips, 158
Pirogoff, N. I., 119

Pitcairne, Archibald, 55, 70
Pizarro, Francisco, 172
Plato, 16, 35
Pliny the Elder, 33, 37, 38, 42, 43
Pomet, 72
Poniatowski, Stanislaus, 72
Pope, Elijah, 78, 94, 113
Porta, Giambattista della, 62, 64
Portal, Antoine, 84, 150, 217, 218
Potter, Francis, 67, 194
Power, Sir d'Arcy, 49
Pravaz, Gabriel, 101, 102, 172, 202
Priestley, Joseph, 20, 70, 74, 77, 78, 80, 82, 124, 178, 179, 180, 181, 221
Prochownick, L., 188
Ptolemy I Soter, King, 36
Pugh, Benjamin, 79
Purmann, M. G., 71, 195
Puységur, Count Maxime de, 76, 83, 88
Pythagoras, 16, 34

Quincke, Heinrich, 106, 175
Quistorp, J. B., 71

Raleigh, Sir Walter, 64, 154
Rameses II, King, 30, 31
Ramsay, Sir William, 191
Ransohof, J. L., 176, 205
Read, R., 184
Réaumur, R. de, 55, 72
Récamier, Joseph-Claude-Anselme, 77, 91
Reclus, Paul, 173
Redard, 146, 166
Rendell-Baker, L., 21
Rhazes, 41, 45

Richardson, Sir Benjamin Ward, 20, 103, 120, 122, 128, 166
Riggs, John M., 95, 126
Robertson, L. B., 198
Robinson, Field, 146
Robinson, James, 101, 117
Rolland, Georges, 146
Rood, F., 161
Roth, 189
Roulin, 92
Roux, C., 119
Rovenstine, E. A., 176
Rowbotham, E. S., 99, 108, 149, 152
Rozier, de, 189
Rudolph II, Emperor, 54
Ruggiero, W. F., 168
Rush, Benjamin, 85
Rymer, S. L., 128
Rynd, F., 94

Saglia, 173
St. Martin, Alexis, 75
Saladin, 47
Salt, 133
Sanderson, J. B., 128, 130
Sansom, A. E., 143
Santorio, S., 54, 65, 71
Sauerbruch, Ferdinand, 107
Saussure, Théodore de, 184
Savigny, 217
Sayre, L. A., 156
Scarborough, Sir Charles, 202
Schäfer, E. A., 160
Scharpff, W., 109, 204
Scheele, Carl Wilhelm, 70, 78, 80, 82, 180, 181
Schleich, Carl Ludwig, 106, 173
Schneiderlin, von, 160
Schomburgk, Sir Robert, 93
Schraff, 172

Schreber, E. von, 83
Schuh, 118
Scoffern, John, 93
Scott, Sir William, 74, 80
Scott, William, 117
Scultetus (Schultz), J., 71, 195
Scurr, C. F., 157
Seguin, 182
Sertürner, Friedrich, 88
Servetus, Michael, 61
Severino, M. A., 14, 67, 68, 164, 165
Shamov, W. N., 198
Shattock S. G., 197
Shearer, William S., 159
Shelburne, Lord, 80, 124, 180
Shelley, Percy Bysshe, 74
Sibley, Francis, 156
Sicard, A., 107, 175, 176
Siebe Gorman & Co., 133
Siebold, C. T. C. von, 118
Silk, J. F. W, 146
Simpson, Sir James Young, 20, 101, 104, 118, 136, 137, 139, 142, 143, 144, 145, 171
Simpson, S, 167
Sims, J. Marion, 146
Singer, Charles, 19, 163
Sivel, 189
Skold, E., 198
Smellie, William, 71, 74
Smilie, E. R., 95, 114
Smith, Edwin, 30
Smith, J. H., 127
Smith, L. W., 167
Smith, P., 160
Smith, Thomas Southwood, 77, 93
Snow, John, 20, 99, 101, 102, 103, 119, 120, 129, 138, 139, 142, 143, 145, 149, 166, 187
Socrates, 34, 35

Soubeiran, Eugène, 92, 135
Souttar, Sir Henry S., 203
Spear, Thomas R., 115
Sprague, A. W., 128
Squibb, E. R., 120, 154
Squire, 101, 117, 118, 119
Stadie, W. C., 190
Stahl, Georg Ernst, 55, 72, 124, 182
Starling, E. H., 107, 200
Stockman, 90
Stokes, Captain, 190
Striker, C., 109, 147
Sturli, A., 197
Swieten, G. L. B. van, 155
Sylvester, Joshua, 63
Sylvius (de le Boë), F., 55, 67, 68
Syme, James, 143

Tait, R. Lawson, 121, 122
Takàts, G. de, 173
Tatum, A. L., 204
Taveau, R. M. de, 158
Taylor, 93
Teter, C. K., 122, 132
Thales of Miletus, 16, 32, 34
Theodoric (Borgognoni), 43, 47, 48
Theophrastus, 36
Thiesing, 146
Thompson, Benjamin (Count Rumford), 74, 87, 183
Thompson, Elihu, 191
Thompson, R. C., 133
Thompson, V. C., 153
Thorsen, 200
Tissandier, G., 189
Tjeser, King, 28
Tocantins, L. M., 199
Topham, W., 94
Tovell, Ralph M., 176

Tracy, S. J., 137
Trendelenburg, Friedrich, 104, 107, 149, 151, 216
Trousseau, Armand, 149
Tuffier, Théodore, 108, 151, 175
Tuohy, E. B., 175
Turner, Matthew, 72, 111
Turner, William, 74, 81
Tutankhamen, King, 30

Valdoni, 158
Valverdi, 64, 171
Venable, James, 94, 113
Vesalius, Andreas, 39, 53, 60, 61, 149, 216
Vespucci, Amerigo, 57
Victoria, Queen, 102, 142
Vinci, Leonardo da, 53, 56, 57
Volta, A., 74
Voltolini, F., 150

Wakely, Thomas, 91
Waldie, David, 136, 137
Waller, Charles, 92, 196
Warburton, Henry, 77, 92
Ward, G. R., 198
Ward, W. Squire, 94
Wardrop, James, 77, 93
Warren, John, 87, 112, 126
Warren, John Collins, 96, 112, 126
Washington, 93
Waters, Ralph M., 108, 144, 152, 204
Waterton, Charles, 92, 155, 156
Watt, James, 80, 86
Wecker, L. de, 68
Weese, H., 109, 204
Weidenfeld, S., 197
Weil, P. E., 198

Weiss, S., 204
Wells, Horace, 78, 95, 101, 113, 114, 115, 126, 127, 185
Wells, Sir Thomas Spencer, 157
Werigo, B., 152
Wesley, John, 74
West, Ranyard, 157
White, S. S., 132, 188
Wiener, A. S., 109, 199
Wilhite, 113
Wilkins, 195
Wilson, George, 95, 185, 186
Wilson, W. Etherington, 175
Windsor, 16
Wintersteiner, O. P., 156
Wohlgemuth, J., 189
Wolffberg, S., 152
Wombwell, James, 94
Wood, Alexander, 102, 172, 202
Wood, H. C., 146
Wordsworth, William, 74, 80, 97
Wren, Sir Christopher, 67, 194, 202
Wright, A., 197
Wright, William, 92
Wylie, W. D., 158
Wynter, Essex, 106, 175

Xenophon, 35

Young, George, 73
Young, Thomas, 87
Yudin, S. S., 198
y'Yhedo, 119

Zaimis, E., 157
Zarate, Augustin de, 172
Zerfas, L. G., 204
Ziemssen, H. von, 175